MW00325910

Philo of Alexandria

Philo
of Alexandria

Jean Daniélou

Translated by
James G. Colbert

 CASCADE *Books* · Eugene, Oregon

PHILO OF ALEXANDRIA

Copyright © 2014 Wipf and Stock Publishers. All rights reserved. Except for brief quotations in critical publications or reviews, no part of this book may be reproduced in any manner without prior written permission from the publisher. Write: Permissions, Wipf and Stock Publishers, 199 W. 8th Ave., Suite 3, Eugene, OR 97401.

Originally published in French as *Philon d'Alexandrie* by Editions du Cerf. Translation of Jean Daniélou, *Philon d'Alexandrie*, Paris: Librairie Arthème Fayard, 1958.

Cascade Books
An Imprint of Wipf and Stock Publishers
199 W. 8th Ave., Suite 3
Eugene, OR 97401

www.wipfandstock.com

isbn 13: 978-1-4982-0550-4

Cataloging-in-Publication data:

Daniélou, Jean

Philo of Alexandria / Jean Daniélou. Translated by James G. Colbert.

xvii + 184 p. ; 23 cm. —Includes bibliographical references.

isbn 13: 978-1-4982-0550-4

1. Philo, of Alexandria. I. Title.

B689 Z7 D48 2014

Manufactured in the U.S.A.

To María

Contents

Translator's Preface

ERWIN GOODENOUGH REMARKS, "THERE is no important writer of antiquity who has been so little studied as Philo Judaeus . . . no one seems to have tried to read Philo, if I may say so, with the grain instead of against it, to understand what Philo himself thought he was driving at in all his passionate allegorical labors."[1] Goodenough himself and even more Harry Austryn Wolfson did an enormous amount to remedy this lack. Of course, since Goodenough and Wolfson, scholarly monographs on Philo continue to appear, and Richard Schenk has recently authored *A Brief Guide to Philo*. Daniélou's *Philo of Alexandria* gives us a historical, philosophical, and religious context of Philo. We almost know him personally by the end.

If it is generally appropriate when translating to give the author's important sources as they appear in published English translations, this is particularly true for Daniélou, who sometimes does not indicate ellipses or who occasionally paraphrases, though using quotation marks. The English speaking world is fortunate to have the Loeb Classical Library, Cambridge: Harvard University Press and London: W. Heinemann, 1971–91 (for the set I consulted). Philo's treatise consists of ten volumes in Greek and English and two volumes in English only that are supplements containing treatises preserved in Ancient Armenian translations. The English translation of volumes I–V is by F. H. Colson and G. H. Whitaker. The English translation of volumes VI–X is by F. H. Colson alone. Ralph Marcus did the translation from Armenian. To these I will

---

1. Goodenough, *By Light Light*, 5.

refer by their Latin titles, books where applicable, and paragraphs as Daniélou does, adding the volume and page of the English translations, e.g. *Philo*, I, 1, or *Philo*, Appendix I, 1.

A useful one volume English translation is available in *The Works of Philo*, done in the nineteenth century by C. D. Yonge and recently updated and corrected by David Scholer.

Within quotations from Philo, material in square brackets is Daniélou's, unless it is explicitly indicated that they are the translator's. Material in curved parentheses appears in the Loeb version.

Incidentally, when checking Daniélou's quotations against the Loeb version, I verified the Greek terms he sometimes includes in his quotations. Daniélou usually mention these terms in the nominative. Where terms appear within quotations, I have tried to present them in the case in which they actually are found in Philo.

Daniélou is not consistent in the abbreviations he uses to refer to Philo's treatises. I have followed the Loeb for Latin names, made my own (hopefully transparent) contracted names, and generally followed the Loeb's English with minor adaptations. I render *Apologia pro Iudaeis* as *Apology for the Jews* rather than the Loeb's *Hypothetica*.

Incidentally, though Daniélou's French text could have stood more editing, the Loeb also manages to refer to both *De Congressu Querendae Eruditionis Gratiae* and *De Congressu Eruditionis Gratiae*; to both *Quod Deterius Potiori Insidiari Solet* and *Quod Deterius Potiori Insidiari Soleat*, and both *Quod Deus Immutabilis Sit* and *Quod Deus Sit Immutabilis*. Let him who is without sin cast the first stone!

Accordingly, the following columns give the Loeb's Latin titles, my contractions, and the English name.

Volume I

De Opificio Mundi	*De Opificio*	*On Creation*
Legum Allegoriae	*Legum Allegoriae*	*Allegorical Interpretation*

Volume II

De Cherubim	*De Cherubim*	*On the Cherubim*
De Sacrificiis Abelis et Caini	*De Sacrificiis*	*On the Sacrifice of Abel and Cain*
Quod Deterius Potiori Insidiari	*Quod Deterius*	*The Worse Attacks the Better Soleat*
De Posteritate Caini	*De Posteritate*	*On the Posterity of Cain*
De Gigantibus	*De Gigantibus*	*On the Giants*

Volume III

Quod Deus Immutabilis Sit	*Quod Immutabilis*	*On the Unchangeableness of God*
De Agricultura	*De Agricultura*	*On Husbandry*
De Plantatione	*De Plantatione*	*On Noah's Work as a Planter*
De Ebrietate	*De Ebrietate*	*On Drunkenness*
De Sobrietate	*De Sobrietate*	*On Sobriety*

Volume IV

De Confusione Linguarum	*De Confusione*	*On the Confusion of Tongues*
De Migratione Abrahami	*De Migratione*	*On the Migration of Abraham*
Quis Rerum Divinarum Heres	*Quis Heres*	*Who is the Heir of Divine Things*
De Congressu Queredae Eruditionis Gratia	*De Congressu*	*On Preliminary Studies*

Volume V

De Fuga et Inventione	*De Fuga*	*On Flight and Finding*
De Mutatione Nominum	*De Mutatione*	*On the Change of Names*
De Somniis	*De Somniis*	*On Dreams*

Volume VI

De Abrahamo	*De Abrahamo*	*On Abraham*
De Josepho	*De Josepho*	*On Joseph*
De Vita Mosis	*De Vita Mosis*	*Moses*

Volume VII

| *De Decalogo* | *De Decalogo* | *On the Decalogue* |
| *De Specialibus Legibus I–III* | *De Specialibus Legibus* | *On Special Laws* |

Volume VIII

De Specialibus Legibus IV	*De Specialibus Legibus*	*On Special Laws*
De Virtutibus	*De Virtutibus*	*On Virtues*
De Praemiis et Poenis	*De Praemiis*	*On Rewards and Punishments*

Volume IX

Quod Omnis Probus Liber Sit	*Quod Probus*	*Every Good Man is Free*
De Vita Contemplativa	*De Vita Contemplativa*	*On Contemplative Life*
De Aeternitate Mundi	*De Aeternitate Mundi*	*On the Eternity of the World*
In Flaccum	*In Flaccum*	*Against Flaccus*
Apologia pro Iudaeis	*Pro Iudaeis*	*Apology for the Jews*
De Providentia	*De Providentia*	*On Providence*

Volume X

De Legatione ad Gaium	*Ad Gaium*	*On the Embassy to Gaius*

Supplement I

Quaestiones et Solutiones in Genesim	*In Genesim*	*Questions and Answers on Genesis*

Supplement II

Quaestiones et Solutiones in Exodum	*In Exodum*	*Questions and Answers on Exodus*

Daniélou refers to *De Explicatione Legum*, which seems to be a collective name for *Legum Allegoriae* and some of the treatises on the patriarchs. He also mentions *De Mundo*, which Yonge regards as identical to *De Aeternitate Mundi*.

Alexandria was the homeland of the Septuagint. (Daniélou has some intriguing comments on Greek translations of the Bible.) Philo, who wrote in Greek used it. One of the differences between the Septuagint, which the Vulgate and translations from the Vulgate follow, is in the numbering of the Psalms. Daniélou himself follows the Hebrew enumeration, even when referring to the Septuagint. It will be noted that both counts total 150. As an exercise upon completion of the present work, the reader might try to imagine Philo giving a homily on the excellence of 150.

To avoid confusion, below is a helpful table that I have adapted from *A Catholic Commentary on Holy Scripture* (Bernard Orchard and others ed., Thomas Nelson and Sons, London, etc., 1953, section 335d):

Hebrew and Contemporary	Septuagint and Vulgate
1 through 8	same
9 and 10	9
11 through 113	10 through 112
114 and 115	113
116	114 and 115
117 through 146	116 through 145
147	146 and 147
148 through 150	same

I have made two terminological decisions. The adjective derived from "Philo" is "Philonic," on the model of "Platonic."

More importantly: the Logos is *it*. In French, Joan of Arc and the kitchen table are feminine. Louis XIV and books are masculine. In English people, animals, some odd plants, and ships have gender. Everything else is "it." The delightful suggestion was made to me that, since in some ways later discussions of the *Shekinah* derive from Philo's reflections upon the Logos, I might call the Logos "she". The trouble, for one thing, is that *Shekinah* is Hebrew for *Sophia*. Philo also uses *Sophia*, and the relations between Sophia and Logos are not quite clear. Besides, I did not want to make him into an early cabbalist. Nor did I think I should make him a Christian by referring to the Logos as "he." Maddeningly, sometimes it sounds very much as if the Logos is a personal being and other times is being described as an aspect of one. Sometimes it is a creature, but sometimes not. I have not dared to try to discern. So the Logos is "it." Although the Loeb's English may sometimes deliberately cultivate an archaic (or perhaps King James version) English, use of it has also forestalled any impulses of mine to render language about God with an eye to medieval metaphysics, and I have thus avoided the final temptation of making Philo into a Thomist or a Scotist.

Author's Foreword

PHILO OF ALEXANDRIA'S LIFE and work have been the object of a number of studies in recent years, especially in the United States and Germany. This interest is due first to the fascination this strange and complex personality continues to cause, with his combination of faith in the Old Testament and Hellenistic culture. It is also due to Philo's testimony about the state of Judaism in the period when Christianity appears—and to the rebirth of lively interest in that environment because of the discovery of the Qumran manuscripts.

But it is odd to see how different authors who have recently dealt with Philo give us conflicting pictures. Hartwig Thyen offered a recent balance sheet of these studies.[1] First of all, there are disagreements about who the man himself was. Völker takes him for a mystic who abandoned the world.[2] Goodenough sees him as an official involved in politics.[3] Wolfson regards him as a philosopher preacher.[4] The same contradictions appear when Philo's writings are interpreted. Völker sees a spiritual exegesis of Scripture without particular speculative concern. By contrast, Wolfson considers the endeavor to be a remarkably coherent philosophical

1. Thyen, "Die Probleme des neueren Philo-Forschung," 230–46.
2. Völker, *Fortschritt und Vollendung bei Philo von Alexandrien*.
3. Goodenough, *The Politics of Philo Judaeus*.
4. Wolfson, *Philo*.

system. Goodenough discovers the transformation of Judaism into a mystery cult.[5] Jonas detects one of the first forms of Gnosticism.[6]

Doubt appears especially in the attempt to situate Philo's fundamental orientation. In the period before 1938, Bréhier,[7] Goodenough, and Pascher[8] see him as the representative of a syncretistic piety with no more than a Jewish coloring. By contrast, Völker and Wolfson present him as a believing Jew, adopting Hellenistic forms of expression. This was already Heinemann's position.[9] Today it seems that Bultmann, Jonas, and Thyen again lean toward a syncretistic interpretation.

The uncertainty seems to stem from this Alexandrian Jew's extraordinary subtlety. We will try to show that first. Many studies appear to commit the error of wanting to look at the work without taking the man into account. Give the prominent position of his family, Philo was in contact with and moved quite easily in widely differing environments. We find him celebrating Passover with the Jewish monks of Lake Mareotis, arguing philosophy at the didaskaleion of Potamo, and negotiating with the Roman Governor Flaccus on behalf of the Jewish community of Alexandria.

Understandably, such flexibility makes him difficult to pin down. Yet the overall sense of his life and of the body of his work leaves no room for doubt. He was passionately devoted to the Jewish community and its faith. His whole activity was dedicated to explaining the Bible to the Jews and defending it before the pagans. Such episodes of his life as we know show him at the service of his brethren in Alexandria.

Yet, this Judaism has no Pharisaical rigidity or zealot fanaticism. Philo is imbued with Greek humanism, with everything the term implies not only about culture but also about good breeding. He is one of the most remarkable products of the παιδεία of his time. His subtle allegories release the faith of his fathers from its Semitic shell to wrap it in the most refined contemporary philosophical forms.

Sometimes that may involve our thinker's showing certain complaisance toward strange doctrines. His enterprise was not risk free. But this Jew of great character and great culture is in no way a syncretist. He enjoys with moderation the bodily goods a refined civilization puts at his

---

5. Goodenough, *By Light, Light.*

6. Jonas, *Gnosis und spätantiker Geist,* 70–121.

7. Bréhier, *Les idées philosophiques et religieuses de Philon d'Alexandrie.*

8. Pascher, Ἡ Βασιλικὴ Ὁδός.

9. Heinemann, *Philons griechische und jüdische Bildung.*

disposition and its intellectual goods with even more moderation. But he takes them for what they are worth, and the absolutely indisputable witness of his work is what he renders to the supreme value of spiritual goods.

Chapter 1

Life of Philo

PHILO THE JEW IS a contemporary of Christ. But he belongs to a completely different world, although not without relation to Christ's world. The life of Christ unfolded within the environment of Palestinian Judaism, among an Aramaic speaking populace that was moved by intense national feeling. By contrast, Philo is the most eminent representative of Diaspora Judaism, specifically in Alexandria, which is the Diaspora's principal home. He was Greek speaking. His citizenship was Roman. A greater contrast is hard to imagine.

By Philo's time the presence of Jews in Egypt was not something recent. Towards the fourteenth century B.C. descendants of Abraham had sojourned there. But after the Exodus nothing seems to have remained of this first group. In fact, the Jewish emigration into Egypt began after the fall of Jerusalem in 681 [sic, translator] and during the following centuries. On the isle of Elephantine vestiges have been found of one of the colonies whose members wrote in Aramaic. But with the foundation of Alexandria, Greek speaking Judaism, properly so-called began. On Josephus's account, Alexander attracted Jews there from the beginning (*Antiquities of the Jews*, XIX, 5, 2).

The colony continued to grow in the last centuries before our era. Philo reports that in his time there were a million Jews in Egypt and one hundred thousand in Alexandria. They lived especially in the Delta quarter to the east of the city. But they were also found in other

1

neighborhoods. When Roman domination replaced the Lagids, the Jews received their own statute and authorization to live according to their customs. They constituted a city apart. They exhibited great loyalty to the Roman Empire. The Empire found support among them, whereas the native population often bore its loss of independence unhappily.

This situation was not unlike that of other Diaspora Jewish colonies. What gave Alexandrian Judaism its peculiar character is that the encounter between Jewish faith and Greek culture took place there. Its most eminent representative is Philo. Alexandria was the center of Greek culture in this period, replacing Athens. Alexandria was where the grammarians edited Homer, Callimacus wrote his poems, and Greek science found one of its great representatives in Euclid.

The Alexandrian Jews adopted this culture, but at the same time they remained loyal to their faith. So their problem was to give that faith Greek expression. This endeavor is embodied above all in the Bible of the Seventy, which would be the foundation of Judeo-Christian Hellenistic literature. We will come back to it. But if the translation of the Bible was the most important manifestation of Alexandrian Jewish literary activity, it is not the only one. Exegetical schools were created where methods of interpretation were applied to the Bible that the Stoics and Pythagoreans applied to Homer. We will also have to discuss that again. To Alexandrian Judaism must be attributed the *Wisdom of Solomon*, which was part of the Alexandrian canon of the Bible. We encounter philosophers like Aristobulus, dramatic authors like Ezekiel the tragedian, and poets like the authors of the Jewish *Sibylline Oracles*.

Philo unites the different aspects of this Alexandrian Judaism within himself: Hellenistic culture, loyalty to Rome, Jewish faith. He belonged to the moneyed high bourgeoisie. We know two of his brothers. The first, perhaps the elder, was an important figure mentioned by Josephus. He was named Caius Julius Alexander. The first two names are characteristic of his Roman citizenship. His birth must be placed around 13 B.C.[1] He was the Alabarch of Alexandria, that is, the person charged by the Roman government with collecting taxes. The protégé of Claudius's mother Antonia, he had ties of friendship with Claudius (Josephus, *Antiquities*, XIX, 5, 1) of whom he was an almost exact contemporary.

His fortune was enormous. Josephus tells us that he furnished the gold and silver to cover the doors of the new Temple of Jerusalem started

---

1. J. Schwartz, "Note sur la famille," 595–96.

by Herod the Great, but unfinished at the time of Christ's death, since the apostles speak of its construction in progress. In 35, when Herod Agrippa I grew bored of life with his uncle Antipas at Tiberiades and needed money to lead a sumptuous existence at Rome, he went to Alexandria to seek out Alexander and borrow a large sum from him. This supposes relations between the Herod family and that of Philo about which we will speak again.

Alexander the Alabarch had two sons, Tiberius Julius Alexander, the elder, is well known.[2] He abandoned the Jewish religion, entered Roman service in 40, and was epistrategus of Syria in 41 and procurator of Judea in 45. Prefect of Egypt under Nero, he repressed a Jewish uprising at Alexandria. He contributed to Vespasian's coming to power. He was second in command of the Roman army during the siege of Jerusalem in 70. Philo mentions him in one of his works, *De Animalibus*. Tiberius Julius was then a cultured young man who had already carried out a mission in Rome. The episode must be situated around 39 before his entrance into Roman service. He must have been about 25. Thus he was born around A.D. 14.

The Alabarch had a second son, Marcus Julius Alexander, undoubtedly born in A.D. 16. He died young in 44. A. Fuks connects him, rightly it seems, with a major Alexandrian exporter of the same name.[3] But Josephus has bequeathed us the most astonishing facet of his biography. He obtained the hand of the Herodian Berenice, daughter of Herod Agrippa I, his father's friend, no doubt thanks to the Emperor Claudius's support. Once more we observe the ties between the families of Philo and of the Herods. As we will explain later on, the episode takes place at Rome in 41, precisely at a time when Philo was there.

Besides the Alabarch, Philo had a younger brother, Lysimachus. He appears in *De Animalibus*, which is a dialogue between two brothers. Schwartz places his birth around 10 B.C.[4] He has often been confused with the Alabarch, as a result of errors in the manuscripts of Josephus. He surely must be identified with one Julius Lysimachus who belonged to the council of the Prefect of Alexandria, Caecina Tuscus. Philo's dialogue informs us that he had a daughter who was betrothed to her cousin Tiberius Julius Alexander.

2. See Goodenough, *The Politics of Philo*, 65–66.

3. Fuks, "Notes on the Archive," 216.

4. Schwartz, "Note sur la famille," 596.

The most interesting point is certainly the connection of Philo's family with the Herod family. The former represented major international Jewish banking, the latter an equally cosmopolitan Jewish aristocracy. The elder Herod, founder of the dynasty, was the kind of oriental kinglet who used to pass part of his life in Rome and there spend his fabulous wealth. One thinks of an Aga Khan. He was connected to Agrippa, Augustus's son-in-law. We will have to speak here especially about his grandson, Herod Agrippa I, and the latter's daughter, the famous Berenice.

For the moment, we only note that the close ties that we observe between the Herods and Philo's family suggest that the two families were related. J. Schwartz assumes this. The connection could only have been through the Hasmoneans, among whom Herod the Great's wife Mariamne was numbered. The link would confirm St. Jerome's report connecting Philo to a priestly line. From that it would follow that the family was Palestinian and that only Philo's father had settled at Alexandria. Support for this is found in the fact, emphasized by Schwartz, of the family's Roman citizenship.[5] This citizenship was impossible for Alexandrian Jews. That implies that Philo's father possessed citizenship before his arrival in the city.

All this data lets us delineate Philo's social and chronological situation with considerable certainty. His birth is often placed around 20 B.C. What we have said allows Schwartz to put it at a latter date.[6] If Alexander the Alabarch was born between 15 and 13, Philo, who came immediately before or after him must have been born around then. Philo seems rather to be the second son. Thus, we can fix his birth around 13 B.C.

Family circumstances might have steered Philo toward business. The highest aspirations were possible for him. From his family's elevated position, he gets a sense of political responsibility. But only at the end of his life do we see him play a role in this order and come into contact with government circles. His interests were directed elsewhere, and primarily toward the philosophical life. His family's position allowed him to get a full education. Frequent allusions in his writings to academic culture, as it was then organized in Alexandria, show that he had passed through all its levels.

He could have been a brilliant rhetorician, the profession at which contemporary culture aimed. But his ideal lay elsewhere. He tells us that

5. Ibid., 601–2.

6. Ibid., 599.

very young "he began to feel the sting of philosophy" (*De Congressu*, 17).[7] He first cultivates grammar, the servant of philosophy, only to prepare himself. Philo identifies with the second of the two great models offered by his contemporary culture, the rhetorician and the philosopher. For him and his contemporaries, philosophy is a conversion. It involves an ascetical effort of detachment that leads to discovering the true meaning of life in the possession of inner goods.

Philo's own testimony confirms that he lead a "philosophical" life.

> There was a time when I had leisure for philosophy and for the contemplation of the universe and its contents, when I made its spirit my own in all its beauty and loveliness and true blessedness, when my constant companions were divine themes and verities, wherein I rejoiced with a joy that never cloyed or sated. I had no base or abject thoughts nor groveled in search of reputation or wealth or bodily comforts, but always seemed to be borne aloft into the heights with a soul possessed by some God-sent inspiration [ἐπιθειασμός], a fellow-traveler with the sun and moon and the whole heaven and universe. Ah then I gazed down from the upper air, and straining the mind's eye beheld, as from some commanding peak, the multitudinous world-wide spectacle of earthly things, and blessed my lot in that I had escaped by main force from the plagues of mortal life (*De Specialibus Legibus* III, 1–2).[8]

This text might have been written by a Platonist of the time, Plutarch for example. It is completely full of Platonic echoes. The divine inspiration, ἐπιθειασμός, recalls the teaching of the *Ion*. The ascension to the heights and participation in the circular movement of the spheres recalls the *Phaedrus*. The observatory, σκοπία, from which one surveys the earthly realm comes from the *Republic* (445 C). All these expressions

---

7. [Translator: this is not in *De Congressu*, 17, which is on *Philo*, IV, 467, nor in other paragraphs whose numbers are likely misprints of 17. Furthermore, *De Congressu* is allegorical and exhortative rather than biographical. In any case paragraphs 17 and 18 do recommend the study of rhetoric and philosophy: "Rhetoric, sharpening the mind to the observation of facts and training and welding thought to expression, will make the man a true master of words and thought, thus taking into its charge the peculiar gift which nature has not bestowed on any other creature. Dialectic is the sister and twin, as some have said of Rhetoric, distinguishes true argument from false and combats the plausibilities of sophistry and thus will heal that great plague of the soul deceit. It is profitable to take them and the like for our early associates and for the field of our preliminary studies."]

8. *Philo* VII, 475, 477.

are found again later in Plotinus, whose resemblances to Philo are striking and still later in the Christian Gregory of Nyssa.

In Philo, as in Gregory, we must not stop at the similarities of expression. Philo gets his way of speaking from Plato. But what he puts
beneath the words is different. For, Philo's God is the God of Abraham.
His mysticism is the outgrowth of Jewish piety. Philo finds the source
of his mysticism not only in the Greek sages he reads, but even more
in his people's religious tradition. Evidently the Bible itself is this source
by which he is primarily nourished. But were there spiritual teachers in
contemporary Judaism who guided him on the path of contemplation?

We know from Philo himself that in his time in Egypt, on the shores
of Lake Mareotis [Mariut], there was a community of Jewish monks, the
Therapeutae. The picture that he gives of their life is remarkable. It is a
valuable document about contemporary Jewish mysticism.

> The houses of the society thus collected are exceedingly sim-
> ple . . . They are neither near together . . . nor yet at a great
> distance . . . In each house there is a consecrated room which is
> called a sanctuary or closet [μοναστήριον], and closeted in this
> they are initiated into the mysteries of the sanctified life . . . They
> keep the memory of God alive and never forget it . . . Twice
> every day they pray, at dawn and at eventide; at sunrise they
> pray for a fine bright day, fine and bright in the true sense of
> the heavenly daylight which they pray may fill their minds. At
> sunset they ask that the soul may be wholly relieved from the
> press of the senses and the object of sense, and sitting where she
> is consistory and council chamber to herself, pursue the quest of
> truth. The interval between early morning and evening is spent
> entirely in spiritual exercise. They read the Holy Scriptures and
> seek wisdom from their ancestral philosophy by taking it as
> an allegory, since they think that the words of the literal text
> are symbols of something whose hidden nature is revealed by
> studying the underlying meaning. They have also writings of
> men of old, the founders of their way of thinking, who left many
> memorials of the form used in allegorical interpretation, and
> these they take as a kind of archetype and imitate . . . (*De Vita
> Contemplativa*, 24–29).[9]

The account of their celebration of the Passover eve, which is the
night before (προέορτος) the great feast, that is to say of the seven weeks
of Pentecost (*De Vita Contemplativa*, 65) is quite remarkable.

9. *Philo* IX, 127, 129.

So then they assemble, white-robed and with faces in which cheerfulness is combined with the outmost seriousness, but before they recline, at a signal from a member of the Rota, which is the name commonly given to those who perform these services . . . Their eyes and hands lifted up to Heaven . . . they pray to God that their feasting may be acceptable and proceed as He would have it. After the prayers the seniors recline according to the order of their admission . . . The feast is shared by women also, most of them aged virgins, who have kept their chastity . . . of their own free will in their ardent yearning for wisdom. The order of reclining is so apportioned that the men sit by themselves on the right and the women by themselves on the left . . . [The couches] are plank beds of the common kinds of wood, covered with quite cheap strewings of native papyrus . . . In this sacred banquet there is, as I have said, no slave, but the services are rendered by free men who perform their tasks as attendants . . . No wine is brought during those days but only water of the brightest and the clearest . . . The table too is kept pure from the flesh of animals; the food laid on it is loaves of bread with salt as a seasoning . . . (*De Vita Contemplativa*, 66–71, 73).[10]

Moreover, this is their ordinary sustenance. They only take it after sundown, having fasted all day (*De Vita Contemplativa* 34). There is no Passover lamb, because they never touch meat.

The President of the company, when a general silence is established . . . discusses some question arising in the Holy Scriptures or solves one that has been propounded by someone else . . . His audience listens with ears pricked up and eyes fixed on him always in exactly the same posture, signifying . . . difficulty by a gentle movement of the head and by pointing with a fingertip of the right hand. . . . Then the President rises and sings a hymn [ὑμνός] composed as an address to God, either a new one of his own composition or an old one by poets of an earlier day who have left behind them hymns in many measures and melodies . . . After him all the others take their turn as they are arranged . . . When everyone has finished his hymn, the young men bring in the tables mentioned a little above on which is set the truly purified meal . . . After the supper they hold the sacred vigil [παννυχίς] . . . They rise up all together and standing in the middle of the refectory form themselves first into two choirs, one of men and one of women . . . sometimes chanting together, sometimes taking up the harmony antiphonally [ἀντιφώνοι], hands and feet keeping time in accompaniment, . . . and rapt with enthusiasm reproduce . . . sometimes the wheeling and counter-wheeling of a choric dance . . . Thus they continue until dawn drunk with the drunkenness in which there is no shame . . . (*De Vita Contemplativa*, 80, 81, 83–84, see also 29, 88).[11]

Philo sees in that "a copy of the choir set up of old beside the Red Sea in honor of the wonders there wrought . . . so filled with ecstasy both men and women, that forming a single choir they sang hymns of thanksgiving to God their Savior, the men led by the prophet Moses and the women by the prophetess Miriam" (*De Vita Contemplativa*, 85, 87).[12] This connection perhaps clarifies the somewhat disconcerting Passover dances. Indeed we know by the Mishnah and already by Jeremiah 31: 3–5 that young Jews dressed in white, danced on the two great feasts of Passover and Tabernacles. Philo's narrative gives us a form of those Passover dances, surely inspired by the choruses of Greek tragedy.

All these details show that Philo had direct knowledge of the Therapeutae. But a wonderful confidence confirms this:

For many a time I have forsaken [καταλιπών] friends and kinsfolk and country and come into a wilderness [ἐρημία], to give my attention to some subject demanding contemplation, and deriving no advantage from doing so, but my mind, scattered or bitten by passion has gone off to matters of the contrary kind. Sometimes, on the other hand, amid a vast throng I have a collected mind. God has dispersed the crowd that besets the soul and taught me that a favorable and unfavorable condition are not brought about by difference of place, but by God who moves and leads the car of the soul in whatever way He pleases (*Legum Allegoriae*, II, 85).[13]

I set aside the testimony about spiritual experience these lines contain. Two things appear in them beyond doubt. The first is that Philo did not ordinarily live away from crowds, and thus that his life ran its course in the midst of them in Alexandria. The second is that he sometimes withdrew into "solitude." Now he describes this solitude in the same terms as that of the Therapeutae. "They flee without a backward glance and leave their brothers, their children, their wives, their parents,

11. Ibid., 163, 165.

12. Ibid., 165, 167

13. *Philo* I, 279.

the wide circle of their kinsfolk, the groups of friends around them, the fatherlands in which they were born and reared . . . And they do not migrate into another city . . . Instead of this they pass their days outside the walls pursuing solitude (ἐρημία)" (*De Vita Contemplativa*, 18–20).[14] Accordingly, it seems quite plausible that Philo spent periods of time among the monks of Lake Mareotis. The exact details that he provides about the Therapeutae confirm that.

While these stays may have been prolonged during his youth, Philo later returned only from time to time. He could not absent himself from the tasks imposed by his position within the Jewish Community at Alexandria. On the one hand, his whole output demonstrates that his life was devoted to commenting on the books of Moses, the Law. The custom of interpreting the Law every Sabbath first developed in Palestine itself. The Gospels give us examples. These commentaries were the origin of the first Christian preaching. This practice spread to Alexandria. Philo alludes to these weekly homilies on several occasions.[15]

As Wolfson has noted, it is quite plausible that Philo gave such lessons: ". . . his writings have the form of sermons or homilies on verses or topics selected from Scripture."[16] The oratorical character of certain passages is evident. Later, St. Ambrose writes homilies inspired by Philo's that are subsequently assembled in continuous treatises. In particular, the collection of Philo's works constituting *Legum Allegoriae* can be included in this the literary genre.[17] They belong to the Haggadic type of moral homily where Old Testament figures are presented as models of virtue. We have similar works at the same period in Palestine in the *Testaments of the Patriarchs*. The *Book of Wisdom* itself already falls within this genre in great measure and has a long homily on Passover.

Thus Philo appears to have been a good preacher, "the founder of the art of preaching as we know it," Wolfson has written.[18] But his importance does not reside exclusively in the quality of his preaching or even in his concern to adapt it to an environment shaped by classical culture. It resides in the philosophical tone given to this predication. For Philo wanted first of all to be a philosopher. The originality of his philosophical

---

14. Ibid., 125.

15. *De Opificio Mundi*, 128; *De Vita Mosis*, 216, etc.

16. Wolfson, *Philo*, I:96.

17. See Thyen, *Der Stil*, 7–11.

18. Wolfson, *Philo*, I:98.

thought has often been overlooked. Wolfson has demonstrated it thoroughly. This originality consists in an attempt to reform traditional Greek philosophy by conforming it to the work of God. And that is done in a way so as to be able to show the superiority of Biblical "philosophy" to pagan philosophy.

At that moment there was a need to establish and teach this Biblical philosophy. Philo indeed found himself in a difficult position, reflected in his work. On the one hand, some Jews continued to confine themselves to completely literal exegesis that was becoming unacceptable to educated minds. But on the other hand, the invasion of Greek philosophy brought its dangers. There was risk of losing sight of the originality of the Biblical message. Philo speaks of the skeptics who identify the story of Iphigenia with that of Isaac. This could lead to apostasy. Philo had the example of his nephew Tiberius. He wanted to show that one could adopt the Hellenic mode of thinking while remaining loyal to Biblical faith.

The *Allegory of the Laws* contains an echo of this philosophical preaching. We can approximate the *Quaestiones* that constitute its survey. The method is still that of Jewish midrash. It is a sustained commentary on Scripture. But the content is philosophical. The union of these two elements is disconcerting. The fragmentary form imposed by the need to follow a historical text keeps the thought's philosophical character from being apparent. Moreover, the exegetes rejected a commentary that continually went beyond the text itself. But that commentary constituted an absolutely original creation, which perhaps made Philo the greatest preacher of his time, in Wolfson's phrase.

The setting for this teaching as well as its form continues to be the Sabbath gathering at the synagogue. Wolfson observes that Philo himself alludes to the Alexandrian Jewish practice of devoting each Sabbath to the "philosophies of the Fathers" as well as problems "related to nature" in the *didaskaleas* (διδασκαλεία) (*De Vita Mosis*, II, 216).[19] This last term may indicate the synagogue itself or an adjoining lecture room. Philo depicts numerous synagogues for us, surrounded by gardens, scattered around Alexandria. But the word *didaskalea* that Clement and Origen pick up is interesting. It shows us synagogue gatherings assimilated to lectures given by philosophers.

This is how Philo appears to us in his maturity: he contains the contrasts of Alexandrian Judaism within himself. He is a believing Jew who

---

19. Ibid., I:79.

faithfully observes the Law, whose fulfillment he defends against pure allegorists. The syncretistic religion that some try to attribute to him is not found in him. But he is not content with fulfilling the letter of that Law. He wants to extract its spirit and nourish his inner life with it. Moreover, he knows the speculations of contemporarily Jews on Genesis. This higher learning, this gnosis is what he seeks. He does so in order to nourish his confreres within the community. Furthermore, he knows how to measure out its teaching according to their level of advancement. In all this, he appears as an eminent rabbi of his time.

But he is a liberal rabbi. He is very open to Hellenistic culture. He is at the opposite pole from the sectarian particularism of certain Palestinian circles. He owes this to his family tradition. He also owes it to his astonishingly open mind. He represents the best in contemporary Alexandrian intellectual circles. He has assimilated all of Hellenistic culture and is a past master in it. He can dispute with Greek philosophers as an equal. His ambition is precisely to show that Jews can rival with Greeks in the very area of culture and thus completely earn their membership in Hellenic civilization.

But, if Jews must be open to the values of Hellenism, it is also necessary to present the eminent worth of the Jewish faith to the Greeks. So Philo's intellectual activity is two-sided. The part of his activity that we have seen is directed to believing Jews. It has an esoteric character. It is carried on within the community. On the other hand, Philo's activity has an apologetic component. He is careful to present the Jewish faith to Greeks so as to make it acceptable. This is what is expressed in other works: *Moses*, the *Explanation of the Laws*, and the *Apology for the Jews*, of which Eusebius has conserved a fragment.

This facet of Philo's activity ought to be situated within the context of Alexandrian Judaism. On the one hand, the Jews were the object of bitter hostility from the Egyptian and Greek pagan population. That hostility was social but also religious in nature. We will return to the particular manifestations of anti-Semitism in Alexandria in which Philo was deeply embroiled. But this hostility was likewise expressed in pamphlets in which the Jewish religion was presented as both crude and dangerous. The story of the patriarchs was ridiculed. The practice of circumcision was mocked. The refusal to worship the city gods was criticized.

This anti-Semitism was in full swing in Philo's time. It is encountered in the priest Cheremon, a Stoic and mystagogue, who was to be Nero's confident. It is particularly represented by the polygraph Apion, whom Philo will encounter again in Rome and who will write a widely circulated pamphlet against the Jews. Flavius Josephus will answer him later in his *Contra Apion*. The attacks are dangerous. They threaten to stir up popular hatred and diminish the standing of the Jews with the authorities. Philo's strives to undermine them. On the one hand, he shows the holiness of the patriarch and the dignity of their customs. That is the precise object of the *Explanation of the Law*. On the other hand, he exalts the greatness of Jewish monotheism, which justifies the refusal to adore gods or emperors.

During this period, therefore, Judaism created a whole apologetic against the pagan religions.[20] In large part Christians of the next generation adopted this apologetic. They were the objects of the same attacks. Celsus will ridicule the story of Jesus. He will accuse Christians of barbaric practices. He will reproach them for disloyalty to the civic cult. Aristides, Justin, Athenagoras, Theophilus, and Origen will take up much of the argumentation of Philo and the Jewish apologists. Paul's speech on the Areopagus already recalls Jewish apologetics. The Christian sibylline oracles pick up themes from the Jewish sibylline oracles.

But to see only a negative apologetic in Philo's exoteric works would be to limit their meaning. The period to which they belong certainly witnesses Jewish proselytism at its peak. The Diaspora appears as the providential measure by which Yahweh is announced to all nations. This attitude reaches its highest expression in Philo. Judaism is presented as the religion of the true God, which all men ought to adopt and which is severed from its national ties. Such cosmopolitanism is very marked in Philo. He accepts the Roman Empire. His ambition is exactly to unite the religion of Israel, Greek culture, and the Roman Empire. He was to attempt on behalf of Judaism what Christianity would achieve four centuries later.

In this matter, Philo's Alexandrian Judaism is far from Palestinian Judaism. For Palestinian Jews, nation and religion are one. The sons of Abraham are the people of God. They bear Rome's political yoke impatiently. This nationalism will grow enormously during Philo's lifetime, animated by the zealots. In the end, even the Essenes will be swept along. The culmination will be the destruction of Jerusalem in A.D. 70. Philo must have had no sympathy for this particularism. It is not by chance that

---

20. Friedländer, *Geschichte der jüdischen Apologetik*, 10ff.; Dalbert, *Die Theologie*.

his nephew Tiberius Alexander is at Titus's side as chief of staff during of the siege of Jerusalem in A.D. 70.

Thus, Philo's apologetic labor bears witness to religious universalism and a deep missionary sense. But for all that, to think he was not concerned with the interests of his people and particularly those of his own community would be to misunderstand his personality. His great moral standing, in particular in pagan circles, and his family connections as well, must have made it difficult for him to avoid involvement in political problems. This went counter to his temperament. Not that he was uninterested in political questions, but he envisaged them on the speculative level. He dreaded direct involvement in practical affairs and having to give up his inclination toward contemplation and study. An appeal to his devotion toward his fellow Jews was required to decide him.

He expressed himself on this painful matter of conscience. After having recalled, in a passage we cited above, how he withdrew into solitude in his youth, he continues:

> But, as it proved, my steps were dogged by the deadliest of mischiefs, the hater of the good, envy, which suddenly set upon me and ceased not to pull me down with violence till it had plunged me in the ocean of civil cares, in which I am swept away, unable even to raise my head above the water. Yet amid my groans, I held my own, for planted in my soul from my earliest days I keep the yearning for culture which ever has pity and compassion for me, lifts me up and relieves my pain. To this I owe it that sometimes I raise my head and with the soul's eye see—dimly indeed because the mist of extraneous affairs has clouded their clear vision—I yet make shift to look around me in my desire to inhale a breath of life pure and unmixed with evil (*De Specialibus Legibus* III, 3–4).[21]

In what period of his life did Philo begin to be introduced to political matters? The text we just quoted seems to indicate that it was fairly early. His literary work indisputably demonstrates wide knowledge of legal affairs. Moreover, this would form part of the attributions of a rabbi. Palestinian rabbis combined edifying exegesis, *Haggadah*, with legal casuistry, *Halakhah*. Whether Philo is linked to these rabbinical traditions is disputed. Heinemann thinks that Philo's legal references relate to Hellenistic law. But that has been challenged. It certainly seems that Philo is a source for the knowledge of contemporary Jewish casuistry.

21. *Philo* VII, 477.

This knowledge of jurisprudence gave Philo a competence that must have marked him for public functions. We have no proof that he exercised as a magistrate in the Jewish community. But Goodenough[22] concludes that he must have been in charge of the legal administration of Alexandrian Jews under imperial control. It may seem difficult to us to reconcile this with his taste for allegorical speculation. But that shows unfamiliarity with rabbinical mentality in which the two aspects were harmonized quite well. David Daube has shown how speculation and casuistry were combined among the rabbis. Also, Philo's complex personality must be recognized. His nostalgia for solitude does not prevent his also having a taste for social life. Perhaps it was not as painful a hardship for him as he seems to tell us.

If we have few details about the beginnings of his political career, at least we are amply informed about its principal episode, the diplomatic mission to the Emperor Caligula with which he was entrusted in order to protest against the acts of violence toward the Jewish community of Alexandria of which the legate Flaccus was guilty. This episode is the subject of two works by Philo, *On the Embassy to Gaius* and *Against Flaccus*. The historian Josephus has narrated the event. It constitutes the most valuable piece of evidence about Philo's life that we possess, because it is situated in A.D. 39. Furthermore, it shows him in contact with Roman circles. It is appropriate to insist on that point.

The episode is situated within the framework of a problem we have not yet raised, the relations between Alexandrian Jews and the native Egyptian population. There was a powerful anti-Semitic current within the latter. It was reinforced by the favor the Roman authorities showed to the Jews. In particular this was the case of Philo's family. We have already mentioned his brother Alexander's relations with the court at Rome for which he was a banker. In addition, he was in charge of collecting taxes at Alexandria. That must not have made him popular among the Egyptian population. But Roman favor ordinarily sheltered the Jewish population from Egyptian harassment.

This had been the policy of Flaccus Avilius, whom the Emperor Tiberius named governor of Egypt around A.D. 32 Philo himself bears witness to Flaccus's good government during his first years. But in 37 a major event, the death of Tiberius and the succession of Gaius Caligula, put his post in danger. Flaccus was part of the entourage of Tiberius. With

22. Goodenough, *An Introduction*, 79.

Caligula, son of Germanicus, another clique acceded to power. Flaccus risked disfavor. Now, at this point something happened which must not have disposed him favorably toward Alexandrian Jews and Philo's family in particular.

This episode involved Herod Agrippa, whose relations with Philo's brother Alexander we have seen. Herod Agrippa was one of Caligula's drinking companions and part of his entourage. That had earned him the disfavor of Tiberius, who imprisoned him. Caligula's accession to the throne meant a change of fortune for Agrippa. Caligula hastened to free him, named him praetor, and gave him his uncle Philip's old kingdom, Abilene, which extends from Chalcis to Damascus in the north of the Trans-Jordan. Agrippa's uncle Herod Antipas was then tetrarch of Galilee. Antipas was also Agrippa's brother-in-law, since he had married his sister Herodias.

Eighteen months after his appointment, Herod Agrippa decided to return to his kingdom. He stopped at Alexandria and stayed at the house of his friend, Philo's brother Alexander. Philo claims Agrippa traveled with great simplicity. But that would be surprising in this personage. It certainly seems that before shutting himself up in his remote kingdom, he could not resist the temptation to dazzle with sumptuosity the Alexandrian friends who had seen his misfortune and had loaned him money. No doubt "the gold and silver buckles" with which his enemies would accuse him of equipping his guards, were not mere legend.

This must not have been at all pleasant for Flaccus. Now that he was on the edge of disfavor, Agrippa's star was rising. However little Agrippa hinted at it, it is understandable that Flaccus was completely bitter. Outwardly, he received Agrippa in the most affable way. That was good politics. But he was totally disposed to take revenge. The pagan population of Alexandria provided him with that revenge. As we have said, this population was hardly favorable to the Jews. The luxury that Agrippa flaunted and his connection to Alexander, who was not popular, were irritants.

Alexandria was the land of mimes. The mimes of Herondas came to us from Alexandria. Agrippa furnished a wonderful subject for the comic writers of his time. Philo tells us: "They spent their days in the gymnasium jeering at the king and bringing out a succession of gibes against him. In fact they took the authors of farces and jests for their instructors and thereby showed their natural ability in things of shame, slow to be schooled in anything good but exceedingly quick and ready in learning the opposite" (*In Flaccum*, 34).[23] These manifestations were reaching their height when the mob seized an innocent lunatic named Carabas and led him to the gymnasium. There, a paper diadem was placed on his head, a mat on his shoulders, a reed in his hand, and the crowd hailed him ironically with the title of king. This scene of derision strangely recalls that of Christ in the pretorium and helps us understand it.

There is no reason to suppose that Flaccus provoked the episode, as Philo suggests. But he surely must have done nothing to prevent it. It is understandable that Philo must have resented the offense. Not only did pagans thus ridicule a Jewish prince, but also the prince was the guest of Philo's brother. The ridicule risked touching Alexander. That can be felt in the report Philo gives about the scene. It is also understandable that he was angry with Flaccus for not having prevented it. "Why did Flaccus show no indignation? . . . For it is evident that if he who could have chastised or at the very least stopped them did nothing to prevent them from acting in this way, they did it with the full permission and consent of him himself" (*In Flaccum*, 35).[24]

In itself the incident was unimportant. But it brought Flaccus close to anti-Semitic elements in the city. That was something new. Now Flaccus's situation was perilous. He could expect nothing from the Jews, partisans of his enemy Agrippa. Support from the city's pagan inhabitants might help him. Some pagan elements hostile to the Jews also saw their advantage in this. Philo names three of them. Denis, about whom we have no other information; Lampon, who was in charge of judicial affairs; and above all Isidore, an intriguer, who headed several secret societies. They pledged their support to Flaccus if he supported them in their attacks against the Jews.

Next began a series of hostile acts against the Jews. The first was a proposal to erect statues to Caligula in synagogues. The idea was astute. The populace's bad reception of his friend Agrippa might antagonize Caligula. This proposal was a clever way of courting him. For Flaccus it was an opportunity to put himself on good terms with Caligula. So he approved the proposal. But it could only be odious to the Jews. "It was," Philo says, "the most abominable infamy." It struck the Jews at their most sensitive point, hatred of idolatry. Their refusal brought closure of the synagogues.

23. *Philo* IX, 321.
24. Ibid.

At that point, Flaccus intervened with an edict in which he declared the Jews foreigners. He was taking a firm position (*In Flaccum*, 8, 53). This edict has provoked heated controversies. Does it mean that the Jews were members of the city, Roman citizens? This is Schürer's thesis. Does it only mean that their residence permits were withdrawn? It certainly seems that the latter hypothesis is correct. The *Letter of Claudius to the Alexandrians* discovered in a papyrus published by Harold Idris Bell seems to demonstrate it.[25] In any case, Flaccus's edict made the Jewish situation completely precarious and put them at the mercy of their adversaries.

Much more was to come. The city of Alexandria became the scene of a veritable pogrom at this point. Philo fixes the date with certainty, noting that it coincided with the mourning prescribed for the whole empire on the occasion of the death of Caligula's sister Drusilla, that is to say, August A.D. 38. The Jews were first driven into one neighborhood, the Delta quarter. Confined in the ghetto, they were dying of hunger. Those who tried to go out were massacred, burned alive, dragged through the streets, or crucified. Women were dragged to the theatre were they were forced to eat pork. Those who refused were put to death.

Far from preventing these abuses, Flaccus encouraged them. He ordered searches to be carried out in Jewish homes to find out whether they had arms. Philo observes that similar searches had been made earlier in Egyptian homes and had turned up results. But nothing was found in Jewish homes. Moreover, the Jews had sent Flaccus a message of congratulation for Caligula, to be transmitted to Rome. That certainly was in 37. But Flaccus, who, at this point, must have been wondering what policy to follow, procrastinated in sending the message forward. When Agrippa came to Alexandria in June 38, Philo complained to him about that and asked him to take charge of making the address reach Rome, explaining the reasons for the delay.

By these maneuvers, Flaccus intended to discredit the Jews along with Agrippa in the Emperor's mind. But he failed to take the latter's standing into account or the Emperor's tenacious grudges. Caligula did not forget that Flaccus belonged to a political clan opposed to him. The maneuvers accomplished nothing. His condemnation was to come. His mandate finished in September 38. Before he set off to give an accounting of his mandate at Rome, Caligula had him arrested at Alexandria during a banquet, by a centurion expressly dispatched from Rome for the purpose.

---

25. Bell, *Jews and Christians in Egypt*, 12–16.

Philo notes that it was the time of the Feast of Tabernacles. That year the Jews were not celebrating because of the persecution against them. But they spent the night in prayer and in the morning, since they no longer had synagogues, they went to the sea shore to glorify God.

Thus ended the dramatic weeks of August–September 38, the most tragic period of Philo's life. They constitute the subject of *In Flaccum*. But in spring 39 another episode in his life will start that is the subject of the *Embassy to Gaius*. The situation of the Jews continued to be precarious. Two major problems concerned them. The first was the presence of the Emperor's statues in their spaces of prayer. The Jews wanted to make it understood that this was incompatible with their faith. The second was their political status. Perhaps they ought to take advantage of the occasion to get themselves granted the rights of citizenship that might have sheltered them from events like those that had just occurred. Lastly, they wanted to give Gaius testimony of their civic loyalty.

So, a delegation was chosen, and Philo was put at its head. This is the clearest evidence of the authority he enjoyed in the Alexandrian Jewish community and allows us to conjecture that his conduct during the pogrom had reinforced his authority even more. Moreover, his family ties to Agrippa and his great culture marked him as the person to establish contact with the court at Rome. The delegation embarked for Italy at the beginning of 40. It must have stayed there until mid 41. So Philo had a long sojourn in Rome at this time. This sojourn was primarily devoted to the mission he had to carry out. But it was also the occasion for contact with intellectual circles in Rome, as we will see.

The mission was particularly difficult. Indeed, Caligula's attitude toward the Jews was in the process of being reversed. He was more and more possessed by megalomania. He demanded divine honors. Philo describes the bizarre manifestations of this state of mind at length. Consequently, Caligula was becoming increasingly hostile toward the Jews, who constituted the chief opposition to his pretensions.

The pagans of Alexandria skillfully took advantage of the Emperor's proclivities. They sent a delegation to Rome at the same time in order to present their point of view. In particular, among its members were two fanatical enemies of the Jews: Isidore, the spokesman of the secret societies, the *thiases*, and Apion, who had published a screed against the Jews to which Flavius Josephus, Agrippa II's friend and historian, would respond. The pagan delegation managed to establish contacts with Caligula's entourage, in particular the Egyptian Helico, who was the Emperor's chamberlain and accompanied him "at hand, to the palestra, to the bath, to the table." He entertained the Emperor with his banter, whose usual butt was the Jews.

So the Jewish ambassadors found the Emperor ill-disposed toward them. After arriving in the spring of 40, they first had to await the return of Caligula, who was in Gaul. The delegates were presented to him at the Campus Martius. He greeted them favorably and had them told that he would receive them. But the audience was put off. Philo, as a person of experience, seeing one after another of the other delegations received, felt that it was a bad sign. The Jews soon understood the reason. One day, when they were at Pozzuoli, accompanying the Emperor's court, always waiting for the audience, the news broke of Caligula's decision to have a statue of himself erected in the Temple at Jerusalem. From that point, everything seemed lost. Was not one of the essential points of their petition the right not to have statues set up in their place of prayer?

Only one possibility was left to the Jewish ambassadors: the influence of Agrippa. This influence had only increased in previous years. His appointment as king of Abilene had irritated his uncle Herod Antipas, who was only tetrarch of Galilee and especially the latter's wife Herodias. They embarked for Rome in August 39. But Agrippa got wind of the matter. He dispatched one of his freedmen, who carried a letter to Caligula in which Agrippa recalled that in 31 Herod Antipas had conspired with Sejanus, who was preparing an uprising against the Emperor. When Antipas appeared, Caligula interrupted him and condemned him for treason. He dethroned Antipas and sent him with Herodias into exile at Lugdunum Convenarum,[26] far from his palace in Tiberiades. Antipas's tetrarchy and fortune were transferred to Agrippa.

Agrippa received the welcome news at Abilene. In 40 he came to see his benefactor. He was at Rome at the same time as the ambassadors from Alexandria. Philo and he met. It is certain that they reflected together on the approach to take. Unhappily, at this moment Agrippa's standing weakened. At the time of the affair of the Jerusalem statue, Caligula sought his advice. This put Agrippa in a tragic dilemma. But Agrippa was a believing Jew. He had the courage to offer the Emperor a defense of the Jewish point of view. Philo has transmitted the long letter Agrippa wrote—in which Philo no doubt collaborated. Caligula was impressed by this frankness. He ordered the statue's installation to be provisionally

---

26. Today Saint-Bernard-de-Comminges in Haute-Garonne.

deferred. But Agrippa's position remained delicate. His dispositions had not changed for all that. He could only give weak support.

The audience finally took place. Philo described it with all the bitterness that it must have caused his wounded dignity. The backdrop was the garden of Maecenas in the proximity of Rome. The ambassadors prostrated themselves before the Emperor. Gnashing his teeth, the Emperor responded: "Are not you those people, enemies of the gods who scorn me and prefer the cult of your nameless God to my cult?" At this he directed a blasphemy at them. Isidore, who headed the Egyptian delegation, lavishing divine titles upon the Emperor, embarked upon fanatical accusations. The Jews exclaimed that they offered sacrifices for the Emperor upon his accession. "You have offered sacrifices for me, but to another. What do your sacrifices matter to me, if they are not directed to me?" answered Caligula.

At the same time, the Emperor continued to visit the villa followed by the unfortunate Jews amid the jokes of the courtiers. After having given orders to the architects, the Emperor turned abruptly to Philo and his companions and asked, "Why do you not eat pork?" This joke provoked general mirth. At the end he asked them to explain their political organization. The Jews began their explanation. But the emperor did not listen and discussed the slabs of rock salt to be placed in the windows. He ended with a less harsh comment: "These imbeciles are more to be pitied than to be blamed."

Philo does not mention his personal role in this audience. But Josephus, who gave us another version, emphasizes it. The text is important, because it is contemporary testimony about Philo. Josephus first emphasizes the accusations made by Apion, who was part of the pagan delegation. Philo assigns the chief role to Isidore. But this does not seem to indicate that there were two audiences. Joseph was especially interested in Apion, against whom he wrote. It was normal for him to underline Apion's role. Philo, by contrast, seems to be more hostile to Isidore.

Accordingly, Josephus writes:

> Many of these severe things were said by Apion, by which he hoped to provoke Gaius to anger at the Jews, as he was likely to be. Philo, the principal of the Jewish embassage, a man eminent on all accounts, brother to Alexander the Alabarch, and one not unskillful in philosophy, was ready to betake himself to make his defense against the accusations; but Gaius prohibited him and bid him begone; he was also in such a rage, that it openly

appeared he was about to do them some very great mischief. So Philo, being thus affronted, went out, and said to those Jews who were about him, that they should be of good courage, since Gaius's words indeed showed anger at them in words, but in reality had already set God against himself (*Antiquities of the Jews*, XVIII, 8, 1).[27]

The fact remained that the mission was headed toward failure. Philo was overwhelmed, so much that, as one can detect in his narrative, he wondered whether he had been clumsy. In any case, he risked having the burden of the failure fall upon him (*Legum Allegoriae*, 46, 369). Their last friends abandoned the Jews, seeing their disgrace. The plight was going to get still worse. Indeed, Caligula ordered the arrest of Philo's brother, Alexander the Alabarch, who was part of the delegation. Alexander was a close friend of Agrippa. The latter had everything to fear.

Then things took a dramatic turn. On January 24, 41, the tribune Chaereas assassinated Caligula. It was a moment of danger. Convoked by the Consuls, the Senate proclaimed the reestablishment of the Republic. The army hailed Caligula's uncle Claudius as emperor. In these circumstances, Agrippa would play a decisive role. It is he who discovered the Emperor's body. To win time he placed it on a bed and declared that the Emperor was still breathing. Then he sought out Claudius and offered his services. He went to the Senate and declared his republican sympathies but asked that Claudius be given their adherence. Sensing that the Senate hesitated, he returned to Claudius and convinced him to proclaim himself Emperor.

At this instant, Agrippa is the leading personality of the Empire. His prestige was at its height. A decree was proposed to the senate to restore the kingdom of his grandfather Herod the Great to him, that is to say, to add Samaria and Judea to what he already possessed. Soon he entered his new capital Jerusalem in triumph. There he met a new problem, Christianity. His grandfather had the Holy Innocents massacred. His uncle had John the Baptist beheaded and sent Jesus back to Pilate with mockery. In 44 Agrippa would have Peter arrested and James beheaded. The Acts of the Apostles describes Agrippa's death, which took place at Caesarea shortly afterwards.

But in January 41 he was at the peak of his glory. His prestige reflected back upon his friends. Alexander was liberated. Was Alexander,

27. *The Life and Works of Flavius Josephus*, 550.

furthermore, not the steward of the possessions of Antonia, mother of the new Emperor? Alexander shared Agrippa's triumph. The connections between the two families became closer through a marriage that constitutes a singular historical nexus. Agrippa gave his daughter Berenice to Mark, the son of Alexander (*Antiquities of the Jews*, XIX 5). Berenice was then thirteen. She enters history with this marriage. It must not have lasted long. Mark having died, she would marry her uncle, Herod of Chalcis. This marriage also must have been brief. At twenty, Berenice was a widow, and would share her kingdom with her brother Herod Agrippa II. The Acts of the Apostles will show her presiding with him over a tribunal that judges St. Paul (Acts 25–26). Then she was to meet Titus.[28]

So Berenice inhabits worlds that we are unaccustomed to combine, Paul's mission, the Empire of the Caesars, Alexandrian Judaism. It is odd for us to think that during that early part of 41, Philo frequently saw the young Jewish princess who was going to become his niece. His situation was now completely reversed. Yesterday the butt of sarcasm at Gaius's court, he became an important figure on the morrow. He must have frequented the highest Roman society. He was part of the Emperor's inner circle. We know well enough that the pious rabbi was a humanist and man of the world to perceive that he found himself perfectly at ease in the new situation.

We have a possible testimony proceeding from the pagan world of Philo's presence in Rome at this date. The treatise *On the Sublime*, so praised by seventeenth century French writers, is well known. This treatise is attributed to the third century rhetorician Longinus. But it has been demonstrated that it was written earlier. Careful studies, in particular those of the great philologist Eduard Norden, have made it possible to demonstrate that it was written in the first century. Certain indicators, among others, praise for the republican regime, even let it be precisely dated in the year A.D. 41.[29]

Now, this treatise contains the first allusion by a pagan author to the Bible. Indeed, a quote from Genesis 9:9 is found in it. The task is to find out through whom the author knew the Book of the Hebrews. At the end of the work, Pseudo-Longinus reports that a philosopher recently questioned him, asking how it happens that in a period so rich in talent, there were so few "natural geniuses." Does not that genius need a

28. See Mireaux, *La reine Bérénice.*

29. Norden, *Genesiszitat.*

climate of freedom and does not tyranny hinder the blooming of genius? Norden has shown that these ideas literally reproduce those of Philo (*De Ebrietate*, 198).

The *Treatise on the Sublime* seems to be very much in the context of the situation of spring 41: it is the period of discussion about the return of the Republic after the excesses of Gaius's tyranny. These questions were discussed in intellectual circles at Rome. Philo was a visible presence in these circles. It is possible that the author of the *Treatise* discussed this with him and that he reports Philo's teaching to us. So, at the time, Philo was in relations with the highest spheres of political and intellectual life. Perhaps in the midst of this worldly life, he felt nostalgia for the desert of Lake Mareotis and for its monks. At any rate, here, we mark the zenith of Philo's career.

It is clear that in these conditions the diplomatic mission must have been completely successful. Moreover, at Alexandria itself the situation had turned around. When they learned of Gaius's death, the Jews had hastened to take up arms—which certainly proves that they possessed some, despite Philo's protestations—and, in their turn, they set about massacring Egyptians and Greeks. Claudius intervened with a series of decrees in which he guaranteed the Jews their rights while inviting both sides to live in peace henceforth. It is certain that Agrippa and Philo inspired these texts. Indeed, they represent the very object of their mission.

The first is an edict that Josephus has preserved, which may date from mid-41 (*Antiquities of the Jews*, XIX, 52). The Emperor recalls that the coexistence of Jews and Alexandrians is of long standing, that the Emperors have recognized the civic rights of both, and that they have acknowledged the right of the Jews to observe their customs. He alludes to the uprising of the Alexandrians against the Jews under Caligula and condemns the latter's attempts to have himself worshipped as a god. He demands that the traditional rights of the Jews be restored and that both sides remain in peace.

Subsequently to that first text, Claudius received delegations of both Jews and pagans coming from Alexandria. He had to listen to complaints from both sides. A second text from 42 is the *Letter to the Alexandrians*, discovered in 1921 and published by Harold Idris Bell.[30] It refers to the Egyptian delegation whose eleven members are named. The first part authorizes the erection of statues and chariot scenes at Al-

---

30. Bell, *Jews and Christians in Egypt*, 23–26.

exandria in honor of the Emperor. But the Emperor asks that no temple be built to him and that there be no high priests devoted to his cult. That is a reaction against Caligula.

The second part alludes to the pogrom of A.D. 38 the Emperor has heard the explanation of the delegation and of the opposing side. This shows that the Jews had also sent a delegation. Claudius exhorts the Alexandrians to live in peace with the Jews and threatens punishments if they begin to persecute them again. He particularly affirms their right to practice their religion. Furthermore, explicitly referring to the counter-attack of A.D. 41, he demands that the Jews be content with the rights that have been acknowledged as theirs, to send no more delegations beside the official delegation, and to live in peace with others.

Thereafter, Claudius showed he had decided to pass from words to deeds. Some years later the Alexandrians made new attempts against the Jews. Again the leaders were Lampo and Isidore. They were summoned to Rome and judged in the presence of Claudius. They tried to place the blame on Agrippa II, son of Herod Agrippa and brother of Berenice. We have rediscovered the papyrus that contains the Acts of this proceeding. Herbert Musurillo has edited them.[31] The trail ends with a death sentence for the two Egyptians. The relentless adversaries of Philo and the Alexandrian Jews saw their careers end tragically. Flaccus had perished. Philo could thus judge that the God of the Jews avenged his persecuted servants.

After his finally successful mission, Philo returned to Alexandria at the end of A.D. 41. We can imagine the reception he received. He had been the savoir of the Jewish community. It remained for him to finish this labor by drawing a lesson from it. It is then that he wrote *In Flaccum*, presumably dedicated to the new Roman governor of Alexandria and the *Legatio ad Gaium* addressed to Claudius. In his fashion, the Christian Apologists of the following century addressed their books to the Emperor. Philo was then over sixty. We know nothing of his last years or of the date of his death.

31. Musurillo, *The Acts of Pagan Martyrs.*

Chapter 2

Philo and His Time

PHILO'S BIOGRAPHY HAS SHOWN him at the crossroad of Judaism, Hellenism, and Roman civilization. We now pose the question of discovering what he knew in these three areas. We begin by seeing how many tendencies collide in the Jewish world, whether Palestinian or Hellenistic. This late Judaism is simultaneously a period of messianic Zealots and cosmopolitan Herodians, of Pharisaic legalism and Essene pietism. We witness an apocalyptic strain flourish there at the same time as the Gnostic interpretation of Genesis. Similarly, many tendencies see the light of day in Greek philosophy. It is a time of eclecticism, as Cicero had shown half a century earlier: Stoicism, Platonism, and Aristotelianism combine in various proportions. Lastly, at the political level, this is a period when the imperial ideology is elaborated but also of republican revolts.

It would be an impossible task to attempt to draw of picture of such a complex world. Equally, it would be meaningless. What matters to us is what Philo in fact deemed important. Thus, as Wolfson has clearly shown, pagan religious trends affected him little. His Jewish faith makes him impermeable to them. He spoke of them only to criticize. To learn what he knew, the best thing is to query him. We ask ourselves which contemporary tendencies he discussed. It happens that there is a group of his works that precisely set out less his ideas than those of his time. These works will be our sources here. We will see what Philo tells us about Jewish pietism, Greek philosophy, and Roman politics.

Philo and the Essenes

The core of Philo's thought is indisputably Biblical. Almost all of his output is Scriptural commentary. He uses the Greek Septuagint translation done at Alexandria itself during the previous centuries. These Biblical sources of Philo's thought are not what interest us for the moment. We will devote a long study to them as well as to the exegetical methods that he found at Alexandria. Our goal is different now. We want to discover what Philo knew about contemporary Judaism. This is the question we put to him. Indeed Philo spoke of Judaism. He wrote an *Apology for the Jews* of which Eusebius has given us important fragments. In the book *Every Good Man is Free*, he presented his ideal of Judaism in contrast with the wise men of Persia, India, and Greece. He devoted two short works to the active and contemplative lives. In all these works, we come up against a massive reality: when Philo wants to present ideal Judaism, he talks about the Essenes.

Moreover, we are also shown the reverse of the coin. Philo's works are very meager in their treatment of other tendencies within contemporary Judaism. We find no echo of the theology of history that was developing an apocalyptic vision, whether in Palestine with contemporary works like the Assumption of Moses or at Alexandria itself with Book II of the Sibylline Oracles, which is slightly earlier than Philo. Remarkably, we find very few traces of the tradition to which the Pharisees adhered that would lead to the *Mishnah* and the *Midrashim*. Heinemann has shown that Philo's legal concepts come from the Greco-Roman environment rather than from the Scribes' *Halakhah*. In Philo we find very few of the edifying elaborations of sacred history that constitute the *Haggadah* that fill a contemporary Jewish current that ranges from the Book of Jubilees to the book of antiquities of Pseudo-Philo.

Thus, for him, the Essenes represent the ideal of contemporary Judaism. We can say that his Judaism has three components: the Greek Bible with its Alexandrian exegesis, Herodian society, and Essene pietism. These three components constitute more of a whole than it might seem. Indeed, as we have already noted, the Herodian circle had geographical contact with the Essenes of Qumran and, furthermore, seemed to be more compatible with these pious monks than with Sadducee politicians or zealot agitators. At the end of his two reports on the Essenes, Philo himself notes that they were protected by even the most despotic of the princes. This is an evident reference to the Herods.

In the first chapter we spoke of contacts with the Herods. In the next one we will speak of Philo's place in Alexandrian exegesis. What interests us here is his testimony about Essene pietism, and we will study this testimony first. Then we will contrast it with the testimony of the Qumran manuscripts. Lastly, we will ask whether Philo's works shows Essene influence. But first we face a preliminary question about the value of Philo's testimony. Indeed, certain authors judge that the depiction of an ideal Judaism in his report has no connection to a particular historical reality. Yet, since he is the first Greek author to speak of the Essenes and the first to give them that name, which is not found in the Dead Sea scrolls, his testimony is of great importance. We must examine the reasons why it is disputed.

The last author to have done so is Henri del Medico. "The Essenes, as Philo called them, would have lived in Palestine. What did he know about them? Philo was born in Alexandria about 30 B.C. [?], and although he did not know Hebrew [?], was named ethnarch [?] by his Greek-speaking coreligionists in Egypt. He left Egypt for the first time at the age of seventy [?], when he had to go to Rome to defend the interests of the community before Caligula. Philo was never in Palestine [?]. Even the short stay in Jerusalem upon his return from Rome is rather hypothetical. Philo seems to make up the virtuous Essenes out of the whole cloth [?]"[1]

In the passage I have marked all the inexactitudes with which the text abounds, the central point that concerns us is that Philo was only in Palestine after his return from Rome, therefore in 41 when he was seventy. Now the text that mentions his stay in Jerusalem is *De Providentia II*; it is related to *De Animalibus*, which is the work of Philo whose date is best established. It is situated around 35. Thus the voyage is earlier. Moreover, Philo, who was really born around 13 B.C., was about forty at the time. Let us add that there is no reason to believe it was his first trip to Jerusalem. Given the attraction Jerusalem exerted at the time of the great feasts, the proximity of Alexandria in relation to Ascalon, the great wealth of Philo, whose brother was a ship-owner, and his ties to the Palestinian Herods, it would be very strange that he should have had no occasion to go to Palestine.

---

1. Medico, *L'enigme des manuscrits*, 79; see 79–81.

There is no reason for us to question Philo's testimony. This is the first point established. But not all the difficulties have been resolved in the identification of the Essenes whom Philo mentions with the Qumran Zadokites. We must, therefore, examine what Philo says. I take the reference of *Quid Omnis Probus Liber Sit*. It begins with three extraordinarily specific indications. The Essenes (Ἐσσαῖοι), as Philo calls them, number around 4000. This indication is valuable in regard to the situations of the Essenes in the time of Christ, which is what Philo describes. It is implausible that it is fictitious. Philo next explains that the name Ἐσσαῖοι that he gives them transcribes an untranslatable Hebrew word that indicates holiness (*Quod Probus*, 75). This indication is also very precise. In fact Ἐσσαῖοι seems to be the transliteration into Greek of the Aramaic *hasa*, which means *pious*, and corresponds to the Hebrew *hasid*.[2] *Essenes* and *Hasidim* are parallel expressions that designate faithful Jews since the second century B.C. This incidentally allows us to observe that Philo certainly knew Hebrew, as Marcus observes.

Philo continues by observing: [they] "have shown themselves especially devout in the service of God, not by offering sacrifices of animals, but by resolving to sanctify their minds" (*Quod Probus*, 75).[3] This passage is one of the most interesting of the report. It contains the observations that the Essenes did not offer bloody sacrifices in the temple but a spiritual sacrifice, which was their priesthood. We first note the last feature, which is an allusion to the priestly origin of the ascetics. What other allusions are there? It was thought that there was a similar condemnation of sacrifices in the *Manual of Discipline*, IX, 3–5. But a better reading of the text excludes this interpretation.[4] There still remains Josephus's affirmation that the Essenes abstained from offering sacrifices in the Temple (*Antiquities of the Jews*, XVIII, 1, 5). Consequently, two things must be distinguished in Philo's text. On the one hand, he observes the fact that the Essenes do not offer sacrifices in the temple. That is completely certain. On the other hand, he interprets this fact as a spiritualization of the cult. That is his personal theory.

Philo next tells us that the Essenes live "in villages" outside the cities. The word κωμηδόν is important. It does not mean that the Essenes were scattered throughout towns, but that they consituted settlements of

---

2. Marcus, "Pharisees, Essenes, and Gnostics," 157.

3. *Philo* IX, 55.

4. See Carmignac, "L'utilité ou l'innutilité," 524–32.

people living together. That can refer to a built up area like Qumran, but it doubtless means that others existed. In any case the essential point is that they lived away from the rest of the Palestinian population, "for they know," Philo tells us, "that their contact would have a deadly effect upon their own souls" (*Quid Probus*, 75).[5] Now, this exactly corresponds to one of the essential themes of the Qumran manuscripts, radical separation of the community from the rest of the people of Israel, considered to be contaminated (*Manual of Discipline*, V, 10, 13–20).

What follows concerns the Essene way of life. Some worked the land or as artisans. They did not seek wealth and lived modestly. They did not make arms or trade. They had no slaves (*Quod Probus*, 76–79). In Philo's eyes, it will be observed, this life of work distinguishes the Palestinian Essenes from the Therapeutae of Egypt. Now this is just what the Qumran documents show us. There is mention of work in the fields and care for flocks (*Damascus Document*, X, 20; XI, 6–7). The document condemns manufacture and commerce (*Damascus Document*, XII, 7–12). By contrast, slaves are explicitly mentioned at least in the *Damascus Document* (XI, 12; XII, 10).

Concerning Essene doctrine, Philo observes: "as for philosophy they abandon the logical part" except in "that which treats philosophically of God and the creation of the universe." By contrast, "the ethical part they study very industriously" (*Quod Probus*, 80).[6] This text is valuable to inform us about what Philo knew of Essene doctrines. On the one hand, he was struck by the interest in moral problems. That completely coincides with the *Manual of Discipline* and the Damascus documents. But the other expression is more odd. The issue is what concerns "the origin of the universe." That seems to me to allude to Greek speculation about the opening of Genesis that would certainly appear to have existed in Judea and may have especially flourished among the Essenes. Further on, we will see that Philo seems to have inherited certain elements of Essene Gnosticism. By contrast, he says nothing about the Messianism and eschatology that have such a large place in the Qumran documents.

Liturgical gatherings take place mainly on the Sabbath, but Bible study is daily. This corresponds to the Qumran regulations. Everywhere that there are ten members, there will be one who studies the law continually." (*Manual of Discipline*, VI, 6–7). Philo notes that there is an order of

5. *Philo* IX, 55.
6. Ibid., 57.

precedence in liturgical gatherings and rules setting down the comportment to be followed (*Quod Probus*, 81). That is one of the points upon which the *Manual of Discipline* insists most. (*Manual of Discipline*, VI, 9–13). A considerable number of rules concern the behavior to be followed during meetings: not interrupt, nor fall asleep, nor spit, nor laugh, nor leave (*Manual of Discipline*, VII, 9–14). Philo's expression seems to sum up this whole part of the legislation.

The program of Essene moral teaching that Philo presents includes "piety, holiness, justice, domestic (οἰκονομία) and civic (πολιτεία) conduct, knowledge of what is truly good, or evil, or indifferent, and how to choose what they should and avoid the opposite, taking for their defining standards these three, love of God, love of virtue, love of men" (*Quod Probus*, 83).[7] This greatly resembles the program proposed at the beginning of the *Manual of Discipline*. One must "practice truth, justice, and law" (I, 5). Good actions and bad actions are described (I, 3). One must withdraw from all evil and adhere to every good work (I, 4–5). The program consists of seeking God (I, 1), practicing the precepts (I, 7), and loving all the Sons of Light (I, 9). In both cases, we have seen this elementary catechesis based on the theme of the two ways and the two commandments that will persist in primitive Christian catechesis and that seems typically Essene.

The details of the precepts present striking points of contact: the state of purity in relation to other people is to be noted (*Quod Probus*, 84; *Manual of Discipline*, VI, 16), which is one of the clearest characteristics and emphasizes the separation from the world. The description of common life is especially important. No one has anything, house, storeroom, money, or clothing, which is not common (*Quod Probus*, 85–86), Now, that is one of the most distinguishing characteristics of Qumran and prevents us from finding, as del Medico does, a description of the Jewish community in general in the portrait of the Essenes (*Manual of Discipline*, VI, 19–20). The *Manual of Discipline* specifies that goods and wages are to be handed over to the treasurer (VI, 19–20). This is another of Philo's reports in the *Apology* in the exact terms: "Each branch when it has received the wages of these so different occupations gives it to some person who has been appointed [ταμίᾳ]" (*Pro Iudaeis*, XI, 10).[8]

7. Ibid., 59.

8. Ibid., 441.

It will be noted that on this occasion Philo observes that the Essenes dwell together "in communities" (κατὰ θιάσους) (*Quod Probus*, 85).[9] The word also appears in the *Apology*: "They live together formed into clubs, bands of comradeship with common meals [κατὰ θιάσους ἑταιρίας καὶ συσσίτια] (*Pro Judaeis*, XI, 5).[10] The Qumran manuscripts again allude to these meals in common (*Manual of Discipline*, VI, 1–4). These communities are likewise designated by the term ὅμιλος (*Apology* XI, 1).[11] Ralph Marcus shows that these terms, which neither Philo nor Josephus employ for other Jewish sects, seem to translate the Hebrew *yahad*, which frequently appears in the Dead Sea Scrolls to indicate the Qumran community.[12] The terms seem to demonstrate that the Essenes had a completely special character, precisely this very close common life, which was that of the Qumran community.

Two frequently misunderstood expressions of Philo also seem to refer to this common life. Philo explains that the Essenes are taught civil life (πολιτεία) and economic life (οἰκονομία) (*Quod Probus*, 83). Lagrange translates this as "family life and civil life."[13] We cannot see what the first translation corresponds to, because Philo does not speak of marriage among the Essenes. In reality, these two phrases, which are part of a brief summary that Philo gives of the *Manual of Discipline,* seem to us to designate two of its parts. Πολίτεια is the totality of the rules concerning the relations of the members of the community among themselves, and οἰκονομία is the rules concerning the use of material goods. We could translate them by "rules of obedience and poverty."

Philo's report ends with a final detail whose exact equivalent is found again in the *Manual*. Philo notes the care that is taken with the sick and the aged who are under the community's charge. Now, the *Damascus Document* contains identical prescriptions. A tax is deduced from salaries to be paid to the common fund (XIV, 13). The goal is to come

---

9. Ibid., 59.

10. Ibid., 439.

11. Ibid., 436.

12. Marcus, "Philo, Josephus and the Dead Sea *Yahad*," 205–9.

13. Lagrange, *Le judaïsme au temps du Christ*, 209. [Translator: I have not been able to find this book. Marie-Joseph Lagrange is author of *Le judaïsme avant Jésus-Christ*. Joseph Bonsirven is author of *Le judaïsme palestinien au temps de Jésus-Christ*; *Palestinian Judaism in the Time of Jesus Christ*, translated by William Wolf. A book by Henri Daniel-Rops with a somewhat similar title is later than Daniélou's study of Philo.]

to the assistance "of the poor and the indigent," of the "elderly," of those affected with leprosy, of "those who have been captives in a foreign land" (XIV, 14–16). Here too the specificity of the report in Philo is such that it practically excludes doubt. Again it emphasizes the group's communal character described both by Philo and the manuscripts.

Such are the data in *Quod Probus*. They attest to Philo's exact knowledge of the Qumran community. The information in the *Apology for the Jews* mostly repeats them, adding particular details like the distinction between winter and summer garments (XI, 12), or the indication of raising bees and tending flocks among practical trades (XI, 8). But on one point it adds a very important characteristic: the explicit affirmation that the Essenes do not marry (XI, 14). The fact that there are no children or adolescents among them can be linked to that. The point is quite unusual. Josephus and Pliny will both observe it. Now, according to the *Damascus Document*, the Zadokites have wives and children (V, 6–7; VII, 6–9). *The Manual of Discipline* says nothing about the matter. Investigations carried out at the Qumran cemetery certainly seem to show that women are buried there.

This leads us to observe that, besides indisputable overall similarities, there are notable differences in the description of the community between Philo and the Qumran manuscripts. They are of two kinds and come under two explanations. On the one hand, we have seen that Philo's *Quod Probus* presents several characteristics that the manuscripts do not, ones that highlight the rigor of the communal regime: prohibition of all oaths (84) and prohibition of slaves. The *Apology* adds celibacy and exclusion of adolescents and children. Now these features contradict what the *Damascus Document* says permitting oaths (IX, 8–16; XVI, 6–12), mentioning slaves, talking about children, and showing us married people. Still it must be noted that the *Manual of Discipline* says nothing of slaves, celibacy, oaths, or children.

That implies differences of time period and orientation. If, as seems plausible, the *Manual of Discipline* shows us the earliest state of the community, we can say that the community subsequently split into two movements. The larger one is that which the *Damascus Document* and Josephus mention. The other, more strict, is what Philo discusses in *Quod Probus*, but it still does not seem to acknowledge an obligation to celibacy when Philo was writing his work. By contrast, it existed after 41 when he wrote the *Apology for the Jews*. Josephus knew this last state. Therefore, it would seem that celibacy appeared late.

This poses the question of knowing what influenced its appearance. If we recall that we are dealing with a period around 40, and if we wonder what influences might give rise to the ideal of virginity in Palestine at that date, it certainly seems that there could only be one, Christianity. That would lead us to think that in Palestine there were mutual influences between Christianity and Essenism at this date.[14] From that might follow the odd consequence that Eusebius was not completely wrong when he believed he recognized Christians in the Essenes described by Philo and Josephus. Indeed, those whom the former's *Apology for the Jews* and the latter's work describe might already have undergone Christian influence. But in this period, Christians and Essenes must not have been so easy to distinguish in outward appearance to a stranger to Palestine.

We can ask whether two other characteristics that differentiate the *Apology for the Jews* from *Quod Probus* may likewise refer rather to Christians than to Essenes so that in the *Apology* we would have a testimony about what Philo tried to say at the end of his life about the development of Christianity in Palestine, which from a distance he confused with Essenism. *Quod Probus* told us that the Essenes fled cities and lived in villages (κωμηδόν) and that they numbered 4000 in all. Now the *Apology for the Jews* shows them as "dwelling in many cities of Judea and also many villages where they form numerous large communities (πολυανθρώπους)" (XI, 1). Living in cities is absolutely opposed to Essene practice. By contrast it describes Christians. Moreover, major growth of the Essenes in this period is not very likely. Their community in fact was pulled in two directions. The Zealots, on the one hand, sweep them along in the revolt against Rome, as Josephus testifies: a sign of this can be seen in the *Apology*'s no longer mentioning the pacifism to which *Quod Probus* bears witness. On the other hand, they were drawn into the Christian orbit, if we are to believe with Cullman that the numerous priest converts mentioned in Acts 6: 7 are Zadokites.

The other characteristic that separates the *Apology for the Jews* from *Quod Probus* is the affirmation that entry into the community is not by birth but free choice (*Pro Iudaeis*, XI, 2). That is why he adds: "Thus no Essene is a mere child nor even a stripling or newly bearded, since the characters of such are unstable" (*Pro Iudaeis*, XI, 3).[15] This does not square with the Zadokites: the community was composed of priestly

14. Daniélou, *Les manuscrits de la Mer Morte*.

15. Philo IX, 439.

families. By contrast, the characteristic seems to correspond to the Christian affirmation that race is not important and that entrance into the community depends only of free choice. Accordingly, the difference between the *Apology* and *Quod Probus* pose a curious problem whose most satisfactory explanation is that there is a reference to Christianity.

With this we have not yet finished with the question posed by the comparison of the information from Philo and the Qumran manuscripts. Indeed, if they describe a community, they at least equally testify to the presence of an eschatological tendency. God sent the Master of Justice to announce that the end of time, foretold by the prophets, had begun. The community left for the desert to prepare itself for the imminent last judgment. The coming of the Messiahs of Aaron and Israel would be its first sign. Then the pagans would be annihilated and the people of God exalted. Now all this—the eschatological expectation, theology of history, messianic tendencies, national exaltation—are totally absent from Philo's information. The practices described are the same, but the spirit is totally different. How are we to admit that Philo could have modified things to this degree?

Yet, this is the solution that imposes itself on us for various reasons. First, there are reasons of prudence. Philo speaks about the Essenes in apologetic writings directed to pagans. He wants to present the Jews in an attractive manner. It is clear that the Zadokite apocalyptic spirit would disconcert and perturb the pagans. Besides, partisan of the Roman Empire that he is, Philo has no sympathy for this facet of the Zadokites. He detests their nationalism. He is not unaware of the notion of an eschatological judgment, but it is foreign to his thought: his ideal is inner. Consequently, it must be admitted that here Philo deliberately sets aside the whole eschatological component of the Zadokite community to retain only its moral characteristics.

One last question remains. Does the rest of Philo's work testify to knowledge of Essene doctrines? We know that the most characteristic Essene doctrine is that of the two spirits, of truth and of iniquity created by God at the beginning and presiding over all human history (*Manual of Discipline*, III, 18–19, IV, 15). These two spirits are mingled in each human. According to whether a person follows one or the other, he places himself in the army of light or of darkness. Here we are not merely dealing with the idea of inner struggle that sets the tendencies of good and evil against each other in the human heart. This last doctrine is that of the two *yeser*, which is found in Judaism before the Essenes.

But what seems peculiar to them is attaching each *yeser* to a spiritual power and attributing to God the establishment of the latter from the beginning. On this point it is difficult to avoid seeing an influence of Iranian magi on the Essenes.

This doctrine is foreign to the totality of Philo's work. As we will see, his angelology is not dualist. It is most unusual to find a text in his work where there is such pronounced dualism. The question arises of knowing whether the text is an allusion to Essene doctrine.[16] It is found in *Quaestiones in Exodum* (I, 23). "Into every soul at its very birth, there enter two powers [δυνάμεις], the salutary [σοτερία] and the destructive [φθοροποιός]. If the salutary one is victorious and prevails, the opposite one is too weak to see. And if the latter prevails, no profit at all or little is obtained from the salutary one."[17] This first part affirms the presence from the start of two opposite powers put by God in man's heart. This doctrine may be Essene. It is found again in Christian works influenced by the Essenes like the Shepherd of Hermes.

But the continuation is still more odd:

> Through these powers [δυνάμεις] the world too was created. People call them by other names: the salutary (power) they call powerful [*potens?*] and beneficent [εὐργετικός];[18] the opposite one (they call) unbounded [*immensa?*] and destructive [κολαστική]. Thus the sun and moon, the appropriate positions of the other stars and their ordered functions, and whole heaven together come into being and exist through the two (powers). And they are created in accordance with the better part of these, namely when the salutary and beneficent (power) brings to an end the unbounded and destructive [κολαστική] nature. Wherefore also to those who have attained such a state and a nature similar to this is immortality given. But the nature is a mixture of both (these powers), from which the heavens and the entire world as a whole have received this mixture. Now sometimes the evil becomes greater in this mixture and hence (all creatures) live in torment, harm, ignominy, contention, battle, and bodily illness together with all the other things in human life, as in the whole world, so in man.[19]

16. See Daniélou, "Démon," columns 163–65.

17. *Philo, Supplement* II, *Quaestiones et Solutiones in Exodum*, 32–33.

18. Ibid., 32. Colson is mistaken in not recognizing here the ordinary expressions in Philo for the δυνάμεις that surround God.

19. Ibid., 33. [Translator: In this passage, the words in round parentheses are from

In any case, this difficult text affirms parallelism between the action of two hostile powers in the cosmos and their action in man. Here two problems must be distinguished. The idea of the two powers established by God at the beginning recalls the *Manual of Discipline*. We observe that Philo seems to assimilate this doctrine to that of the powers who surround God that is familiar to him. We can connect this to *Quaestiones in Exodum*, II, 68, where Philo teaches that the favorable power whose proper name is Benevolent (εὐεργετικός) is subordinated to the creative power and that the legislative (νομοθετική) power is joined to the royal (βασιλική) power. See also *De Sacrificiis Abelis et Caini*, 38, 131–33. These similarities assure the passage's Philonic authenticity. But the doctrine of powers in our text still has a dualistic character foreign to Philo's overall work.

Moreover, the action of the two opposing powers not only in human souls and in history but also in the cosmos has no equivalence in Essene doctrine. By contrast, it has striking similarity to the doctrine we find in Plutarch, a pagan author slightly posterior to Philo. In *De Iside et Osiride* Plutarch explains: "nothing that is in nature is free from mixture and everything comes to us from two opposed principles" (45). He shows this is common to several traditions. He mentions Iranian dualism, the benevolent and malevolent influence of the stars in the Chaldeans, the different Greek dualisms, the two souls in Plato's *Laws*. Then he adds, "I will devote myself to reconciling the theology of the Egyptians and Plato's teaching" (*De Iside et Osiride*, 48). He then interprets Osiris as the source of all that "the earth, wind, water, sky, and stars is orderly, constant, and salutary, and Typho with all that is perishable and harmful in the body of the universe, irregularities and seasonal bad weather, solar eclipses, the occultation of the moon" (*De Iside et Osiride*, 49).

It is not that Plutarch is the source of our passage. By contrast, it is very plausible that Philo and he applied the same procedure, one to the exegesis of the Bible and the other to the exegesis of Egyptian myths, and that they used lecture notes where different dualist interpretations of philosophers and religious traditions were brought together. Indeed, several characteristics of Philo's text recall that of Plutarch. One of the titles of the harmful power is *immensa*, which seems to translate ἄπειρος. Now, Philo's text says that for Anaxagoras and Pythagoras the source of evils is the ἄπειρον (48). The reference to heavenly disorders with the mention of solar eclipses (κρύψεις), occultation of the moon (ἀφανισμοί),

---

Marcus's translation; those in square brackets are from Daniélou's text.]

seasonal bad weather (ἀωρίαι) is met again amid textbook arguments against Providence in *De Providentia* II, 71, another of Philo's works about which we will speak below. It certainly seems that Philo alludes to Greek philosophical doctrines here.

The continuation confirms it: "This mixture [μῖξις] is in both the wicked and the wise man, but not in the same way. For the souls of foolish men have the unbounded and destructive rather than the powerful and salutary (power), and it is full of misery when it dwells with earthly creatures. But the prudent and noble (soul) rather receives the powerful and salutary (power) and, on the contrary, possesses in itself good fortune and happiness, being carried around with the heaven [μετεωροπορῶν], because of kinship [συγγένεια] with it."[20] These last expressions allude to Plato's *Phaedrus* and are frequent in Philo. But here again, he evidently uses a source alien to his thought. The idea of the family relationship of the soul with the heavens, likewise the idea that destinies are determined by the proportion of good and evil in the soul are foreign to Philo's thought—and also to Essene doctrine.

By contrast, the conclusion brings us back to the introduction: "The force which is the cause of destruction strives, as it were, to enter the soul, but is prevented by the divine beneficences [θέιαι εὐεργεσίαι], from striking (it), for these are salutary. But those from whom the favors and gifts of God [αἱ τοῦ θεοῦν τοῦ χάριτες] are separated and cut off suffer the experience of desertion and widowhood."[21] Here again we find the Essene idea of the two spirits disputing for the soul and the soul opening itself to one or the other. Thus, it seems that the strange passage has two sources, both alien to Philo: on the one hand, the Essene explanation of the two spirits and their action upon the soul; on the other, a dualistic philosophical explanation proceeding from Egyptian philosophical schools. Once again, it seems here that Philo has retained a moral trait of Essene teaching but has divorced it from its eschatological context and replaced that context with a cosmological explanation.

The Philosophers of Alexandria

Philo interpreted the Bible with the categories of Greek philosophy. Thus, our problem is to find out what this philosophy is. This is not

20. *Philo* X, 33–34.

21. Ibid., 34.

accomplished easily. Pohlenz devoted a chapter to Philo in his book on Stoicism. Wolfson views Philo as a Platonist. Wendland ties him to Aristotle. Festugière is satisfied to speak about eclecticism. In that, Philo is certainly the reflection of the period of the early Empire to which he belongs. Schools tended to be confused with each other following a trend that began in the previous century. Posidonius had opened classical Stoicism to Platonic influences. Antiochus of Ascalon had integrated Stoic and Aristotelian elements into Platonism. These diverse influences persist into Philo's period.

Nevertheless, certain currents can be distinguished. Stoicism, properly speaking, seems to hold sway at Rome. Seneca is its chief representative. With him, it deliberately assumes a moralistic orientation that Epictetus and Marcus Aurelius will take up again. But Seneca is a little younger than Philo. The Stoicism exactly contemporary to Philo is more oriented toward religious traditions and their symbolic interpretation. This is interesting, because we find a similar tendency in Philo. Two names in particular must be mentioned. The first is that of the African Cornutus, who lived in Rome under Tiberius and Claudius and was the teacher of the poets Perseus and Lucan. We possess his *Greek Theology*, which is a symbolic interpretation of mythological data.

For us, Chaeremon is the most interesting figure, because he is Alexandrian. Egyptian in origin, he was head of the Alexandria School of Grammarians and director of the *Museion*. The letter of Claudius to the Alexandrians mentions him as one of the members of the delegation sent to Rome in 53.[22] Later, he was tutor to Nero before Seneca. He is linked to Stoicism. But at the same time, he was an Egyptian scribe rooted in his country's religious traditions.[23] He was a violent anti–Semite. Josephus cites selections from an anti-Jewish work of his to refute them, in which Chaeremon reports that Isis appeared to Amenophis to inspire him to expel the Jews from Egypt in the time of Moses (*Contra Apion*, 37–38).

Confronting the Stoic mystagogy, we see the eclectic Platonism initiated by Antiochus of Ascalon continue in this period. Antiochus had lived in Alexandria before succeeding Philo of Larissa as the head of the school at Athens. But, as R. E. Witt has noted,[24] "He left a group of followers at Alexandria who continued his tradition." At the end of the first century B.C.,

---

22. Bell, *Jews and Christians in Egypt*, 29.

23. See Reitzenstein, *Zwei religionsgeschichtliche Fragen*, 96–100.

24. Witt, *Albinus and the History of Middle Platonism*, 25.

the chief representative of this eclectic Platonism was Eudoxus who, like Antiochus, joined Stoic and Aristotelian elements in his Platonism. Essentially, this means that he combined curiosity about the cosmos inherited from Posidonius plus Aristotle's psychology with the Platonic dogma of the distinction of God and the world of the spirit and of matter.

This school was still functioning in the period in which Philo pursued his studies under Augustus. Diogenes Laertes (*Proemeium*, 21) speaks of an eclectic sect (ἐκλεκτικη) founded by Potamon that was in the line of Antiochus.[25] Ammonius, teacher of Plutarch, who is a little later than Philo, belonged to the school. Now, as we will see by examining Philo's philosophical writings, this eclectic Platonism is exactly the philosophy we find in him. Philo combats Stoic theses, but is impregnated with Stoic thought. Thus, it is plausible that he attended the school of Potamon.

Arius Didymus must be considered close to the school, although not directly connected to the Academy. He is characteristic of institutional philosophy that was established then and would retain its position in general culture until the end of Hellenism. Didymus is not tied to any school but presents the opinions of the great philosophers. This does not mean that he takes no positions. In fact, he seems influenced by Antiochus of Ascalon. In particular, he believes in the transcendent existence of the world of ideas.[26] The point is important for us, because the same will be true for Philo. A native of Alexandria, Didymus was attracted to Rome by Augustus.

Lastly there was Aristotelianism, but Aristotelianism principally of the early, still Platonizing Aristotle, whose works are now lost. The treatise *De Mundo* represents this tendency.[27] Festugière has shown that *De Mundo*'s use of the esoteric works of the founder of the Lyceum, published by Andronicus of Rhodes only towards 40 B.C., excludes an earlier date of composition.[28] The work seems to be influenced by Arius Didymus,[29] and furthermore is one of Philo's sources. This would let us

25. Ibid., 25–26.

26. Ibid., 27.

27. It must be compared with Pseudo-Ocellus whom Philo explicitly quotes. See Heyden-Zielewicz, *Prolegomena in Pseudocelli*, part 1, 38. According to this author (73), the work dates from the beginning of the first century A.D.

28. Festugière, *Le Dieu Cosmique*, 477. This is vol. 2 of *La Révélation d'Hermès Trismégiste*.

29. Ibid., 492–96.

situate it around A.D. 1–20. There is no reason to hold, as Pohlenz still does, that the Alexander to whom it is addressed is Philo's nephew Tiberius Alexander.[30] But it belongs to an environment close to Philo and beyond doubt Alexandrian.[31]

We see the common atmosphere of these different philosophical works that are situated in the reigns of Augustus and Tiberius. But we have more direct evidence that helps us become acquainted with Philo's philosophical environment. Within his work there is a group of writings that are completely distinct. They are the treatise on the *Eternity of the World*, preserved in Greek, the two books *On Providence*, and the dialogue *On the Soul of Animals* preserved in Armenian.[32] The treatise that *Every Good Man is Free* can be placed within this group. What is peculiar about these works, especially the first ones, is that they are all purely philosophical. Pagans might have written them. That is why their Philonic authenticity has been doubted. However, it seems indisputable. Bousset has found the right explanation, showing that we are dealing with class notes, where Philo sums up the teaching received rather than setting out his own ideas.[33] These are primary sources, but for Alexandrian philosophical education.

The treatise *On the Eternity of the World* is quite typical in this sense. There we find affirmations that absolutely contradict Philo's thought as we encounter it in the remainder of his work. The world is presented as uncreated (*De Aeternitate Mundi*, X, 53).[34] The fixed stars are "visible gods" and the notion that they might perish is declared "mischievous ravings" (*De Aeternitate Mundi*, IX, 46).[35] The world is "uncreated and therefore is indestructible" (*De Aeternitate Mundi*, XIII, 69).[36] God did not exist before the world. He is called the Soul of the world (*De Aeternitate Mundi*, XVI, 84).[37] Clearly, it would be absurd to attribute these opinions

---

30. Ibid., 479.

31. See Adriani, "Note sul Trattato," 208–22.

32. [Translator: *On the Soul of Animals* is not contained in the Loeb Library edition.]

33. Bousset, *Jüdisch-christlicher Schulbetrieb*, 134–52.

34. *Philo* IX, 221.

35. Ibid., 215, 217.

36. Ibid., 193. [Translator: Daniélou has "the cause of its own existence."]

37. Ibid., 245. [Translator: This is stated as the opinion of adversaries. I do not find the explicit denial that God existed before the world, but by implication, if the world is eternal, as is repeated a number of times, God does not exist before it.]

to a pious Alexandrian Jew. Besides, the literary similarities to the rest of the philosophical corpus are striking. Bousset has shown[38] that the key to the enigma is in the final section: "We have described to the best of our abilities the arguments transmitted [παρειλήφαμεν] to us to maintain the indestructibility of the world. In what follows we have to expound the answers given in opposition to each point." (*De Aeternitate Mundi*, XXVII, 150).[39] That does not mean, as has been said, that a second part disputing incorruptibility ought to be opposed to a first one defending it. But the sense is that Philo wanted to report what he had heard on the matter, reserving its discussion for later.

So understood, everything makes sense. Philo explains that there are three opposing opinions (*De Aeternitate Mundi*, III, 7–12).[40] The Aristotelians take the world to be both ungenerated and uncorruptible. The Stoics see a succession of generated and corruptible worlds.[41] We will note that Philo observes that Moses shared this last opinion. Now, oddly, the only opinion presented in fact is the first. But that makes perfect sense if the work echoes contemporary philosophical teaching. Indeed, the Aristotelian position seems to be the common position at this time. It is the one that Pseudo-Ocellus, whom Philo explicitly quotes, teaches in the same period. The Stoics Panetius and Boethus of Sidon adhered to it, as Philo will note (*De Aeternitate Mundi*, XV, 76).[42] Seneca will hold it a little later.

The very detail is constantly paralleled in contemporary philosophical works. At the start of his treatise Philo studies the different senses of the word κόσμος:

> In one sense the world or Cosmos [κόσμος] signifies the whole system [σύστημα] of heaven and the stars including the earth and the plants and the animals thereon; in another sense the heaven only. It was on heaven that Anaxagoras . . . The third sense, which is approved by the Stoics is something existing [οὐσία] either reduced or not reduced to order [διακεκοσμημένη], and time, they say, is what measures its movements (*De Aeternitate Mundi*, II, 4).[43]

38. Bousset, *Jüdisch-christlicher Schulbetrieb*, 136.

39. *Philo* IX, 291.

40. Ibid., 191, 193.

41. On the persistence of this debate in the Church Fathers see Corsini, "Sources de l'Hexameron," 94–103.

42. *Philo* IX, 239. For Pseudo-Ocellus see 3, 12, on p. 193.

43. Ibid., 187, 189. [Translator: Daniélou here cites the Latin edition of Cumont,

Philo will adhere to the first definition, according to which the world is the "whole system [σύστημα] of heavens and the stars including the earth and the plants and animals thereon" (*De Aeternitate Mundi*, 2, 4).[44] Now, *De Mundo* gives two of these definitions: "This world is the collection [σύστημα] that the sky and earth fill with all the kinds of beings they contain. In another sense world is also said of the order and arrangement [διακόσμησις] of universal nature" (*De Mundo*, 2, Festugière, 461).[45]

Let us take Arius Didymus now: "According to Chrysippus, the world is the collection [σύστημα] formed by sky and earth with the kinds of beings they contain,[46] or the collection [σύστημα] formed by gods and men and all that has been made for the good of these two kinds of beings. In another sense, it is God who is called the world, God in virtue of whom good order [διακόσμησις] of the world is formed and achieved." (figure 31; Festugière, 492). We see that *De Mundo* and especially Philo have set aside the definition of Arius Didymus, who only gathered earlier δόξαι. But the substance is the same in the three authors.

So, the work introduces us into the philosophy that predominated in Alexandria at the time. It is interesting to analyze it to become familiar with both the positions and spirit of this philosophy. The arguments in favor of the incorruptibility of the world are first that corruption ought to have an external or an internal cause. Now, both are impossible. Indeed nothing is outside the world but God, and it would be absurd that God should destroy the world. On the other hand, if the corruption comes from within, the part would be more powerful than the whole, which is equally absurd. Philo then quotes *Timaeus* 32 c, according to which the elements of the world, being simple, cannot be dissolved. This entails incorruptibility (*De Aeternitate Mundi*, VI, 27–28).[47] Aristotle would add that only what is generable is corruptible, and therefore, what is incorruptible is ungenerated. Philo pursues this argument: "When the assembled things are in the combined state of existence they have accepted conditions of disorder in exchange for their natural order and move away into positions opposite to the natural . . . But when they are dissolved they return to the condition proper to their nature." (*De Aeternitate Mundi*,

---

Philo De Aeternitate Mundi, 2.]

44. *Philo* IX, 187, 189.

45. [Translator: I take it that Daniélou is referring to an edition of *De Mundo*, in Festugière, *Le Dieu Cosmique*.]

46. Posidonius gives this definition (Diogenes Laertes VII, 138).

47. *Philo* IX, 203, 205.

VI, 31).[48] This order of the world is what is immutable, although it is continually deployed in combinations that are mutable. Moreover, would it not be impious to think that "the fixed stars, that mighty host of visible gods" must perish (*De Aeternitate Mundi*, IX, 46)?"[49]

Another argument starts from time. Time, according to the Stoic definition is "the measurement" [διάστημα] of cosmic movement. So it is absurd to think that the world could have existed without time. But time could not have begun, because to affirm that there was a time when time did not exist is still to affirm time. So the world also did not begin. And let us not say with the Stoics that time could as well be that of the world that will follow the ἐκπύρωσις as that of our world. Because if this world deserves the name κόσμος that we give it, its transformation by fire would no longer be an order but a disorder [ἀκοσμία]" (*De Aeternitate Mundi*, X, 52–54).[50]

Philo mentions another argument of the Aristotelian Critolaos: "If the world has been created, the earth must have been so too . . . and if the earth was created, so certainly must have been the human race, but man is "uncreated and his race has existed from everlasting as will be shown, therefore the world also is everlasting" (*De Aeternitate Mundi*, XI, 55).[51] On this occasion Philo first attacks the poets who depict the first men emerging adult and armed from the earth. That is contrary to the law of nature according to which man must first be a baby, a child, and an adolescent. So there is no beginning where man would have issued from something else, but the chain of generation is eternal. Likewise, if this earth could produce men at one moment, it ought to be able to do so still. Or else its power is diminished. But everything proves the opposite. It is always Pandora, she who scatters all gifts (*De Aeternitate Mundi*, XII, 63).[52] Therefore, if human generation is eternal, the world of which it is part is also eternal. Critolaos himself reasoned thus: that which causes existence is eternal; now the world itself causes its existence; therefore it is eternal.

Philo was led to pose the question of evolution: was there not a place to consider that the world, like the individual, develops from infancy to

48. Ibid., 207.

49. Ibid., 215. On the origin of this last argument in young Aristotle's περί φιλοσοφία, see Festugière, *Le Dieu Cosmique*, 239–40. Likewise for the antecedents see Heyden-Zielewicz, *Prolegomena*, 30–32.

50. *Philo IX*, 221, 223.

51. Ibid., 223.

52. Ibid., 227. On the Aristotelian origin see Heydin-Zielewicz, *Prolegomena*, 47–50.

maturity? To our author, "Such things are impious not merely to speak but even to think" (*De Aeternitate Mundi*, XIV, 73).[53] Indeed, one would have to think that not only the body, but the *logos* of the world, would grow and thus that at the beginning of creation the world was not yet rational. The impiety there is thinking that the world has not always been perfect. Here, the deeply anti-historical bent of Aristotelico-Platonist thought is radically affirmed. It certainly seems that it was the thought of Philo himself, for whom history plays no role.

Continuing his inventory, Philo mentions that since the εἰμαρμένη is eternal, so is the world (*De Aeternitate Mundi*, XV, 74). Then he recalls that the Stoics Panetius and Boethus of Sidon have themselves rejected the ἐκπύρωσις (*De Aeternitate Mundi*, 15, 25). He quotes Boethus's arguments: there are no external or internal causes for the corruption of the world. So it has nothing as its cause, which is absurd. Or again, in the moment of the ἐκπύρωσις what will God do? He indeed, is like the driver and pilot of the universe, helping sun, moon, stars, and planets, air and other parts of the cosmos and working with a view to the conservation of the whole and of its flawless organization in conformity with right reason. If everything is suppressed, will we live a life without life in idleness and inactivity? What would be more absurd? If you take its continuous activity from the soul, you destroy it. Now, God is the soul of the world (XVI, 83–84).

To these positive reasons Philo adds criticisms of the doctrine of ἐκπύρωσις: fire needs matter to exist; it cannot subsist alone (*De Aeternitate Mundi*, XVII–XVIII). The different elements are complementary (*De Aeternitate Mundi*, XX, 104–5). Even more, they are transformed into each other (*De Aeternitate Mundi*, XXI, 107–9). Thus, the disappearance of one is only its transformation into another (*De Aeternitate Mundi*, XXI, 110–11). He mentions the opinion of Theophrastus according to whom those who deny the incorruptibility of the world are misled by the unevenness of the earth's surface, the drop of the ocean, the dissolution of each part of the universe, the corruption of every animal species on earth. The arguments are: for the first point, that if the earth had always existed, today it would be completely leveled by erosion, the mountains leveled by rain; for the second that new islands would appear showing that the sea is evaporating; for the third, that a reality all of whose parts

---

53. *Philo* IX, 235.

are corruptible is itself corruptible; for the last, the late appearance of civilization.

Taking his inspiration from Theophrastus, Philo responds to these objections. First the earth, like trees, has its growth and decay. Sometimes the mountains are elevated by the impulse of fire, sometimes they are wiped out under the weight of water (*De Aeternitate Mundi*, XXV, 124–127) Similarly, if it is true not only that islands have eroded but that submerged cliffs have become dry land, the reverse also occurs. On dry land, not only riverbanks but also interior regions have been swallowed up and continents turned into seas are filled with innumerable ships. Thus, it is told that Sicily used to be part of Italy, but that floods broke (ἀνερράγη) the isthmus uniting them whence the name of Reggio (Ῥήγιον) given to the city founded on the strait. Was not the island of Atlantis larger than Libya and Asia, swallowed up in a day and a night to make room for an ocean (*De Aeternitate Mundi*, XXVI, 132–42)?[54]

In the third place, the corruptibility of different beings that are in the world is not a proof that the world itself is corruptible, but they are changes and transformations of a whole that itself does remain corruptible. Finally, to the objection drawn from the recent character of civilization, Philo anticipating Spengler, answers that we know a recent civilization, but that others have preceded it. Indeed, catastrophes, whether fire that destroys those who live in the mountains or water that drown the plains-dwellers, have destroyed almost all humanity in certain periods, so that it has been necessary to reinvent everything from scratch.[55] The part of the work that has come down to us ends with these answers.

It will be noted that the sequence of arguments is not very coherent. More precisely, certain themes reappear on different occasions: for instance the contrast of external and internal causes of corruption (*De Aeternitate Mundi*, chapters V, XVI and XIV), the enumeration of different modes of corruption (*De Aeternitate Mundi*, chapters VI, XVI, and XXII), the affirmation that God could not destroy the world (*De Aeternitate Mundi*, chapters VII, XVI, and XX). In a perceptive analysis, von Arnim[56] concludes that we have the reuse of the same scheme that must go back to Critolaos, the second occurrence of which comes from

54. Ibid., 283. According to Strabo (II, 160 bc), Posidonius considered the disappearance of Atlantis to be historical.

55. This comes from Aristotle's youthful treatise *On Philosophy*. See Festugière, *Le Dieu cosmique*, 222 and 590.

56. Arnim, *Quellenstudien zur Philo*, 38–39.

Boethus and Panetius, the third perhaps from Pseudo-Ocellus. Thus, in this curious work we are really given lecture notes on the problem.

We have a completely similar case in *De Providentia* I. Philo left us two treatises on Providence. Wendland established their authenticity. The second is a dialogue in a finished literary form about which we will speak later. By contrast, the first seems to be a set of fairly heterogeneous notes. Bousset has done an analysis of it.[57] It first contains a short series of theses intended to establish the contradictions into which those who deny Providence incur (*De Providentia*, I, 2–4). Then come three sections that Bousset has thoroughly distinguished, which differ both in theme and in philosophical sources. In the first, Philo shows that the world is not eternal but has a beginning and an end. The other two deal with the objections against Providence.

Thus, the first part of *De Providentia* has the same theme as the treatise *On the Eternity of the World*. But the position is exactly the contrary. In *De Aeternitate*, Philo explained the Aristotelian viewpoint. Now he presents the Stoic vision. It is obviously absurd to think that this responds to two stages of his thought. Moreover, it is clear that his own position is different. As Bossuet has thoroughly shown, the only solution is to view these two works as documents about Philo's teachers, not about him,. The previous treatise describes the Aristotelianism Philo knew in Alexandria, to which, moreover, the treatise *On the World* attests. *De Providentia* I familiarizes us with Stoic teaching as Chaeremon might have received it at Alexandria. Moreover, the theme of Providence was Stoicism's most cherished tenet, which it passionately defended against the Epicureans.

But, before dealing with Providence, the work first criticizes the Aristotelian thesis of an uncreated and incorruptible world:

> It happens that some judge that the world exists eternally and without beginning, so that there is no notion of creation but that the world possesses perpetual existence and cannot be dissolved . . . Indeed they say that it is fitting that divinity not remain inactive, because that is a mark of sloth and idleness. Therefore, they say, God established the universe without beginning. They do not understand the absurdity of such a hypothesis (*De Providentia*, I, 6).[58]

---

57. Bousset, *Jüdisch-christlicher Schulbetrieb*, 137–38.

58. [Translator: The Loeb's *Philo* IX has only the fragments of *De Providentia* conserved in Greek. Daniélou uses the longer *De Providentia et De Animalibus*, translated into Latin from Armenian by J.-B. Aucher.]

Now, this argument was employed in the opposite sense in the treatise *On the Eternity of the World*, where the necessity of God's always acting was presented as an argument in favor of the eternity of the world. The contradiction could not be more explicit.

Furthermore, Philo next takes up the arguments that the treatise *On the Eternity of the World* offers in favor of the world's eternity in order to refute them. That work contrasted the parts of the world, which are corruptible, and the whole, which is not. It is affirmed, on the contrary, that if the parts have a beginning, the whole has one too (*De Providentia*, I, 9; that if the parts are corruptible, the whole is likewise corruptible (*De Providentia*, I, 15–20). The idea that human generation could go back infinitely is presented as absurd (*De Providentia*, I, 11). The author is particularly drawn to the thesis according to which creation simply consists in arranging preexisting formless matter (*De Providentia*, I, 7–8). Matter itself has a beginning. For that Philo bases himself both on Plato and Moses (*De Providentia*, I, 20–22). But he likewise appeals to Zeno (*De Providentia*, I, 22). Nevertheless, he criticizes the Stoic position that considers the world to be an animal (*De Providentia*, I. 22).

The next part of the treatise develops two successive arguments in favor of Providence. In the first, Philo, carrying out the plan he proposed in his preamble, shows that the contemplation of the world establishes the existence of Providence (*De Providentia*, I, 24–36); providence among men is found in the shepherd, the pilot, the physician (I, 25); it is found in the government of the body by the spirit (ἡγεμονικόω) (*De Providentia*, I, 28); in the existence of the arts, music, philosophy, geometry (*De Providentia*, I, 32); in the harmony of the world (*De Providentia*, I, 33): "And these things manifest the development of an immutable order (τάξις καὶ ἀκολουθία) moving the universe in the manner of a soul by the law of Providence" (*De Providentia*, I, 33). Indisputably, all that bears a Stoic stamp.

Next comes a refutation of Epicurean attacks against Providence, which also echoes Stoicism. The argument is from the existence of events that overwhelm the world (*De Providentia*, I, 37): floods, hail that destroys crops, disasters striking just and unjust alike. Philo responds by noting the educational value of trials (*De Providentia*, I, 54), emphasizing that they do not affect the wise man, who is detached from external goods (*De Providentia*, I, 56). Many secondary characteristics bear witness to the Stoic source here. For instance the comparison of man to a microcosm will be noticed, contrasted to the macrocosm that is the world (*De Providentia*, I, 40) or the concept of man as citizen of the world *De Providentia*, (I, 40), The paragraph on the Stoic ideal of the wise man recalls Seneca (*De Providentia*, I, 70–76).

But we find that after number 79 Philo changes abruptly to a last topic, the critique of fatalism and astrology. There we have a bit of anti-Stoic polemics. So, as Bousset notes, the treatise's composite character is apparent in the juxtaposition of different sources. Having explained Stoic doctrine, Philo offers a refutation of its most debatable position. As David Armand has shown,[59] this segment's significance is that, with Cicero's *De Fato*, it constitutes one of the oldest anti-fatalistic testimonies going back to the Platonist Carneades, the adversary of Chrysippus, a position which was destined to become standard in the Church Fathers.

Accordingly, once more Philo's argument is valuable documentation of a feature of the philosophy of his time. He first shows that the opinion that puts responsibility for human action on the stars is an easy excuse for those who do evil (*De Providentia*, II, 77–78). Then comes a series of four arguments. If everything is governed by fatality, there is no longer responsibility. Consequently, there are no longer guilty parties, and criminals cannot be condemned (*De Providentia*, I, 79–80). There are no longer laws, right, justice, or judges" (De Providentia, I, 82). In the second place, the laws by which nations are governed are the same for all their members. Therefore, they are not determined by individual horoscopes (*De Providentia*, I, 84–86). Bardesane, the Christian philosopher of Edessa, will take up that argument. In the third place, catastrophes annihilate everyone in a region: must we say that they were all born under the same star (I, 87)? Finally, how can a person's horoscope be determined when the moment of his conception is unknown (I, 87)? Then comes a conclusion that parallels the introduction. Philo defends the idea of an end of the world. But he is not inspired by the Stoic conception of a cosmic necessity that results in the ἐκπύρωσις by gradual desiccation. The end of the world has a moral character: it is a judgment of God. This already appears in *De Providentia*, I, 23. Evil grows in the measure that men turn away from God (*De Providentia*, I, 89).

> By what right will the world try to persist when providence has given so many demonstrations of its forbearance? The elements of the world persist against their liking in fear and trembling before the wrath of Providence. The angels set over the world will

59. Armand, *Fatalisme et liberté dans l'antiquité grecque*, 81–96.

abandon it when it is struck by the judgment it deserves . . . The beauty of the world is withdrawn from it. Man, the citizen of the world, perishes with the world, conquered by evil (*De Providentia*, I, 90).

It certainly seems that in this strange passage the Stoic notion of the end of the world is interpreted in the Jewish perspective of the Judgment. But several curious elements are to be noted. The first is the pessimistic vision of growing evil and general apostasy.[60] It recalls the visions of the contemporary Jewish apocalypses. The notion will also be observed that the elements put up with the sins of men against their liking, which recalls Romans, 8:20. Lastly, the theme of angels in charge of administering the earthly creation and abandoning it will be found again in a whole Christian tradition.[61]

The two treatises we have studied so far are slightly elaborated recollections in which we find the echo of philosophical teaching received by Philo at Alexandria. The matter is approached differently in another pair, *De Providentia* II and *De Animalibus*. We are still dealing with purely philosophical works that echo contemporary discussions in the schools. But the form is different. We have dialogues in the Platonic fashion. These texts are interesting because of the data they give about Philo—which guarantees their authenticity. As we have seen, *De Animalibus* matches Philo and his younger brother Lysimachus. His nephew Tiberius Alexander plays an important role in it. In the other dialogue, Philo confronts an Alexander. The character's identity is debated. But the closeness to *De Animalibus* would make us opt for Tiberius Alexander.

The dialogues are generally viewed as Philo's youthful work. Nevertheless, Pohlenz has disputed this opinion. He sees the mature expression of one side of Philo. This view seems completely valid to us. It is confirmed by the chronological data finished by *De Animalibus*. As we have seen, there is the matter of Philo's nephew and his betrothal. If Tiberius Alexander was born around 10, the dialogue takes takes place toward 35. Tiberius Alexander has already carried out a mission at Rome. Therefore Philo is about fifty years old. He is at the height of his powers. This is the period when he plays an important role at Alexandria. He is brought into relation with pagan circles. That seems to us to fit his maturity much better than his youth, when his concerns are more mystical and when

60. Daniélou, "Le comble du mal."
61. Daniélou, *Les anges et leur mission*, 148–51.

he mixes less with the world. Moreover, we observe that these several treatises including *De Aeternitate Mundi* and *De Providentia* have points of contact with the *Explanation of the Laws*, directed to the pagans, which seems to us to come from the years between 30 to 40 AD.

This brings us to the important point, Philo's close relations with pagan circles in his maturity. We should not forget his family's close contacts with official Roman circles. In reality, Philo's environment is paganized in large part. In particular, his nephew Tiberius Alexander will become an apostate and embrace paganism. Both dialogues include precisely Tiberius Alexander. We can see in them the echo of discussions Philo in fact had with his nephew, whose formation had been mainly pagan and who was won over by the philosophical ideas of his time—by Epicureanism, it seems, as his criticism of Providence and his materialism attest.

Thus, under a different form, we still very much find the echo of the philosophy of the time here. *De Providentia II* shows us Alexander approaching Philo late in the evening, since darkness has already fallen. Alexander has not slept the previous night, so agitated is his mind from an argument about Providence. This does not suppose a previous work at all, but only represents a theatrical device. Alexander marshals all his objections against Providence, a good part of which we have already met in *De Providentia* I. The evil prosper, and the good suffer misfortune: what would we say about a legislator who governs like that (*De Providentia*, II, 3)? He cites as examples Polycrates and Dionysius on one side, Socrates and Zeno on the other. Philo answers by showing God's patience toward the guilty (*De Providentia*, II, 15), the significance of earthly goods (II, 24), and the utility of tyrants as executioners (II, 31).

Against the notion of Providence Alexander then cites the fact that the poets show us the gods carrying out innumerable infamies. Saturn, son or Uranus, mutilates his father (*De Providentia*, II, 35). Jupiter, dispossessing Saturn, throws him into Tartarus. Mars is an adulterer, Mercury a thief (*De Providentia*, II, 39). Philo's answer here is interesting. First, he recommends that we attend to what is most seemly in the poets (*De Providentia*, II, 40). Then he shows that their narratives must be interpreted allegorically. "What is said of Vulcan must be attributed to fire, what concerns Juno to air, what relates to Hermes to language" (*De Providentia*, II, 42). If "the rules of allegory" are not observed, one falls into absurdity. Now this is the interpretation that Stoics like Cornutus gave and that Philo himself will apply to the Bible. Finally, we must not ask the poets to be philosophers. Everyone must stay within his limits (II, 42).

The subsequent discussion is interesting from another point of view. Alexander affirms that neither the laws of the spirit nor place nor time nor the void affirmed by the Stoics are created by God.[62] so to what is Providence reduced (*De Providentia*, II, 52–54)? Now, Philo does not dispute this affirmation. Therefore, he accepts the Aristotelian position here. But he shows the action of Providence in the organization of the world (*De Providentia*, II, 55–58). But, says Alexander, this disposition of the elements is the work of a determinism. Besides, it shows no finality. What use is the immense expanse of ocean (*De Providentia*, II, 60–61)? Philo answers that the properties of the elements are the work of Providence (*De Providentia*, II, 62). As for the sea, it serves to nourish gods and men: the gods by the evaporation that feeds sun and stars; men by the dew spread over the earth (*De Providentia*, II, 64–65). Furthermore, the sea serves for navigation (*De Providentia*, II, 66). The idea that the sun is fed by the sea comes from Heraclitus (Plutarch, *Placita*, II, 17) and had been taken up by Posidonius (Macrobius, *Saturnalia*, I, 23).

The end of the work consists of the expansion of these last words. Alexander successively alludes to the disorders of the heavens (occultation of the moon, eclipses (*De Providentia*, II, 71)[63] to the winds that cause shipwrecks (*De Providentia*, II, 87), to the rain that falls on the sea (II, 88), to plagues, famines and floods (*De Providentia*, II, 90), to serpents (*De Providentia*, II, 92). Along the way interesting references are made to contemporary scientific knowledge, for instance the explanations of the Milky Way considered as a reflection of starlight,[64] as the joint of the heavens, as the old path of the sun, as the path of Geryon's flocks, as the milk from Juno's breasts (*De Providentia*, II, 89). Philo offers counter arguments: the eclipses serve for predictions (*De Providentia*, II, 100); serpents' venom has medicinal uses (*De Providentia*, II, 104). Moreover the primary ends of Providence may bring secondary occurrences that Providence does not directly want (*De Providentia*, II, 79–102).

The last part of the dialogue is particularly interesting because of all of the data it offers about contemporary science. Its curiosity is a characteristic of the period. We find it in the treatise *De Mundo*. Posidonius especially made it fashionable. This literature likewise makes *De Animalibus* of interest. The theme under discussion, animal souls, is a school

---

62. For this enumeration, see Arnim *Stoicorum veterum Fragmenta*, II, 158.

63. See Plutarch *De Iside et Osiride*, 49.

64. This is Posidonius's definition (Macrobius, *Commentarium in Somnium Scipionis*, I:15).

topic. Philo certainly seems to undertake it only to set out a received opinion. "I am an interpreter, not a teacher. Those who communicate their own knowledge to others speak as doctors. But those who report to others exactly what they have heard are interpreters" (*De Animalibus*, 7).[65]

Like the previous dialogue, this one alludes to an early conversation. Tiberius Alexander, who is still a young man (*adolescens*), has given a brilliant discourse to a gathering where there were Romans and Alexandrians, in which he developed the idea that beasts have souls. Lysimachus has a copy of the lecture. He reads it to Philo. This discourse is a collection of curious anecdotes about animal intelligence that has many points of contact with Pliny the Elder's *Natural History*, which is slightly later. We see parrots greet important people and horses compute. The skill of spiders and bees is praised (*De Animalibus*, 19–20). Goats walk tightropes and play ball. Elephants learn to sign their names. Certain animals can be presented as models of virtue, but others are promiscuous, cowardly, or cruel (*De Animalibus*, 66).

We are not dealing with a real philosophical discussion but a brilliant bit of erudition. Philo's answer is going to distinguish what is simply instinct from obvious intelligence. He takes Alexander's examples and discusses them. But the *Dialogue*'s interest is that it falls within a very popular literary genre of the period, stories about animals. Pliny the elder will devote his *Natural History* to them, Seneca his *Quaestiones Naturales*. In the Greek world , during Philo's time, Alexander of Myndos was writing his *History of Animals* and his *Recollection of Wonders*, which Aelian will use in the following century. Here too, Philo can be viewed as a simple witness to Alexandrian culture of his time and to the topics that culture appreciated.

Philo and Roman Politics

The two personality types we have described so far through the picture that Philo gives us of them were the Jewish monk and the Greek philosopher. The third is the Roman emperor. These, indeed, were components of the world in which Philo lived. These were also the circles in which his family's cosmopolitan character made him move. Therefore,

---

65. [Translator: *De Animalibus* is not one of the works in the Loeb library. It is not *De Agricultura*. It is one of the works preserved in ancient Armenian.]

here we do not address Philo's political ideas any more than in the previous paragraphs we were concerned with his philosophical ideas. We
will see that later. For the moment, we will ask about the world he knew.
Now here Philo appears to us in a new light, as an informant about
imperial ideology.

In the *Embassy to Gaius*, written under Claudius and perhaps addressed to that emperor, we saw that Philo reports the political role he
played in the last months of Caligula's reign. [Translator: Caligula is the
nickname of Gaius Julius Caesar Augustus Germanicus, emperor 31–41
AD. Claudius is Tiberius Claudius Caesar Augustus Germanicus, emperor 31–54 AD.] But the first part of the *Embassy to Gaius* begins with
a portrait of Caligula that is a political document of the first importance
and offers details that are not in Suetonius or Cassius Dio. Thus, he tells
us that young Tiberius, grandson of the Emperor of the same name and
Caligula's cousin, was driven to suicide by Caligula and not murdered.
He gives us numerous details about the role of Macro and his wife Ennea
in the rise of Caligula and about how Caligula led them to do away with
themselves. Philo found himself at Rome immediately after these events.
He knew men who had been directly involved in them, especially Herod
Agrippa I. Consequently, his testimony is very valuable.

But what interests us here is not historical detail, but the imperial
ideology. With Caligula, the doctrine making the emperor a demi-god
comes into full flower. We have seen how much this doctrine was the
source of conflicts with the Jews just as with Christians later. We know
that Caligula was surrounded by Egyptian servants who smothered him
with flattery. The doctrine of royal divinity was traditional en Egypt. We
can wonder whether it was not suggested to the emperor by the flattery
of his courtiers.[66] But also, in certain first century neo-Pythagoreans like
Diotogenes, Sthenidas, or Ecphantus, we find an image of the king in
which he is regarded as belonging to a different species from the rest
of humanity.[67] These authors may have been influenced by the Egyptian
ideal. They were known in Roman circles. Caligula, as he became half-
mad, may have wanted to give literal meaning to their speculation.

It is in this perspective that the ideas Philo presents in *The Embassy
to Gaius*[68] take on their full importance. They let us follow the devel-

---

66. Piganiol, *Histoire de Rome,* 249.

67. Louis Delatte, *Les traités de la royauté d'Ecphante, Diotogène et Sthénidas,* 151ff.

68. Bréhier, *Les idées,* 19–20 (reference to the edition, Paris: J. Vrin, 1925, 1950).

opment of the imperial ideology in Caligula's mind. A first passage, in fact, shows us the royal idea as the neo-Pythagoreans conceived it. It is a speech of Macro:

> You ought not to be like those around you or anyone else at all . . . always and everywhere remembering [your] sovereignty [ἡγεμονία], that [you are] as a shepherd [ποιμήν] and master of a flock. . . . What should he do who has learned the highest and greatest art? And the best and greatest art is the art of government that causes the good deep soil in lowlands and highlands to be tilled, and all the seas to be safely navigated by merchant ships laden with cargoes to effect the exchange of goods which the countries in desire for fellowship render to each other . . . Accordingly having under Nature's escort risen to the highest post in the stern, and the tiller placed in your hand, steer to security [σωτηρίως], the common ship of mankind rejoicing and delighting in nothing so much as in benefiting [εὐεργετεῖν] your subjects (*Ad Gaium*, VII, 43–44, 47–50).[69]

In this text there are features that become common after Plato's *Laws*, for instance, the comparison of the king to a pilot. But others more directly evoke neo-Pythagorean theoreticians: the king must not resemble anyone else; he is for the whole of humanity what God is for the universe; power is the highest art. Bréhier could write that Macro's speech is believed to be taken from Diotogenes.[70] Goodenough completely supports Bréhier's conclusion except that he sees this royal ideology as already widespread in the Hellenic world.[71] The terms σωτηρίως and εὐεργετεῖν should be especially noted in Macro's speech. The king is the σωτήρ, the one who saves the universe from ruin.[72] Macro attributes to him the prosperity of agriculture and commerce. He is also the *Evergetes*, the source of goods. Philo has already connected the two terms (*Ad Gaium*, IV, 22). It should be added that Philo takes inspiration from this neo-Pythagorean ideology in his image of the ideal offered in *Moses*.[73]

This is the ideology that we find, although deformed, in the notion of kingship that Caligula constructs. For us, the interest is that through

69. *Philo* X, 23, 25.

70. Bréhier, *Les idées*, 22.

71. Goodenough, *The Politics of Philo*, 46. See the bibliographical information on this page.

72. Ibid., 97.

73. Bréhier, *Les idées*, 21

this deformation, many of the features of the period's ideology may be discerned. This is already true in the speech that Philo gives Caligula in answer to Macro. We see the idea appear that the king has not been taught by anyone. This knowledge is the privilege of the royal lineage. Caligula first proclaims that he possesses it from the royal line to which he belongs. But he goes further. There are:

> [There are] kinglike potentialities [βασιλικαὶ δυνάμεις] for government . . . For just as the seminal forces [ἐν τοῖς σπερματοκοῖς] preserve similarities of the body in form and carriage and gate, and of the soul in projects and actions, so we may suppose that to the governing faculty they contain a resemblance in outline. And then does anyone dare to teach me, who even while in that womb, that workshop [ἐγαστήριον] of nature, was modeled as an emperor [αὐτοκρατώρ], ignorance dare to instruct knowledge? How can they who were but now common citizens have a right to peer into the counsels of an imperial [ἡγεμονική] soul? Yet in their shameless effrontery they who would hardly be admitted to rank as learners [μυσταί] dare to act as masters [ἱεροφαντεῖν] who initiate [τελεῖν] others into the mysteries of government" (*Ad Gaium*, VIII, 53–56).[74]

So kings form a race apart that has its own characteristics transmitted genetically and not by education. The Stoic flavor of the excerpt will be noted in the allusion to the λόγοι σπερματικοί. Thus there is a seed of royalty like that of other traits. The phrase ἐργαστήριον τῆς φύσεως will also be noted. It is found again in the treatise *On the Eternity of the World*, as a quote from an unknown author (*De Aeternitate Mundi*, XII, 66) as well as in *Moses*, II, 84, and the *Explanation of the Laws*, III, 33, 109. This emphasizes that the ideas in the discourse are certainly Philo's.

Only this royal race possesses the secrets of government. These are a mystery hidden from ordinary mortals. The king is the hierophant and interpreter. Royalty assumes a sacred character here. The king appears not as just belonging to a higher realm than ordinary people but to a strictly divine sphere. Goodenough observes that this passage is "an exposition of current royal philosophy in the form Philo could employ in his allegory of the patriarchs and that he admitted in theory for kings. But when Gaius grounds his pretensions not on his official position but on his peculiar nature and configuration, Philo deems it sacrilegious."[75]

---

74. *Philo* X, 29.

75. Goodenough, *The Politics of Philo*, 106.

After Macro's death, Gaius found another mentor in the person of his father-in-law, Silanus (*Ad Gaium*, IX, 62). But Gaius no longer accepted advice. Among the reasons Philo give, one interests us. Caligula claimed that he was, "the wisest and most temperate of men and also the bravest and justest" (*Ad Gaium*, 9; 64).[76] We recognize the four Aristotelian virtues here. The royal ideology had as a theme that the king had to be the most virtuous of men. It is a theme Philo takes up frequently. The king is firstly one who commands his passions. It is because he is the model of virtues that he deserves to serve as the rule for others.[77] But we see the reversal Caligula has made. The Pythagoreans said, "The wise man is king." Caligula declares, "The king is wise." The king possesses all virtues because he his king. Thus the notion Caligula forms of royalty is a distorting mirror, where we meet the Hellenic idea transposed into a caricature. The theme is the same, but the application is totally different.

This deformation reaches its climax in the extraordinary passage where Gaius affirms himself equal to the gods. Here again, in reality, he only takes up a current theory, Diotogenes's claim that the king is an imitator[78] of Zeus. We will see that in Philo's response to Caligula's position, he does not question the principle but only disputes the application. Here again, Caligula's doctrine is a witness of the current royal ideology, but used to justify the most extravagant pretensions. Therefore, as Bréhier has thoroughly shown, in Caligula's theories we may seek the deformed expression of contemporary philosophical accounts of royal ideology about which Philo offers us testimony.

An astonishing passage must be quoted: "Those who have charge of the herds of other animals, ox herds, goat herds, shepherds, are not themselves oxen, nor goats or lambs but men to whom is given a higher destiny and constitution, and in the same way I who am in charge of the best of herds, mankind, must be considered to be different from them, and not of human nature but to have a greater and diviner destiny" (*Ad Gaium*, XI, 76).[79] And again, "he no longer considered it worthy of him to abide within the bounds of human nature but overstepped them in his eagerness to be thought a god" (*Ad Gaium*, XI, 75). Now, Bréhier has definitely shown that "Philo himself admits the reasoning that he as-

---

76. *Philo* X, 33.

77. Goodenough, *The Politics of Philo*, 91.

78. Bréhier, *Les idées*, 19.

79. *Philo* X, 39.

signs to Caligula, when that bad emperor assimilates himself to the gods. Moreover, the words are an almost exact presentation of a passage from Plato (*Laws*, IV, 713 d).[80] Accordingly, Philo does not dispute that there is something divine in royalty. He grants that to royalty along with his contemporaries.[81] Philo will transpose this to Moses.[82] But he criticizes the application that Caligula makes of it.

This application finally becomes madness in Caligula: "He had firmly sealed in his mind and carried about with him, poor fool, a mythical fiction as if it was an indisputable truth . . . and was emboldened to publish to the multitude his most godless assumption of godship [ἐκθέωσις]" (*Ad Gaium*, XI, 77).[83] Philo then describes to us Caligula presenting himself in public attired in the accoutrements of the gods, something we know otherwise from Suetonius. "He [tr. Caligula] began first of all to liken himself to the so-called demi-gods, Dionysus and Heracles and the Dioscuri, treating Trophonius and Amphiaraus and Amphilochus and their like and their oracles and celebrations as laughing-stocks compared to his own power. Then, as in a theater, he assumed different costumes at different times, sometimes the lion skin and club, both overlaid with gold, to adorn himself as Heracles, sometimes caps on his head when he made himself up as the Dioscuri, or again as Dionysus with ivy, thyrsus and fawn's skin" (*Ad Gaium* XI, 78–79).[84] Suetonius confirms this. "His entourage having pointed out to him that he had been elevated above princes and kings, from that moment he assumed the majesty of the gods (IV, 22) . . . Often he was seen with a golden beard, holding the symbols of the gods in his hand: the lightening bolt, the trident, or the physician's caduceus" (IV, 52).[85]

We should note that on this point Suetonius reports that one day, hearing several kings dispute among themselves, Caligula quotes a verse of Homer to them: "Let there be one commander, one master [εἷς βασιλεύς] only" (*Iliad*, II, 236)[86] One of the kings answered that Caligula

80. Bréhier, *Les idées*, 21–22.

81. Goodenough, *The Politics of Philo*, 107: "Caligula did no more than apply the Hellenistic theory."

82. See Lacombade, *Le discours sur la royauté de Synésios de Cyrène*, 92.

83. *Philo* X, 39.

84. Ibid., 39, 41.

85. For the *Caduceus* see *Legum Allegoria*, 13, 94,

86. Homer, *The Iliad*, translated by Robert Fagles, 106. [Translator: Daniélou cites line 204, which seems to be wrong. Odysseus is rallying the army, lines 234–38:

was even above royalty. It is odd to note that Philo quotes this verse from Homer (*De Confusione Linguarum*, 170) and so does *De Mundo*, 6.[87] It constitutes one of the elements of royal ideology. *De Mundo* sees an expression of divine monarchy in it. But the unity of humanity under a single emperor appears as the created reflection of that monarchy. Later, Eusebius will take up the concept to apply it to the Christian empire. But it takes shape in Philo's era. We may add that Cassius Dio tells us that the king who told Caligula that his royalty was essentially different from that of kings was Herod Agrippa I. All this shows how the speculation about royal ideology has a place in the circles to which Philo belonged.

The fact remains that Philo rejects Caligula's pretense to affirm himself as a demigod and more than a demigod. But even there Philo remains within the royal ideology.[88] Indeed, what he retorts to Caligula is that rather than attiring himself in the outward trappings of the gods, he ought to imitate their virtues. Thus Heracles cleansed the world of the monsters that harmed it. Dionysus gave the world wine that comforts soul and body. The Dioscuri "made inequality, the source of injustice, vanish in equality, which is the fountain of justice" (*Ad Gaium*, XI, 81–85).[89] Likewise, when Caligula makes himself equal to the great gods themselves, here too, he ought to have imitated their virtues (*Ad Gaium* XIII, 93—XV, 113). The praise Philo gives to pagan divinities in these passages has been noted. It is clear that this relates to his developing an ideology taken from contemporary paganism and that he does not take it up on his own account. He testifies to the contemporary royal ideology.

All this lets us conclude that Philo is a valuable source for us about the royal ideology as it was established in his time. The Alexandrian neo-Pythagoreans had established this ideology in the first century before our era to exalt the Lagid and Seleucid dynasties. But a new question is posed with the Roman Empire. The notion of universal monarchy spreads. The neo-Pythagorean ideology begins to be transferred to the Emperor at Rome. It

---

"How can all Achaeans by masters here in Troy?
Too many kings can ruin an army—mob rule!
Let there be one commander, one master only,
endowed by the son of crooked-minded Cronus
with kingly scepter and royal rights of custom."]

87. Peterson, *Theologische Traktate*, 52–57.

88. On the use of divine titles given to emperor see Louis Delatte, *Les traités de la royauté d'Ecphante, Diotogène et Sthénidas*, 145–48

89. *Philo* X, 41, 43. On ἰσότης see Goodenough, *The Politics of Philo*, 87.

is completed with a concept of monarchy that *De Mundo* interprets theologically as the unity of God and that is transferred to the political sphere. Caligula gives evidence the development of the ideology, as does Philo. Both echo contemporary speculations developing in the Roman Empire.

Did Philo adopt this ideology himself? It is certain that the pictures he gives us of the ideal king in *Moses* or of the ideal procurator in *De Josepho* are inspired by it.[90] But there it belongs to pagan wisdom and philosophy. Philo knew pagan wisdom, Greek philosophy, and Roman imperialism. His work bears evident traces of their influence. But he did not adopt them unchanged. In the apologetic work that have been the material for this chapter and that are addressed to pagans, Philo's goal is to show them that the idea they expressed is really found in the Jews. Thus, the true wise man of Stoicism is the Essene monk. The true philosophy according to neo-Aristotelianism is that of the Bible. The true statesman according to neo-Pythagoreanism is Moses. Philo remained deeply Jewish. As Wolfson has rightly seen, Philo remakes Greek philosophy according to the demands of the Jewish faith. But before approaching his personal thought, as we will do now, it is important to situate it in relation to the world whose inheritance he received.

Before leaving the different figures of the environment in which Philo lived, we could ask ourselves whether the works that we have studied and that describe those figures explicitly are the only ones where they are treated. That is not at all the case. In reality, we often meet them while studying Philo's personal work. Certainly, that endeavor is a symbolic interpretation of the Bible. But this symbolism has the goal of detaching the characters he describes from their historical context in order to make them universal types. Thus, Philo's work is continually full of allusions to customs of his time. It is one of his most picturesque features, one that must have provided great flavor for his listeners and readers. Behind the Bible heroes they recognized figures that were familiar to them: Joseph the politician, Abraham the philosopher, Jacob the ascetic. In this work that to the reader seems full of abstract allegories, Philo has really made an extraordinary experience of life pass in front of us, which must have made the work astonishingly real for his contemporaries. We must not forget it when studying his developments.

90. See Heinemann, *Philons griechische und jüdische Bildung*, 201.

3

The Bible at Alexandria

I N THE PREVIOUS CHAPTER, we have studied the picture of his time
that Philo gives us through his apologetic works. But, if Philo's activity
seems varied, interpretation of the Bible and almost exclusively of the
Pentateuch remains the essential part of his work. Philo is a believing
Jew for whom the whole truth is contained in God's word. The Bible is
where he seeks true wisdom, true philosophy, and true politics. Thus,
Philo appears to us as a very important witness on Biblical exegesis in the
New Testament period. In this chapter we will study his biblical writings,
his method of interpretation, and his place in the history of Alexandrian
exegesis. It will remain for us afterwards to expound the theology and
mysticism that he extracts from the sacred text.

Philo's Exegetical Work

In what concerns the Bible, Philo's output consists of three great commentaries on the Pentateuch, one more literal, the *Exposition of the Law*;
the second more allegorical, the *Allegorical Interpretation*; the third,
gathering different exegetical writings, the *Quaestiones*. Do these three
commentaries correspond to three stages of his life? Attempts to arrange
them chronologically have led to contradictory results. Massebieau puts
the *Exposition* first, the *Allegorical Interpretation* next.[1] Cohn ultimately

1. Massebieau and Bréhier, "Essai sur la chronologie," 25–64, 164–85, 167–289.

concluded the reverse.[2] Besides, the difference between the treatises does not seem to stem from an evolution in Philo's thinking for which we have no proof, but, as we have seen, rather from the fact that the *Allegorical Interpretation* is an echo of his preaching in the synagogue, while the *Exposition* originates in an apologetic aimed at pagans. Therefore, the order in which they were composed has little importance and cannot be determined at present.

The Exposition of the Law

The *Exposition of the Law*[3] first of all includes a treatise *On Creation* that is like a cosmological introduction. It is an important work for Philo's theology. It shows the creation of the pre-existing intelligible world in the Genesis narrative (*De Opificio*, 17–22), whose unity is the Logos. The seven days do not mark a succession but an order. The whole world appeared complete at the same time. Likewise, man in the image of God is the idea of man created in the intelligible world (*De Opificio*, 69). By contrast, the second narrative of human creation corresponds to the creation of a particular man made of earth and spirit. In this work Philo weaves together the cosmologies of the *Timaeus* and Genesis.

After this cosmological introduction, Philo presents the figures of the great patriarchs who expressed the perfection of the Law within themselves. Only two of these treatises remain, *De Abrahamo* and *De Josepho*. At the beginning of the former Philo explains: "These are such men as lived good and blameless lives, whose virtues stand permanently recorded in the most holy scriptures . . . for the instruction of the reader" (De *Abrahamo*, 4).[4] In some way these men are the divine Law (ἔμψυχος).[5] "First he [tr. Moses] wished to show that the enacted ordinances are not inconsistent with nature; and second that those who wish to live in accordance with the laws as they stand have no difficult task . . . so that one might properly say that the enacted laws are nothing else than memorials

2. Cohn, "Einleitung und Chronologie," 387–435.

3. [Translator: *The Exposition of the Law* is not a treatise but a series of treatises. *De Opificio Mundi, De Abrahamo, De Isaaco, De Jacobo, De Josepho, De Premiis et Poenis, De Specialibus Legibus, De Decalogo,* and *De Virtutibus. De Isaaco* and *De Jacobo* are lost. As the names suggest, it is more literal than *Allegoriae Legum*. It does not include *De Vita Mosis.*]

4. *Philo* VI, 7.

5. See Richardson, "The Philonic Patriarch," 515–26.

of the life of the ancients" (*De Abrahamo*, 5).[6] On the one hand, they show that the commandments are not in disagreement with nature and that they are not so difficult. The written laws would only be commentaries on their lives." Here we find the Greek theme of the unwritten law, to which Sophocles and Cicero appeal and which Philo reduces to the Jewish Law. The life of Abraham is presented as the symbol of conversion. The Chaldeans mistake the world for God (*De Abrahamo*, 69). By contrast, Abraham is the one to whom God's transcendence has appeared (*De Abrahamo*, 77). The apparition at Mambre is commented upon in a remarkable way. The person in the middle is He Who Is; the other two are his powers, the creative power (θεός) and the royal power (κύριος). The completely pure soul attains unity; others are detained in the shadows (120 ff).[7] There must have been a treatise on Isaac next and another on Jacob, the perfect person and the improving person. These treatises are lost. We have only their summary at the end of the *Exposition of the Law*. It is possible that Christians destroyed the treatise on Isaac.

De Josepho is a rather peculiar work. For Philo, Joseph is always the type of the "politician." In certain treatises like *De Somniis*, he is presented rather pejoratively. Politics is the realm of opinion and persuasive speeches whose goal is not the search for truth but for power. The perspective is different in *De Josepho*. Perhaps, the difference is because Philo directs himself to pagans here. In Joseph he describes the politician, but the ideal politician. Our author presents the kind of Roman governor dreamt of by the Jews. He constitutes the fourth race. His training as a shepherd was the best preparation for him to be the guardian of peoples (*De Josepho*, 2). We also find this in *Moses*. Joseph also exemplifies other characteristics of the perfect politician: he is a good administrator, and he has authority (*De Josepho*, 54). Here again we find the themes of Hellenistic royal ideology about which we have spoken.

One can associate these treatises with a work that is not part of the *Exposition of the Law* but belongs to the same kind of exegesis, *Moses*. This is a biography of Moses taken from the Pentateuch with certain borrowing from Jewish tradition. Philo is inspired by the Hellenistic ideal. Moses is presented as the ideal type of king according to the Pythagorean conception. He is a child of great beauty (*De Vita Mosis*, I, 9). He receives a complete education according to the Hellenistic ideal: arithmetic,

---

6. *Philo* VI, 7.

7. [Translator: I have removed Daniélou's quotes around this last sentence, which I do not find in *Philo* VI, 63, 65. The gist is given in *De Abrahamo*, 122.]

music, and geometry. This is found again in Stephen's discourse in the Acts of the Apostles 7:22. The second book successively presents Moses as legislator, in as much as he gives the Decalogue, as priest, and finally as prophet. In all this, Philo's goal is to show Moses as the incarnation of the ideal of the Hellenistic world, to present Moses in a way so as to gain acceptance for him from the pagans Philo is addressing. Allegorical elements intervene in some measure in the explanation of the tabernacle and of the vestments of the high priest. But that is traditional at Alexandria and is already found in the Greek book of *Wisdom*.

After this series of exemplary figures, the *Exposition of the Law* takes up the study of Jewish legislation. "Having related in the previous treatises the lives of those whom Moses judged to be men of wisdom, who are set before us in the sacred Books as founders of our nation and in themselves unwritten laws, I shall now pass in due course to give full descriptions of the written laws" (*De Decalogo*, 1)[8] The main treatises are *De Decalogo* and the series entitled *De Specialibus Legibus* that deals successively with circumcision, the (divine) monarchy, temple, priests, sacrifice, and oaths. Philo then takes up the symbolism of the feast days. It is one of the most interesting chapters of the treatise. We will analyze it in great detail because it constitutes a valuable document both about contemporary Judaism and about Philo's method.

Firstly, every day is a feast day for the wise man. That is a Hellenistic ideal that we find again in Christianity. Then, Philo studies the Sabbath in regard to which he develops the dignities of the number seven.

> Some have given to it the name of virgin, having before their eyes its surpassing chastity. They also call her the motherless, begotten by the father of the universe alone, the ideal form of the male sex with nothing of the female . . . Some give it the name of the *season* [καιρός] judging its conceptual nature from its manifestation in the realm of sense. For seven is a factor common to all the phenomena which stand highest in the world of sensible things and serve to consummate in due order transitions of the year and recurring seasons. Such are the seven planets, the Great Bear, the Pleiades, and the cycles of the moon . . . For seven reveals as completed what six has produced, and therefore it may be quite rightly entitled the birthday of the world . . . (*De Specialibus Legibus* II, 56, 57, 59).[9]

8. *Philo* VII, 7.

9. Ibid., 343, 345.

This passage is characteristic of Philo. The Jewish theme of the seventh day is interpreted in function of the Pythagorean symbolism of seven.[10] We will meet the explanation of mysterious attributes of the number seven again.

After the Sabbath, the third feast is the monthly observance after the new moon. Then comes "the crossing-feast, which the Hebrews in their native language call *Pascha*" (*De Specialibus Legibus* II, 145).[11] In Philo, in fact, as in the Septuagint, *Pascha* is translated by διάβασις or διαβατήρια in an evident reference to crossing the Red Sea, whereas Theodotion will translated it as ὑπέρβασις, which evokes the Jewish first born spared by the Exterminating Angel. Moreover, Philo clearly defines the feast "a reminder and thanks-offering for that great migration from Egypt." He distinguishes the *Pascha* from the celebration of the unleavened bread, although they are observed together. He notes that this other feast has two meanings, one peculiar to the Jewish people, the remembrance of the departure from Egypt, and the other concerning all humanity, which relates to the harmony of the cosmos. In the second meaning the symbolism of the unleavened bread comes from the feast's coinciding with the spring equinox and thus being the anniversary of creation.

> In the spring equinox we have a kind of likeness and portraiture of that first epoch in which this world was created . . . So every year God reminds us of the creation of the world by setting before our eyes the spring when everything blooms and flowers . . . The feast begins at the middle of the month, on the fifteenth day, when the moon is full, a day purposely chosen because then there is no darkness, but everything is continuously lighted up as the sun shines from morning to evening and the moon from evening to morning and while the stars give place to each other no shadow is cast upon their brightness. Again, the feast is held for seven days . . . The first is the beginning of the feast and the end of the preceding past, the seventh is the end of the feast and the beginning of the coming future (*De Specialibus Legibus*, II, 151, 155, 156, 157).[12]

---

10. See Armand Delatte, *Études sur la littérature pythagoricienne*, 158–222. Already a century before Philo, Aristobulus, an Alexandrian Jew, had preceded him in this allegory of seven (Eusebius, *Preparatio Evangelica*, XIII, 12).

11. *Philo* VII, 395.

12. *Philo* V, 399, 401, 403.

Lastly, Philo connects a third feast with the paschal group, the one he calls "the first grains, the holy sheaves." It takes place on the day that follows the first, therefore the second of the seven days of the paschal fast.[13]

Next, the text speaks of Pentecost, which is the week of weeks and the feast of the first fruits of the harvest. In this context he specifies the concept of first fruits at great length (*De Specialibus Legibus*, II, 180). Then comes the *Hieromenia* or Feast of the Trumpets, which is the New Year's feast at the beginning of September. The Feast of the Fast follows it. This is the name Philo gives to the Day of Atonement (*Kippur*).[14] For him it is the holiest feast. It expiates the sins of the year that is ending and wins grace for the coming year (*De Specialibus Legibus*, II, 190). It takes place ten days after the beginning of the year (*De Specialibus Legibus*, II, 200). Finally, the feast of Tabernacles, *Scenopegia*, corresponds to the fall equinox. Philo interprets it either as a seasonal feast, the celebration of the completion of the grape harvest, or as the commemoration of the crossing of the desert by the ancestors of the Jewish people. All this symbolism is encountered again in the Fathers.[15] Notably absent are references to the feast of the Dedication and to Purim, feasts of recent origin and peculiarly Palestinian and national.

The end of the *Exposition of the Law* contains first of all the Treatise on Virtues. It begins with the last part of *De Specialibus Legibus* devoted to Justice. Then comes the treatise on Strength, on Goodness (φιλανθρωπία), on Penance and on Nobility. They are helpful for a study of the relations between Biblical and Hellenistic morality. There we find the first sketch of treatises on virtues that Christian theology would continue. Lastly, after showing the positive aspects of the Law, Philo dedicates a treatise to punishments and rewards. There is no eschatology. Philo describes the virtues of the patriarchs. He contrasts them with the punishments for sinners similarly envisaged at a purely temporal level.

13. See Pedersen, *Israel*, II:303 and 410.

14. [Translator: Daniélou's footnote seems to remit to the *Acts of the Apostles*. Philo's treatment of Rosh Hashanah, including trumpets, and Yom Kippur in *De Specialibus Legibus* is at 188 and 193; *Philo* VII, 188, 193.]

15. See Daniélou, "La Fête des Tabernacles," 262–79.

The Allegory of the Laws

In the *Exposition of the Law*, the exegesis remains close to the literal meaning. By contrast, in the *Allegorical Interpretation*, we encounter a work that is much more symbolic in nature. But at the same time, Philo expresses his ideas there much more. It is the primary work both for his theology and for his spirituality. That is why we will insist on it less here, since we will utilize it more in our systematic presentation. The first treatise is titled *Allegorical Commentary of the Holy Laws According to the Hexameron*. It is a commentary on chapters 2 and 3 of Genesis. In reality it is a treatise on anthropology mainly inspired by Aristotle and the Stoics, whose doctrine Philo rediscovers in Scripture thanks to the allegorical method. The work's structure is very puzzling. It begins without introduction, to the degree that it was thought that the beginning had been lost. But Fr. Delcuve in an unpublished thesis has shown that the book has a very subtle organization and in particular that it has neither beginning nor end . . . The essential theme, on the one hand, is the distinction of intelligible man or the idea of man and man as he is made, and moreover, the doctrine of knowledge, the relations of intelligence (Adam) and sensation (Eve) and those of will, ἡγεμονικόν, and the passions (animals). We meet all this again in Origen and Ambrose.

This predominantly philosophical treatise is misleading. The successive works are Philo's masterpieces. The first is *De Cherubim*. The two cherubim of the Paradise narrative are God's two powers, the creative power and the providential power. The fiery sword is the Logos, which is a fire that obtains good and destroys evil (*De Cherubim*, 28). But above all, this is the treatise where Philo develops his theory of the radical dependence of all things in relation to God. "In possession all things are God's, and only as a loan do they belong to created beings . . . And if we recognize that we have but their use, we shall tend them with care as God's possessions, remembering from the first, that it is the master's custom, when he will, to take back his own" (*De Cherubim*, 109, 118).[16] *De Sacrificiis Abelis et Caini* shows us φιλαυτία in Cain, which is the sin opposed to εὐχαριστία. The three sins against the action of grace are forgetfulness, pride, and the attitude that, while grace comes from God, we merit it. This might well be a controversy against certain Jews. The reason is remarkable: "'Not for thy righteousness . . . but . . . that he [God] might establish the covenant which he swore to our fathers' (Deuteronomy,

16. *Philo* II, 73, 79.

9:5). Now the covenant of God is an allegory of His gifts of grace" (*De Sacrificiis Abelis et Caini*, 57).[17]

The next treatise *That the Worse Attacks the Better* takes the occasion of the story of Cain and Abel. The basic idea is that man cannot know the invisible God. No soul is capable of knowing its creator. But thinking that this knowledge was useful, God breathed something divine into the soul. This is what explains man's aptitude to know everything. He does not stop with the world. He sees a limit there to his tireless course. The mind would not push beyond it "had it not been an inseparable portion of that divine and blessed soul?"(*Quod Deterius*, 90).[18] *De Posteritate Caini* contains one of Philo's two principal passages on negative theology, texts on which Gregory of Nyssa would directly depend:

> When therefore the God-loving soul probes the question of the essence of the Existent Being, he enters on a quest of that which is beyond matter and beyond sight. And out of this quest there accrues to him a vast boon, namely to apprehend that the God of real Being is apprehensible by no one, and to see precisely this, that He is incapable of being seen [ἰδεῖν ὅτι ἐστὶν ἀόρατός]"(*De Posteritate Caini*, 15–16).[19]

De Gigantibus refers to Genesis 6:2. It is a treatise on angels. "They are consecrated and devoted to the service of the Father and Creator whose wont it is to employ them as ministers and helpers, to have charge and care of mortal man" (*De Gigantibus*, 12).[20] *De Ebrietate* brings us to Noah, like *De Sobrietate, Quod Deus Immutabilis Sit, De Plantatione*, and *De Agricultura*. *De Confusione Linguarum* is above all a treatise on the Logos, who is called "*God's First-born*, the *Word*, who holds the eldership among the angels, their ruler as it were. And many names are his, for he is called, *the Beginning*, and the *Name of God*, and his *Word*, and the *Man after His Image*, and *he that sees*, that is, *Israel*" (*De Confusione Linguarum*, 146).[21] *De Migratione Abrahami* is an essential text from the spiritual point of view.[22]It must be distinguished from *De Abrahamo*,

---

17. Ibid., 137.

18. Ibid., 263.

19. Ibid., 337.

20. Ibid., 451.

21. *Philo* IV, 89, 91.

22. Philon d'Alexandrie, *La migration d'Abraham*, Greek text and French translation by René Cadiou.

which belongs to the other cycle. The great theme is "going forth" as origin of the spiritual life.

> God begins the carrying out of His will to cleanse man's soul
> by giving it a starting-point for full salvation in its removal out
> of three localities, namely, body, sense perception, and speech.
> "Land" or "country" is a symbol of body, "kindred" of sense-
> perception, "father's house" of speech . . . Nay, thou must change
> thine abode and betake thee to thy father's land, the land of the
> Word that is holy and in some sense father of those who sub-
> mit to training: and that land is Wisdom, abode most choice
> of virtue-loving souls. In this country there awaiteth thee the
> nature which is its own pupil, its own teacher . . . That nature
> is entitled Isaac . . . And the fountain from which the good
> things are poured forth is the companionship of the bountiful
> [φιλόδωρου] God (De Migratione Abrahami, 2, 28–29).[23]

The treatise *Who is the Heir of Divine Things?* is equally important in order to understand the doctrine about the Logos:

> To his word, His chief messenger, highest in age and honor, the
> father of all has given the special prerogative, to stand on the
> border and separate the creature from the creator. This same
> word both pleads with the immortal as suppliant for afflicted
> mortality and acts as ambassador of the ruler to the subject
> (*Quis Heres*, 205).[24]

We also find a rich spiritual doctrine in the ἡσυχία, the harvest (*Quis Heres*, 14). *De Congressu Quaerendae Eruditionis et Gratiae* concerns the marriage of Abraham and Hagar. Hagar is the figure of profane culture, of παιδεία, *De Congressu* is the primary text on Philo's conception of secular culture. The subsequent treatises continue to follow Abraham's life. They are *De Fuga et Inventione* (story of Ishmael) and *De Mutatione Nominum*. Two treatises come last: *De Somniis* deals with Joseph's dreams. In it we find first of all a very complete theory of dreams. We know this was a favorite topic of Hellenistic science. Moreover, it is a valuable source for Philo's mysticism. He reports how he received inspirations several times.

> Friend, it would seem that there is a matter great and precious of
> which thou knowest nothing, and this I will ungrudgingly shew

23. *Philo* IV, 133, 149. [Translator: I have not found the Greek phrase λόγος κατὰ προσφοράν that Daniélou indicates is in the first part of the passage translated here, which also appears earlier than he indicates.]

24. Ibid., 389.

thee, for many other well-timed lessons have I given thee. Know then, good friend, that God alone is the real veritable peace, free from all illusion, but the whole substance of things created only to perish is one constant war (*De Somniis*, II, 242–53).[25]

The Quaestiones

The last group of Philo's writings is made up of a third commentary on the Pentateuch, differing from the others in form and spirit. They are the *Quaestiones* on Genesis and Exodus. They are not continuous commentaries; rather interpretations of difficult passages are given. We now only possess the *Quaestiones* in Armenian. Aucher translated them into Latin in 1830.[26] They were not included in the Cohn-Wendland edition of Philo.[27] But Ralph Marcus translated them into English in 1953 with valuable notes. This is an important text where Philo gives the most esoteric side of his thought. Moreover, the *Quaestiones* are very interesting because for each passage Philo sets out the earlier literal and allegorical explanations. Thus it is also a valuable work for the history of allegorical exegesis before Philo.

Philo's Bible: the Septuagint

The Greek translation of the Bible, called the Septuagint or version of the seventy, is the foundation of Hellenistic Jewish religious culture. It established what was to become Philo's language, as well as that of the New Testament and the Greek Fathers.[28] The familiar legend reported by the letter of Aristeas describes how, in the third century, B.C., Ptolemy Philadelphus charged 72 old men with translating the Pentateuch. In reality we only know that this translation was made at Alexandria around this period. The other books of the Old Testament were translated during the following two centuries by different authors, as can be observed by the difference in translations of the same words. The versions are also quite

---

25. *Philo* V, 557.
26. Philo of Alexandria, *Paralipomena Armena*.
27. *Philonis Alexandrini, Opera Quae Supersunt*, edited by Cohn and Wendland.
28. See Dodd, *The Bible and the Greeks*.

uneven in literary value. Some attempts have been made to determine the order of translation.[29]

Whatever we make of this diversity, the Septuagint forms a whole that the Christian Church has considered the official translation of the Bible. But, was it so for the Jews? We know that in the first and second centuries of our era there would be new translations like Aquila's in Palestine, Theodotion's in Asia Minor, and Symmachus's among the Judeo-Christians. But this seems to have been the case much earlier. Indeed in Philo, the same Old Testament passages are cited now according to the Septuagint, now according to another translation. Peter Katz has recently maintained that this other translation represented a later revision by a Christian of the school of Antioch.[30] But another hypothesis is possible.

Indeed, Paul Kahle holds that there were never official translations of the Bible among the Jews.[31] The only official text was the Hebrew text. Taking up an idea of Manson, he thinks that in synagogue gatherings, the Hebrew text was always read first and then it was translated. The situation would have been the same as in the Catholic Church before the second Vatican Council where the official Latin alone was read first, then one of many existing translations. This would explain the presence in Origen's *Hexapla* of the second column, which is the transposition of the Hebrew text into Greek letters. This practice even seems to have existed in primitive Christianity acording to the opening of Melito of Sardis's Easter Homily. Moreover, this was what happened in Palestine with Aramaic. The Targumin are standard translations.

Certainly, this theory contains some truth. Indeed we have other examples of these variations outside of Philo. Josephus often departs from the Septuagint. It has been observed that his translation resembles the one Lucian of Antioch used in the third century. An ancient papyrus from the second century with this translation has been found. It thus pre-dates Lucian. It is also found in Theophilus of Antioch in the second century. Furthermore, it has been observed that quotations in Justin, who was born in Palestine in the second century, offer a different text from the Septuagint. A manuscript of the Minor Prophets has just been found in the desert of Judea that gives the text utilized by Justin.[32] If we then take

29. See Katz, "Septuaginta Studies in Mid Century," 176–208.

30. Katz, *Philo's Bible*.

31. Kahle, *Die hebräischen Handschriften*, 30ff.; also "Problems of the Septuagint," 328–38.

32. Barthélémy, "Redécouverte d'un chaînon manquant," 18–30.

the New Testament, we observe that the Psalms are quoted according to the Septuagint but that for Isaiah, while Luke follows the Septuagint, Matthew refers to a completely different text.[33] This is particularly striking for Isaiah 42 (Matthew 12:18). Now, we possess no other instance of this text utilized by Matthew.

These facts show us beyond doubt that there were several Greek versions of the Bible before the Christian era. Indeed, the geographical distribution of the translations will be noted. There was an Antioch version, and Asian version, and one or several Palestinian versions. It would be important to identify Matthew's Greek version of the Bible to situate the origins of his Gospel. Consequently, the Septuagint would have appeared as the Alexandrian version. Moreover, it is certain, as the papyruses have shown, that the Septuagint presents dialect characteristics or allusions that are definitely Egyptian. Swete has collected several in his introduction to the edition of the Septuagint.[34] Gerleman has added others.[35] Furthermore, this translation, at least in what concerns the law, was able to attain special authority.

The fact remains that Philo's exegesis is based essentially on the Septuagint. Therefore, that is what interests us here. Now the translation of the Septuagint bears traces of concerns peculiar to Judaism of this period and interprets the text in the direction of these concerns. In this regard, the Septuagint marks a transition between the Old and New Testaments, a stage in the theology of Judaism. There we find Judaism's concerns and at the same time the background of Philo's theology.

In the first place, as regards God we note the emphasis placed on universalism. Yahweh Sabaoth is translated Κύριος Παντοκράτωρ as in Job, Ecclesiastes, and I Kings. Isaiah keeps Θεὸς Σαβαώθ and the Psalms give Κύριος δυνάμεων. That is certainly within the meaning of the Hebrew expression, but conveys a development from the "God of Hosts" of Israel. The Septuagint insists on the idea of creation: "Who is a rock if it is not our God" is translated "Who will be a creator" (II Samuel 22:32).[36] Likewise the term eternity, which is not present in Semitic vocabulary, is in-

---

33. See Kilpatrick, *The Origins of the Gospel According to St. Matthew*, 56; also Stendahl, *The School of St. Matthew*.

34. *The Old Testament in Greek according to the Septuagint*, edited Swete.

35. Gerleman, *Studies in the Septuagint*, vol. 1: *Job*.

36. [Translator: Daniélou follows the usage of referring to I and II Samuel and I and II Kings instead of I–IV Kings. His II Samuel is II Kings in the other usage, and his I Kings is III Kings in the other usage.]

troduced by the Septuagint to distinguish God from the gods of different nations: "God is greater than man," the Hebrew text says. The Septuagint translates: "He that is above mortals is eternal," αἰώνιος (Job 33: 12; see also Job 34:17).

We also encounter a concern in Judaism with eliminating anthropomorphic expressions or actions unworthy of God. For that reason, the Septuagint, like the books of Jubilee, employs three procedures. In Exodus 24:10, "They saw the God of Israel" is replaced by "They saw the place (τόπος) where the God of Israel stood." Now, it is remarkable that this expression will be a very frequent substitute for "God" in the Tannaitic rabbis. Here, one expression is replaced by another that safeguards divine transcendence. A second procedure consists in replacing imaginative expressions by abstract ones. There are innumerable examples. The "hand of God" becomes the "power of God" (Isaiah 55:24). "Buckler" becomes "help" (Psalm 7:11). "Rock" becomes "support" and "stone" becomes "help" (Psalm 18:3). Finally, a third procedure, consistent throughout the Jubilees, is to attribute to angels what the Hebrew attributes to God. Exodus 4:24 states, "On the way Yahweh came to meet him and wanted to slay Moses." The Septuagint has, "the angel of the Lord." See also Judges 6:14 and 16.

We have similar attempt to soften the Biblical text in Isaiah 6:9. The Hebrew says, "Go and tell this people. You listen and do not comprehend. You see and do not understand." This is said of a positive action of God, who hardens the hearts of the wicked by the very manifestations of truth and veils a profound doctrine.[37] Now, the Septuagint completely erases the role of God, who limits himself to foretelling the blindness of the Jews: "Ye shall hear indeed, but ye shall not understand; and ye shall see indeed, but ye shall not perceive." It is worth noting that the text is quoted seven times in the New Testament and that Matthew and Acts follow the softened meaning of the Septuagint, whereas Mark and John remain faithful to the rigorist tone of the Hebrew (Matthew 13:14; Acts 28:26; Mark 4:12; John 12:40).[38] Likewise, the translation of Job attenuates the paradox of the misfortunate just man.[39]

Along with divine transcendence, the two most characteristic doctrines of Judaism are its eschatology and angelology. Regarding the

---

37. Feuillet, "Isaiah," col. 653.

38. See Skringar, L'aveuglement final dans Isaïe," 306ff.

39. Gerleman, *Studies in the Septuagint*, vol. 1: *Job*, 50–59.

former, we can note that the doctrine of resurrection is emphasized by the Septuagint, for example in Isaiah 26: 19 and in Daniel 12:2. A supplementary phrase is added to the book of Job 42:17: "It is written that he will rise again with those whom the Lord raises up." Similarly, resurrection is suggested in Job 19:25.

In angelology something similar occurs. In Deuteronomy 32:8 the Hebrew gives: "When the Most High assigns a portion to the nations . . . he gives the boundaries of the peoples, after the number of the children of Israel" (*beni Israel*). The Septuagint translates: "according to the number of the angels of God," which is an evident trace of the *haggadah* about the angels of nations that we have in the Apocalypses. We meet the angels again at the end of that same canticle of Moses in a verse that has no Hebrew parallel: "Rejoice ye gentiles with his people, and let all the sons of God strengthen themselves in him"[40] (Deuteronomy 32:43), where we find the parallel between sons of God or angels and nation. At 33:2 the Hebrew reads: "From his right hand shot forth flashes of light." The Septuagint renders this, "On his right hand *were* the angels with him."

In the Septuagint, besides Deuteronomy, the doctrine on angels appears in the Psalms. The first passage gives us the doctrine of the angels of the forces of nature. It is Psalm 104:4.[41] The Hebrew declares: "Of the winds he makes his messengers." The Septuagint interprets: "Who makes his angels spirits." In other passages we find a rectification of the text in a monotheistic direction. This occurs where mention is made of the *Elohim*. "All the gods prostate themselves before him" (Psalm 97:7)[42] is rendered "Worship him all ye angels." "In the presence of the gods, I wish to sing psalms" (Psalm 138:1)[43] is translated into "I will sing my psalms to thee before the angels." More important is Psalm 8:5. "You makest him a little less than God" is translated "You makest him a little less than the angels." The theme of transcendence appears here. Now, the Letter to the Hebrews bases itself upon the Septuagint text in these three passages to mark the superiority of Christ over the angels, despite his having been lowered for a time beneath them (Hebrews 1:5–8, 13). Here Paul's

40. [Translator: Daniélou has "angels" instead of "sons of God."]

41. [Translator: In the Septuagint's own numeration, which is followed by the Vulgate, this is Psalm 103.]

42. [Translator: In the Septuagint, Psalm 96.]

43. [Translator: In the Septuagint, Psalm 137.]

doctrine develops not the Hebrew but the Septuagint.[44] Manna is considered the food of angels by Psalm 78:25 in the Septuagint,[45] whereas the Hebrew only mentions the Strong. Now, in the Greek book of Wisdom 16:20, we read: "Thou feedest thine own people with angels' food." The *Beni Elohim* of Genesis 6:2 are understood to be angels and the verse to refer to the fall of the angels (See Job 1:6).[46]

Besides these characteristics stemming from Jewish concerns, we find the desire in the Septuagint to adapt the Bible to Hellenistic culture. First of all this involves the transformation of practices with an overly Semitic character. Gerleman has shown this clearly in Job, one of the books where it is most evident.[47] The book is adapted to Greek taste. (The Greek version is one fifth shorter than the Hebrew.) The vision of nature is more scientific and less animistic. "The stars sang" is replaced by "the stars were made" (Job 38:7). *Sheol* is translated as *Hades* or even as *Tartarus*, which is more literary and found only in Job. The name of one of Job's daughters, Keren Happuch (Job 42:14), which means "box of antinomy," is translated "Amalthaea's horn." The desert jackals (Job 30:29) become sirens. We see the Phoenix appear as a symbol of long life (Job 29:18).

The description of Leviathan and Behemoth (Job chapters 40 and 41) is particularly curious. Whereas the Hebrew text is more realistic, the Greek is more mythical. Instead of "under the belly of the [crocodile] are broken potsherds," the Greek translates "and all the gold of the sea under him [the dragon] is like an immense *quantity of* clay." Gerleman rightly sees there an allusion to the dragon that guards treasures.[48] He has been formed "to be sported with by my angels" (Job 41:24). "Sinners have made him an object of commerce" is translated "And do the nations feed upon a him" (Job 40:25),[49] which is found again in the Apocalypses. We have something other than mistranslation here. There is a genuine adaptation.

44. See Venard, "L'utilisation des Psaumes," 257ff.

45. [Translator: In the Septuagint, Psalm 77.]

46. [Translator: The *Septuagint*, however translates υἱοὶ Θεοῦ literally despite the traditional interpretation.]

47. Gerleman, *Studies in the Septuagint*, vol. 1: *Job*.

48. Ibid., 40.

49. [Translator: Illustrating Daniélou's point about the different lengths of Greek and Hebrew Job, there are at least two enumerations of Job chapters 40 and 41. Daniélou gives this verse as 30, which it is in the Jerusalem Bible. It is missing from the New King James, where chapter 40 ends at verse 24.]

Alongside the cultural adaptations, we must acknowledge the influence of Hellenistic thought with which the Alexandrian translators were permeated.[50] It affects several important passages. In the creation narrative (Genesis 1:2) the Biblical *tohu-bohu* is translated ἀόρατος καὶ ἀκατασκεύαστός which represents an expression taken from the *Timaeus* to designate prime matter.[51] In the creation of man, the Biblical *demut* is translated ὁμμοίωσις, which certainly also seems to be a reference to Plato and will orient all Philonic and Patristic speculation in a different direction from that of the Bible.[52] In Exodus 3:14, the revelation from the burning bush, "I Am Who Am," affirmation of divine sovereign subjectivity, is translated into Platonic language: Ἐγω ἔιμι ὁ ὤν, which orients it in the direction of ontological essentialism. Song of Songs 1:8 gives: "Tell me oh thou whom my hear loves, where you lead your sheep to pasture. If you do not know, fairest among women, follow in the footsteps of the flock." The Septuagint translate this as, "If thou know not thyself" (Ἐὰν μὴ γνῶς σεαυτήν). Origen will emphasize the similarity to a Platonic expression (*In Canticum*, ii).

Lastly, some other themes can be related to Alexandrian Jewish theology, as we find it in Philo. Psalm 110, the paradigmatic messianic psalm, gives in its third verse: "Your people offers itself to you in the day when your army gathers with the sacred vestments, from the womb of the morning you have the dew of young warriors." Now the Septuagint translates: "With thee is dominion in the day of thy power, in the splendors of thy saints (angels), I have begotten thee from the womb before the morning." The theme of the Messiah pre-existing in the society of the angels is a favorite of this period. The apparition of παρθένος to translate *alma* in Isaiah 7:14 is less surprising, if we recall that the theme of virginal maternity is frequent in Philo. The distinction of the spirit of piety and the spirit of fear that continues the seven gifts, where the Hebrew text only recognizes six (Isaiah 11:3) is completely in agreement with Philo's catalogues of virtues.[53]

---

50. See Heinisch, *Griechische Philosophie und Altes Testament*.

51. *Timaeus* 51 A. See however, Horovitz, *Untersuchungen über Philons und Platons Lehre*, 118.

52. *Theaetetus*, 176 A.

53. Drummond, *Philo Judaeus or the Jewish Alexandrian Philosophy*, has studied this question (I:156 ff.).

Alexandrian Exegesis before Philo

Not only does Philo employ the Alexandrian translation of Scripture, but also his exegesis is situated in a tradition that seems to have been rich and varied. We still have some traces of this Alexandrian exegesis before Philo. On the one hand it consists of edifying elaborations of sacred history parallel to the Palestinian Haggadah, but utilizing Hellenistic literary forms. We find this in apologetic narratives like those of Artapan and Eupolemus, in the *Tragedy of Exodus* by Ezekiel the tragedian, and above all at the end of the Wisdom of Solomon.

Of greater importance is the existence of an allegorical exegesis that itself presents different traits. The letter of Aristeus, which is certainly from the second century B.C., offers an allegorical interpretation of dietary prohibitions in Leviticus that we will find again in Philo (*De Specialibus Legibus*, IV, 116) and in Christian authors (Barnabas, X, 4), and that falls within a kind of pastoral exegeses concerned with drawing edifying lessons from legal precepts.[54] In this regard, as Hartwig Thyen has correctly seen,[55] it is interesting to note that allegorical exegesis of a moral type, far from being esoteric in nature, stems on the contrary from a concern for practical application. That is why it is found principally in homiletic literature in Philo and later in Origen.

But among Philo's precursors, we find a different sort of allegory in Aristobulus. Only a few fragments of this author have survived. His literary activity ought to be situated at the end of the first century before Christ. Thus, he is an immediate predecessor of Philo[56] His most important surviving fragment concerns the beginning of Genesis. The seventh day, identified with the first, is a symbol of wisdom from which all light comes. Here we are faced with speculations about the beginning of Genesis that are influenced by the Pythagorean number symbolism that we meet again in Philo and that fall under a completely different scholarly allegorical approach from the previous one.

The best way to become acquainted with the situation at Alexandria in this area is to interrogate Philo himself, as we have done for philosophy. We find, in fact, that he frequently refers to exegetes of different tendencies against whom he sets himself. Thereby, he himself introduces us

---

54. See S. Stein, "The Dietary Laws," 141–54.

55. Thyen, *Der Stil*, 80.

56. See Dalbert, *Die Theologie der hellenistisch-jüdischen Missionsliteratur*, 102–3.

into the controversies that existed in Alexandria in his time.[57] We grasp their extreme complexity. It is not always easy to identify the group to which he alludes in the context of what we otherwise know. But at least we have an overview.

The adversaries are firstly those who can be called extreme literal-ists. Shroyer has studied their position in an article.[58] In reality, distinct types can be recognized under this name. First of all, there are simple people, the ignorant, who by taking everything literally end up in absur-dities. The following passages envisages them:

> Then [Genesis 6:6] he [Moses] says that "in the beginning God made the heavens and the earth," taking "beginning" not as something, in a chronological sense, for time there was not be-fore there was a world. Time began either simultaneously with the world or after it . . . And since the word "beginning" is not taken as the chronological beginning, it would seem likely that the numerical order is indicated, so that "in the beginning He made" is equivalent to "He made the heavens first" (*Quod Im-mutabilis*, 21–22).[59]

Philo appears not as an allegorist but an exegete of the true literal mean-ing against a crude interpretation of it.

Philo gives some examples of these materialistic interpretations at the beginning of *De Opificio*. "He says that in six days the word was cre-ated, not that its Maker required a length of time for His work, for we must think of God as doing all things simultaneously . . . Six days are mentioned because for the things coming into existence there was need of order" (*De Opificio*, 13).[60] Here his criticism envisages anthropomor-phic interpretations. Moreover, these interpretations are directly envis-aged further on. We are dealing with the expression *In the beginning*:

> Then he [Moses] says that "in the beginning God made the heaven and the earth," taking "beginning" not, as some think, in a chronological sense, for time there was not before there was a world. Time began either simultaneously with the world or after it . . . And since the word "beginning" is not taken as the chrono-logical beginning, it would seem likely that the numerical order

---

57. See Edmund Stein, *Die allegorische Exegese des Philo*.

58. Shroyer, "Alexandrian Jewish Literalists," 261ff.

59. *Philo* III, 21.

60. *Philo* I, 13.

is indicated, so that "in the beginning He made" is equivalent to
"He made heaven first" (*De Opificio*, 26–27).[61]

In these passages we see a concern for reflective interpretation against
materialist interpretations

Similarly, in the *Quaestiones in Genesim*, Philo criticizes unacceptable interpretations. Thus, regarding Genesis 8:1, "God brought a wind
upon the earth and the water stayed [tr. receded]," Philo writes:

> Some would say that by "spirit" is meant the wind through which
> the flood ceased. But I myself do not know of water being dimin-
> ished by a wind. Rather is it disturbed and seethes. Otherwise vast
> expanses of the sea would long ago have been consumed. Accord-
> ingly (Scripture) now seems to speak of the spirit of the deity, by
> which all things are made secure (*In Genesim*, II, 28).[62]

When these literal interpretations deal with God, they lead to real
impiety. Thus, in regard to the expression, "Cain went forth from the face
of God," Philo writes:

> Let us here raise the question whether in the books in which
> Moses acts as God's interpreter we ought to take his statements
> figuratively, since the impression made by the words in their
> literal sense is greatly at variance with truth. For if the Existent
> being has a face . . . what grounds have we for rejecting the impi-
> ous doctrines of Epicurus, or the atheism of the Egyptians, or
> the mythical plots of play and poem of which the world is full?
> For face is a piece of a living creature, and God is a whole not a
> part" (*De Posteritate Caini*, 1).[63]

Moreover, regarding these "simple" folk, Philo has only pity. Still, their
case is fairly serious, because it is a source of scandal. Indeed, this naive
interpretation leads some Jews to stop taking Scripture seriously and to
abandon the faith.

Accordingly, regarding "tunics of skin," Philo declares: "Some may
ridicule the text when they consider the cheapness of the apparel of
tunics, as being unworthy of the touch of such a creator" (*In Genesim*,

---

61. Ibid., 21, 23. [Translator: Daniélou has "le monde" where Colson and Whitaker have "heaven." Since the Greek says οὐρανόν here, it would seem that Colson and
Whitaker are right.]

62. *Philo, Supplement I*, 106.

63. *Philo II*, 329.

I, 53).[64] Philo first defends the literal sense, showing the superiority of poverty over wealth. Then he goes on to the spiritual sense. Others mock the change of name of Abram to Abraham:

> Some of the uncultivated, or rather, of the uninitiated and of those who do not belong to the divine chorus ridicule and reproach the one who is blameless in nature, and say reproachfully and chidingly, "Oh, what a great gift! The Ruler and Lord of all has graciously given one letter, by which He has increased and made greater the name of the patriarch, so that instead of having two syllables it has three." Oh what great devilishness and impiety (it is) that some presume to bring forward slanders against God, being deceived by the superficial aspects of names, whereas it would be proper to thrust their minds into the depths in search of the inner facts for the sake of greatly possessing the truth. And yet these (names) which are ready to hand (and) which someone is said to have granted (in) writing –why do you not believe that (they are) the work of Providence and that this is to be honored? (*In Genesim*, III, 43).[65]

Philo then takes up the study of the letter A. But we see that here again, he defends the true sense of Scripture, the literal sense, which is the name's symbolism against a crudely materialist view.

A final example is that of Esau's selling his birthright for a mess of pottage. Philo tells us:

> I know that things of this kind provide (occasion for) ridicule and mocking derision to uncultivated men and those who lack consistency of character and do not recognize any form or appearance of virtue and attribute their own uneducatedness and stupidity and perversity and thoughtlessness to the Holy Scriptures, which are more truthful than any other thing. And the reason for this is that just as the blind merely touch and approach and come near to bodies by touch but are not able to perceive their color, shape, form, or any other particular property whatever, so also uneducated, untrained, and untaught men, blinded in soul and thick-skinned, dwell on the literal meaning only rather than on the (content of the) narrative and touch and deal only with the words and the literal text. But they are unable to look into the inner (meaning) at the intelligible forms. And the literal meaning contains a not insignificant reproof of the

---

64. *Philo, Appendix* I, 30.
65. *Philo, Appendix* II, 234.

intemperate man for the admonition of those who can be cured
(*In Genesim*, IV, 168).[66]

Here again, it is worth noting that Philo condemns stupid literalism in the
name of intelligent literal meaning. The spiritual sense only comes later.

A second kind of extreme literalists are the syncretists. These are
learned men. But they no longer see the transcendence of the Bible and its
difference from other religions. They are the ancestors of certain modern
representatives of the school of history of religions. They assimilate Jewish institutions to pagan customs and lose sight of their transcendence.
Regarding comments on Abraham's sacrifices of animals divided into two
groups, Philo remarks:

> But I am not unaware that all such things give occasion to idle
> calumniators to reject the Sacred Writings and to talk nonsense
> about them. Thus they say that in the present instance nothing
> else but the sacrificial victim is described and indicated by the
> dismembering and dividing of the animals and by the inspec-
> tion of the entrails (*In Genesim*, III, 3).[67]

Philo offers a remarkable answer to these criticisms:

> But such people, it seems to me, are (in the class) of those who
> judge and evaluate the whole by only one part, and do not,
> on the contrary, (judge) the part by the whole . . . Accordingly,
> the Legislation is in some sense a unified creature, which one
> should view from all sides in its entirety with open eyes and
> examine the intention of the entire writing exactly, truly, and
> clearly, not cutting up its harmony or dividing its unity (*In
> Genesim*, III, 3).[68]

Or again, the Old Testament narratives are related to myths. This
posture is clearly depicted in *De Confusione Linguarum*:

> Persons who cherish a dislike of the institutions of our fathers
> and make it their constant study to denounce and decry the
> Laws find in these [about the tower of Babel] and similar pas-
> sages openings as it were for their godlessness. "Can you still,"
> say these impious scoffers, "speak gravely of the ordinances as
> continuing the canon of absolute truth? For see your so-called
> holy books contain also myths, which you regularly deride when

66. Ibid., 453–54.
67. Ibid., 178.
68. Ibid., 178–79.

you hear them related by others" (*De Confusione Linguarum*, 2).[69]

The issue is the comparison between the tower of Babel and the Homeric episodes of the giants piling Pelion on Ossa to storm heaven.[70] Philo next alludes to another myth that the adversaries of Moses relate to the confusion of tongues, according to which in the beginning beasts and men spoke the same language.[71] He shows that in the simple literal sense there is no parallel to these two passages. Thus, for the second: "Now Moses, say the objectors, brings his story nearer to reality and makes a distinction between reasoning and unreasoning creatures, so that the unity of language for which he vouches applies to men only" (*De Confusione Linguarum*, 9).[72] It is noteworthy that through Eusebius we know the men to whom he refers in the first case. They were syncretistic Jewish writers who likened Biblical narratives to Homeric myths (*Praeparatio Evangelica*, IX, 11 and 17).[73]

Especially deserving of attention is Philo's refutation of these comparative scholars who liken the sacrifice of Isaac to human sacrifices in pagan religions:

> But quarrelsome critics who misconstrue everything and have a way of valuing censure above praise do not think Abraham's action great or wonderful, as we suppose it to be. They say that many other persons, full of love for their kinsfolk and offspring, have given their children, some to be sacrificed for their country to serve as a price to redeem it from wars or drought or excessive rainfall or pestilence, others for the sake of what was held to be piety though it is not really so. Indeed they say that among the Greeks men of the highest reputation, not only private individuals but kings have with little thought of their offspring put them to death and thereby saved armed forces of great strength and magnitude . . . Barbarian nations, they add, have for long admitted child sacrifice as a holy deed and acceptable to God, and this practice of theirs is mentioned by the holy Moses as an abomination [Deuteronomy 12:31] . . . Again they point out that in India the gymnosophists even now when the long incurable

69. *Philo* IV, 11.

70. Abydenos made the identification according to Eusebius, *Praeparatio Evangelica* IX, 14, as well as Eupolemus, *Praeparatio Evangelica* IX, 17.

71. Josephus, *Antiquities of the Jews*, I:1, 4.

72. *Philo* IV, 15.

73. This is also what we find in the *Sibylline Oracles*.

disease of old age begins to take hold of them, even before they are completely in its clutches, make up a funeral pile and burn themselves on it . . . And the womenfolk when the husbands died before them have been known to hasten rejoicing to share their pyre; and allow themselves to be burned alive with the corpses of the men. Why then, they ask, should we praise Abraham, as though the deed which he undertook was unprecedented when private individuals and kings and whole nations do it when occasion calls? To their malignity and bitterness I reply as follows. Some of those who sacrifice their children follow custom in so doing, as was the case according to the critics with some of the barbarians . . . These give their children partly under compulsion and the pressure of higher powers, partly through the desire for glory and honor, to win fame at the time and a good name in the future. Now those who are led by custom to make the sacrifice would not seem to be doing anything great . . . Where the gift is made through fear no praise is due . . . And if anyone throws away a son or daughter through desire for glory he will be justly blamed . . . We must therefore examine whether Abraham, when he intended to sacrifice his son, was mastered by any of these motives, custom or love of honor or fear. Now in Babylonia and Mesopotamia and with the nations of the Chaldeans with whom he was brought up and lived the greatest part of his life the custom of child slaughter does not obtain . . . Surely, too, he had nothing to fear from man . . . Nor was he under the pressure of any public misfortune . . . What praise could there be in a solitude? . . . That the deed really deserves our praise and love can easily be seen in many ways. First, then, he made a special practice of obedience to God, a duty which every right-minded person holds to be worthy of all respect and effort (*De Abrahamo*, 178–92).[74]

Accordingly, the comparative approach is wrong, because it associates things that are really different. But even if these things were similar, because of the approach's excessive literalness, it would still be wrong to classify the Biblical narratives as fables. So, for example, we must acknowledge that the story of Eve's creation is fictional (μυθῶδες). "For how could anyone admit that a woman, or a human being at all, came into existence out of a man's side?" (*Legum Allegoriae*, II 19),[75] Likewise, the serpent of Genesis is also presented as fictional (μυθῶδες) in *De Agricultura*, 97. Philo explains how figurative interpretation allows us to set aside the

---

74. *Philo* VI, 89, 91, 93, 95.

75. *Philo* I, 239.

mythical element.[76] The same goes for those who interpret the tree of life as if, just as some plants are fatal, others transmit immortality. But, Philo adds, they do not know how such plants have this salutary power. That is why here again we must resort to the figurative sense (*In Genesim*, I, 10).

But these literalists, whether unintelligent because of ignorance or hostility, are not the only ones Philo knows. There is another infinitely more respectable kind and, for our author, more dangerous because of that very thing. They are the kind of Jews who practice literal exegesis intelligently but refuse to acknowledge another type. Here Philo no longer defends the literal meaning against deformation but the allegorical interpretation against pure literalism. Indeed, we frequently see him talking about persons who are experts in explaining the letter of Scripture. Regarding a passage in Leviticus 14:36, where it is said that when leprosy is in a house, the priest ought to start by taking away all of the objects in it for fear they may become impure, Philo writes: "Now whether in the plain and literal sense of the ordinance these things are consistent with each other is a matter for those who are used to such questions and find pleasure in them. But *we* must say positively that no two things can be more consistent with each other than that, when the priest has entered, the belongings of the house are defiled" (*Quod Immutabilis*, 133).[77] We see that here these specialists explained difficult passages through a subtle exegesis without recurring to allegory. Philo alludes to exactly this subtlety with the name he ordinarily gives them, σοφιστής, which means, "clever man, scholar." Accordingly about Exodus 22:26, Philo writes: "Let what has been said and other considerations of the same kind suffice for the self-satisfied pedantic professors [σοφισταί] of literalism, and let us in accordance with the rules of allegory make such remarks on this passage as are appropriate" (*De Somniis*, I, 102).[78]

These are the same personages that Philo seems to mean in an odd passage of *De Cherubim*. He is getting ready to explain the paradigmatic allegorical mystery, the marriages of the Patriarchs as figures of the birth of virtues:

76. But in *Quaestiones in Genesim* I, 32, he justifies the literal sense by the power of God and by the exceptional circumstances at the beginning of the world.

77. *Philo* III, 77. [Translator: Daniélou renders the second sentence as a denial that the passage is consistent. But the whole context, which makes a point somewhat similar to St. Paul's affirmation that with the law sin comes into the world, supports the Loeb rendering of Colson and Whitaker.]

78. *Philo* V, 351

> The virtues have their conception and their birth pangs, but when I purpose to speak of them, let them who corrupt religion into a superstition [δεισιδαίμονες] close their ears or depart. For this is a divine mystery and its lesson is for the initiated who are worthy to receive the holiest secret, even those who in simplicity of heart practice the piety which is true and genuine, free from all tawdry ornament. The sacred relation is not for those others who under the spell of the deadly curse of vanity, have no other standards for measuring what is pure and holy but their barren words and phrases and their silly usages and ritual (*De Cherubim*, 42).[79]

These last traits let us situate these personages: their subtleties in literal exegesis, their complications in the Halakah are exactly the characteristics of the Palestinian scribes. Wolfson[80] is completely right in seeing here a description of rabbinical exegesis as we will find it in the Talmud, which represents a tendency totally hostile to Philo.

We observe that, to the contrary of what occurred earlier, Philo does not condemn the method. Literal exegesis is good and necessary for him. He always begins with it in the *Quaestiones*. We saw him reject the mythological explanation in regard to the episode of confusion of tongues. On the contrary, he has no objection to the episode being taken literally as an explanation of there being different languages. "I would not censure such persons, for perhaps the truth is with them also" (*De Confusione*, 190).[81] But he invites us not to stop there and to go on to figurative interpretation (*De Confusione*, 190). Consequently, his position seems quite clear. Literal exegesis is good, but one must not halt there. Thus, regarding the four wells found by Isaac's servants, Philo writes:

> It may be that men of narrow citizenship will suppose that the lawgiver delivers this very full discourse about digging wells, but those who are on the roll of a greater country, even this whole world, men of bigger thought and feeling, will be quite sure that the four things propounded as a subject of inquiry to the open-eyed lovers of contemplation are not four wells, but the four parts of this universe (*De Somniis*, I, 39).[82]

---

79. *Philo* II, 33, 35.
80. Wolfson, *Philo*, I:6.
81. *Philo* IV, 113, 115.
82. *Philo* V, 315.

Here we have a new meaning: the literalists are μικροπολῖται. They are shut up in the narrowly national, literal sense of scripture, whereas the interpretation of others is universalist.

Accordingly, what Philo reproaches is not their science in the literal sense; it is the scorn for everything that goes beyond the literal meaning. Here we can recall an expression we passed over without emphasis. When they hear someone speak of allegory, they frown (*De Somniis*, I, 102) sowing their lack of confidence and their disdain. Philo shows us these people again: "But since it is our purpose to examine the more allegorical meaning after the literal, I must say what is needful on that also. Perhaps some of the more thoughtless will laugh at my words" (*De Josepho*, 125).[83] If we recall that Philo's treatises are surely in part synagogue sermons, we have very lively vignettes here, where we see different groups reacting during the homily, and Philo taking them aside and inviting them to leave, "Let them go away," when he is about to delve into more mystical interpretations.[84]

The different kinds of literalist make up a first group of Philo's opponents. But they are not the only ones. Indeed we have observed that if Philo was opposed to a purely literal interpretation of the law, he nevertheless maintained the importance of this interpretation. So, he encounters a second kind of adversary at the opposite extreme, pure allegorists, those who deny on the one hand, the literal sense of the Law, seeing in it only pure symbol and, on the other hand, reject observance for a purely spiritual religion. The chief text on this point is found in *De Migratione Abrahami*:

> There are some who, regarding laws in their literal sense in the light of symbols of matters belonging to the intellect, are over-punctilious about the latter, while treating the former with easy-going neglect. Such men I for my part should blame for handling the matter in too easy and off-hand a manner: they ought to have given careful attention to both aims, to a more full and exact investigation of what is not seen and in what is seen to be stewards without reproach. As it is, as though they were living alone by themselves in a wilderness, or as though they had become disembodied souls, and knew neither city nor village nor household nor any company of human beings at all,

---

83. *Philo* VI, 201.

84. See again *De Somniis* II, 301; *Philo* V, 579.

overlooking all that the mass of men regard, they explore reality
in its naked absoluteness (*De Migratione Abrahami*, 89–90).[85]

We see the meaning of the text. Philo again does not reprimand the
search for the spiritual sense and for intelligible goods. To the contrary,
we will see the value he attributes to them. But he condemns the attitude
of those whom this search for spiritual goods leads to neglect humble
external observances.

> It is quite true that the seventh day is meant to teach the power
> of the Unoriginate [ἀγένητος] and the non-action of created be-
> ings. But let us not for this reason abrogate the laws laid down
> for its observance, and light fires or till the ground or carry loads
> or institute proceedings in court or act as jurors or demand the
> restoration of deposits or recover loans, or do all else that we are
> permitted to do as well on days that are not festival seasons. It
> is true also that the feast is a symbol of gladness of soul and of
> thankfulness to God, but we should not for this reason turn our
> backs on the general gatherings of the year's seasons. It is true
> that receiving circumcision does indeed portray the excision of
> pleasure and all passions, and the putting away of the impious
> conceit, under which the mind supposed that it was capable of
> begetting by its own power: but let us not on this account repeal
> the law laid down for circumcising. Why, we shall be ignoring
> the sanctity of the temple and a thousand other things, if we are
> going to pay heed to nothing except what is shewn us by the in-
> ner meaning of things. Nay, we should look on all these outward
> observances as resembling the body, and their inner meanings
> as resembling the soul. It follows that, exactly as we have to take
> thought for the body, because it is the abode of the soul, so we
> must pay heed to the letter of the laws. If we keep and observe
> these, we shall gain a clearer conception of those things of which
> these are the symbols" (*De Migratione Abrahami*, 91–93).[86]

We see that this passage is remarkably clear and balanced. In it
Philo explicitly affirms against the allegorists that spiritual interpretation of the Law in no way dispenses from literal observance. The perfect man is one who combines the two, neither pure literalist nor pure
allegorist. Moreover, says Philo, the true friends of virtue "are valiant
guardians of the laws which their father, right reason, has laid down,
and faithful stewards of the customs which their mother, instruction,

85. *Philo* IV, 183.
86. Ibid., 183, 185.

has introduced" (*De Ebrietate*, 80).[87] Accordingly, the personal religion that Philo calls the natural law must be joined with the social religion that he calls the positive law. Finally, in the passage from *De Migratione*, we note the two reasons Philo provides to justify the observance of the letter of the Law. The first is man's social nature: pure allegorists are asocial beings. The second is man's corporeal nature: pure allegorists are incorporeal souls. Now, this will be the reason Origen will offer later to justify the visible cult.

Along with this extreme allegorism that he rejects, Philo knew exegetes in contemporary Alexandria who preceded him in the healthy use of allegory. A passage in *De Specialibus Legibus* deals with Passover. Philo first recalls that the law mandated that Passover be celebrated yearly, "to remind them of their duty of thanksgiving . . . But to those who are accustomed to turn literal facts into allegory [δι' ἀλληγορίαν], the Crossing-festival suggests [αἰνίττεται] the purification of the soul" (*De Specialibus Legibus*, II, 146–47).[88] Here we have a spiritual interpretation connected to tradition. Elsewhere, speaking of the cherubim on the ark, Philo writes: "Some hold that, since they are set facing each other, they are symbols of the two hemispheres, one above the earth and one under it" (*De Vita Mosis*, 98).[89] Similarly in *De Josepho*: "I have heard, however, some scholars give an allegorical exposition of this part of the story in a different form. It was as follows. The king of Egypt, they said, was our mind, the ruler of the land of the body" (*De Josepho*, 151).[90]

Philo sometimes designates these exegetes with the more precise name of natural philosophers: "I have also heard some natural philosophers (φυσικοί) who took the passage allegorically, not without good reason. They said that the husband was a figure of the good mind . . . The wife, they said, was virtue, her name being in Chaldean *Sarah*" (*De Abrahamo*, 99).[91] Likewise in *De Posteritate Caini*: "Well, if God has not a face,.. the only thing left for us to do is to make up our minds that none of the propositions put forward is literally intended and to take the path of figurative interpretation so dear to philosophical souls" (*De Posteritate*, 7).[92]

---

87. *Philo* III, 80.

88. *Philo* VII, 397.

89. *Philo* II, 497.

90. *Philo* VI, 213.

91. Ibid., 53.

92. *Philo* II, 331.

The term does not have our modern meaning. To understand it, we must recall what φύσις, nature, is for Philo.[93] Essentially, it is opposed to θέσις, that which is established by man. Θέσις is the totality of positive laws which constitutes the literal meaning and are peculiar to the Jewish people. By contrast, the universal realities that are symbolized by these laws are φύσις. The person who stays within the θέσις, the literalist, is an inhabitant of his little city (μικροπολίτης). He who knows their spiritual meaning, on the contrary is a κοσμπολίτης.

Through Philo, we perceive that these allegories constitute several different tendencies. In *Quaestiones*, we often see him give several possible interpretations. Thus for the tree of life: "Some believe that as plants are corporeal and subject to death, so also some have life and immortality . . ."—This is the literal interpretation that is mythological and that must rightly be rejected.

> For some say that the tree of life is the earth, for it causes all things to grow for the life of both man and all other things. Wherefore He apportioned a central place to this plant; and the center of all is the earth. And some say that the tree of life is a name for the seven circles which are in heaven. And some say it is the sun because it is, in a sense, the midst of the planets and is the cause of the seasons, by which all things are produced. And some have said that the tree of life is the government of the soul . . . And the center, in one meaning, is the chief and head, as is the leader of a chorus. But worthy and excellent men say that the tree of life is the best of the virtues in man, namely piety, through which pre-eminently the mind becomes immortal (*In Genesim*, 10).[94]

If we take up this text again, we see that Philo gives interpretations that respond to four principal headings. First of all there is the literal sense that we have already seen. Next, there is a cosmological interpretation: the tree of life is a figure of earth or the fourth heaven or the sun. That was the Stoic sort of interpretation. In pre-Philonic Judaism, it was typical, and we meet it again in Philo. Then comes the psychological interpretation: the tree of life is a figure of the spirit, the highest part

93. On φύσις and νόμος, see Heinimann, *Nomos und Physis*, (according to the fifth century B.C. Greek philosophers). See also Greene, *Moira*. [Translator: I surmise that Daniélou got his information about Greene's book from an article by Édouard Des Plantes, S.J., in the 1949 volume of *Recherches de Science Religieuse*.] It may be observed that this doctrine of θέσις as inferior to φύσις will cause difficulty for positive revelation.

94. *Philo, Appendix* I, 6–7. See also *Legum Allegoriae*, 1, 49.

of the soul. This interpretation was also classical before Philo. Several times he has shown us people who see this spirit in Pharaoh, or the spirit of sensation in Abraham and Hagar. Finally come the *optimi viri*, the perfect, the really initiated, for whom the interpretation is mystical: it is the mystery of perfect virtue and union with God. This exegesis is especially dear to Philo.

We can observe that the distinction of these different tendencies captures what we know otherwise about pre-Philonic Alexandrian exegesis, to which we will refer shortly. Cosmological exegesis appears in the book of Wisdom and in Flavius Josephus, as we will see further on. It even seems to be announced in figurative monuments, particularly in what concerns the seven-branched candlestick.[95] Moral exegesis characterizes synagogue homilies, whose echo is found in the Letter of Aristeus. Lastly, mystical exegesis corresponds to what we have found in Aristobulus. Josephus's account leaves no doubt that it is what the Therapeutae practiced.

95. See Goodenough, *Jewish Symbols*, IV:75–80.

Chapter 4

Philo's Exegesis

AFTER ALL WE HAVE just said, Philo's theoretical position in the field of exegesis seems quite moderate and truly exemplary. On the one hand, wherever possible, he safeguards the proper literal sense. On the other hand, he often discerns with great accuracy the cases in which the literal meaning is figurative, as in the case of the narratives at the beginning of Genesis as well as in certain anthropomorphisms. Lastly, he affirms that the literal explanation of the text is not everything, that the text also contains a spiritual meaning. So far we are completely in agreement with him. Why then does his endeavor ultimately disappoint us from the exegetical viewpoint, setting aside the theological and mystical viewpoint? It is because of the practical application of this double exegesis. Indeed, both literal and spiritual exegesis alike suffers from a fundamental flaw. The defect in literal exegesis is that Philo interprets the Biblical text in function of a purely Hellenistic culture. The defect of the spiritual exegesis is that Philo totally lacks a sense of history and that instead of showing Old Testament events as the figure of eschatological events, the way the contemporary Apocalypses did, he sees in them the sensible reflections of an atemporal, intelligible world.

Literal Exegesis

Let us first discuss literal exegesis. For Philo, it consists of putting all of contemporary Hellenistic science at the service of understanding Scripture.[1] The idea in itself is sound. St. Augustine will still hold it. This is what Henri-Irenée Marrou shows in his thesis on *St. Augustine and the End of Classical Culture.*[2] We could do exactly the same study on Philo, and we would end with the same result. In particular, we come to the astonishing discovery that for the ancients science essentially consists of the handing on of a certain number of techniques and not at all in discovery and progress. This placing science at the service of exegesis often ends in confusion that perennially befalls harmonization. But beyond that, a conception that appears in Philo will dominate all ancient and medieval exegesis, and therefore it is worth our while to pause for a moment.

Above, we quoted a text where Philo told us that the true friend of virtue is able to maintain fidelity to its mother, παιδεία, and its father, right reason. In that text παιδεία was associated with literal fulfillment of the law as opposed to its spiritual observance. This shows us that from the start there is a link between literal meaning and παιδεία. Παιδεία is the realm of everything received through teaching, transmitted by tradition. In *De Migratione Abrahami*, 39, Philo sees symbolism in the fact that hearing is how truths are transmitted to us indirectly, whereas wisdom is compared to the eye, which is direct contact with reality. So παιδεία has value (*De Mutatione*, 228). It represents a necessary stage, and in that it is like literal meaning. But it is only an inferior stage (*De Ebrietate*, 186), which is nothing alongside wisdom, and something that ought to be left behind. This likewise connects it to literal meaning.

The content of παιδεία is quite diverse. It encompasses all we learn. First of all, therefore, παιδεία will include the Jewish Law. We will not insist further on this, because it is evident. We will only observe that for Philo the law is essentially the Torah, the Pentateuch. He makes the Pentateuch alone the object of his commentary. In the *Exposition of the Law* he cites it alone. In other commentaries there are some references to the Psalms and to the books of Kings, but they are very rare. A quote from Samuel is presented as from "former times" (*De Migratione Abrahami*, 38).[3] Philo still regards the other books as inspired (*De Confusione*,

1. See Festugière, *Le dieu cosmique*, 528.
2. Marrou, *Saint Augustin et la fin.*
3. *Philo* IV, 153.

149). Goodenough thinks they are inspired for Philo but not in the same sense.[4] It is hard to tell.

What place, on the other hand, do we see Philo allot to Jewish oral traditions? Indeed a characteristic of Palestinian Rabbinical practice was to establish an entire legislative tradition alongside the law to settle hard cases. This is called Halakah. Furthermore, there were wondrous or edifying traditions with which Scripture had been embellished and which constituted Haggadah. We find no trace, so to speak, of the latter in Philo. The aspects that are cited are insignificant and could come from another source. At the beginning of *Moses*, Philo certainly writes: "I will . . . tell the story of Moses, as I have learned it, both from the sacred books . . . and from some of the elders of the nation" (*De Vita Mosis*, I, 4).[5] But these elders may perfectly well be the authors of Old Testament books other than the Pentateuch. For Halakah the matter is more complicated. Heinemann only records a few traces of it.[6]

Moreover, παιδεία is Hellenistic culture. Philo often elaborated upon the importance he attributed to it, but in particular he devoted a treatise to it, *De Congressu Quaerendae Eruditionis et Gratiae*. This is an allegorical commentary on the union of Abraham, who is the symbol of beginning, with Hagar, the symbol of profane culture in contrast to Sarah, who is wisdom. Thus it is indeed fitting to first acquire human culture. "For, just as in houses we have outer doors in front of the chamber doors, and in cities suburbs through which we can pass to the inner part, so the school course [ἐγκύκλιος παιδεία] precedes virtue" (*De Congressu*, 10).[7] This *encyclios paideia* is the school curriculum as all antiquity knew it,[8] whose parts Philo enumerates: grammar, rhetoric, dialectic, music, geometry (*De Congressu*, 15–19), to which astronomy and physics must be added. Philosophy, history, natural sciences, and law constitute higher education, which does not form part of the *encyclios paideia*.

Philo greatly values this culture. It is necessary. But it is only a stage. It is the handmaiden of Philosophy:

---

4. Goodenough, *By Light, Light*, 77–80.

5. *Philo* VI, 279.

6. Heinemann, *Philons griechische und jüdische Bildung*. In the contrary direction see Belkin, *Philo and the Oral Law*.

7. *Philo* IV, 463.

8. See Marrou, *Histoire de l'éducation*.

> When first I was incited by the goads of philosophy to desire her I consorted in early youth with one of her handmaids, Grammar, and all that I begat by her, writing, reading and study of the writings of the poets, I dedicated to her mistress. And again I kept company with another, namely Geometry . . . Again my ardor moved me to keep company with a third; rich in rhythm, harmony and melody was she, and her name was Music. . . . For some have been ensnared by the love lures of the handmaids and spurned the mistress, and have grown old, some doting on poetry, some on geometrical figures . . . and forget their pledges to Philosophy (*De Congressu*, 74–78).[9]

Furthermore, Philosophy itself is not the summit. It is subordinated to wisdom as the liberal arts are subordinated to it.

> Wisdom is the knowledge of things divine and human and their causes. And therefore just as the culture of the schools is the bondservant of philosophy, so must philosophy be the servant of wisdom. Now philosophy teaches us the control of the belly and the parts below it, and control also of the tongue. Such powers of control are said to be desirable in themselves, but they will assume a grander and loftier aspect if practiced for the honor and service of God (*De Congressu*, 79–80).[10]

Now, wisdom is the spiritual understanding of scripture. All profane culture, in elucidating literal meaning, has the object of preparing the way to contemplation. We are going to take some examples of Philo's utilization of different sciences.

First comes grammar. It involves two parts: learning to read and explaining the authors. When we see Philo reflecting on the letter *a*, in the context of its addition to the name Abram, he refers to the first part: "For the first written element of sound is *a*, both in order and in power. Second, it is a vowel and the first of the vowels, being fitted on to them like a kind of head. And third, it is not naturally one of the long vowels, and not naturally one of the short ones, but one of those which have both these (quantities)."[11] References to explanations of authors are more important. On the one hand, as to how content shows that grammar is useful for virtue, Philo explains: "It will teach us also to despise the vain delusions of our empty imagination by shewing us the calamities which

---

9. *Philo* IV, 495, 497.

10. Ibid., 497, 499.

11. Ibid., 234–35.

heroes and semi-gods who are celebrated in such literature are said to have undergone" (*De Congressu*, 15).[12]

That is an obvious reference to the authors explained, in particular Homer. Moreover, we know that the ancients did not distinguish between history and mythology. Indeed, we see Philo quote Homer frequently. So, to take only the *Questions and Answers on Genesis* commentary on Genesis 15: 18, "To your descendants I have given this land from the river of Egypt to the great river," he connects it to a verse in Homer to show that the expression "river of Egypt" is customary for the Nile (*Odyssey*, XIV, 258). Commenting on Genesis 18:2, "When he saw them, he . . . ran to meet them," he connects the passage to *Odyssey*, XVII, 485, "When he saw him, he ran before him." A little further on, he compares the hospitality Abraham provides for the three angels of Mambre to what Menelaus bestows on Telemachus. "A guest remembers all his days that host who makes provisions for him kindly" (*Odyssey* XV, 74–75).[13] It is evident that the Greek text of the *Septuagint* resonated in Philo's mind with Homeric verses that he knew by heart. Likewise, if he criticizes the myths from the doctrinal viewpoint, as we have seen, he uses them for literary purposes. Thus Proteus and Tantalus (*De Specialibus Legibus*, IV, 81) are used as figures of desire. Among the tragedians, Euripides is quoted some twenty times.[14]

But Philo has not just taken certain examples for the explanation of authors. What is much more important, he has adopted their method. As we know, this method involved the reading of the text and its discussion (the Roman *emendatio*). We find few traces of the *emendatio*. Philo takes the Septuagint text as it is without asking whether it contains errors. By contrast, commentary occupies a major place in him. Properly speaking, it is the explanation of the text. Philo's method is as follows. He looks for a reason for every anomaly, for example, in Leviticus 18:6 "the repeated word, 'a man, a man'" (*De Gigantibus*, 33),[15] or the phrase in Genesis 15:5, "He led him forth" (*Legum Allegoriae*, III, 40).[16] Similarly, he carefully distinguishes synonyms (Exodus 16; *Legum Allegoriae*, II, 105). Etymology is a typical figure. If in general he gives the Hebrew etymology, he

12. Ibid., 465.

13. Homer, *The Odyssey*, 269.

14. For more detail see Siegfried, *Philo von Alexandria als Ausleger*, 137–55 and following.

15. *Philo* II, 461.

16. *Philo* I, 327.

comes to interpret the Hebrew word according to the Greek root: thus
Euphrates by εὐφραίνουσα (*Legum Allegoriae*, I, 72), Leah by λεῖος (*Legum
Allegoriae*, II, 59), and above all *Pascha*, which he usually interprets by
διάβασις, is also explained by πάσχειν (*Quis Heres*, 192).

After grammar comes rhetoric, the art of speaking. It is what gives
its character to ancient culture, more oriented to expression than to depth
of ideas. Rhetoric is something inferior for Philo. Joseph the politician
is its symbol. Nevertheless, he uses it often. We can say that part of his
task consists in recounting sacred history to the Greeks by putting it into
their style. Here exegesis often becomes simple oratorical development.
Rhetoric especially holds sway in the *Explanation of the Law*. I will give
two examples. First, Jacob's speech when he hears of the death of Joseph:

> Child, it is not your death which grieves me, but the manner of
> it. If you had been buried in your own land, I should have com-
> forted and watched and nursed our sick-bed, exchanged the last
> farewells as you died, closed your eyes, wept over the body as it lay
> here, given it a costly funeral and left none of the customary rites
> undone. Nay, even if it had been on foreign soil, I should have said
> to myself: "Man, be not downcast that nature has recovered the
> forfeit that was her due." Separate countries concern the living:
> every land is the tomb of the dead. Death comes early to none,
> or rather it comes early to all, for few are the years of the longest-
> lived compared with eternity. And, indeed, if you needs must have
> died by violence or through premeditation, it would have been a
> lighter ill to me, slain as you would have been by human beings,
> who would have pitied their dead victim, gathered some dust
> and covered the corpse. And then if they had been the cruelest
> of men, what more could they have done but cast it out unburied
> and go their way, and then perhaps some passer-by would have
> stayed his steps, and, as he looked felt pity for our common nature
> and deemed the tendance of burial to be its due. But as it is, you
> have become, in common phrase, a rich banquet for savage car-
> nivorous beasts who have found my own flesh and blood to their
> taste and feasted thereon . . . Many desperate calamities I have
> seen and heard: thousands of them have I experienced myself,
> but trained to moderate my feelings at such I remained unmoved
> [μετριοπαθεῖν]. But none was more unbearable than this event
> which has overturned and destroyed the strength of my soul. For
> what sorrow could be greater or more pitiful. My son's raiment
> has been conveyed to me, his father, but not a part of him, not a
> limb, not a tiny fragment (*De Josepho*, 23–27).[17]

17. *Philo* VI, 153, 155.

Here we re-encounter classic themes of Greek rhetoric: the corpse left without burial in *Antigone*, Oedipus's unheard of misfortunes in old age.

Let us consider the narrative of the departure from Egypt:

> Thus caught between the enemy and the sea, they despaired each of his own safety. Some thought that the most miserable death would be a welcome blessing, while others, believing it to be better to perish by the elements of nature than to become a laughing-stock to their enemies, purposed to throw themselves into the sea, and loaded with heavy substances, sat waiting by the shore, so that when they saw the foe near at hand they might leap down and easily sink into the depths. But while in these helpless straits, they were at death's door with consternation, the prophet, seeing the whole nation entangled in the meshes of panic, like a draught of fishes, was taken out of himself by divine possession and uttered these inspired words: "Alarm you needs must feel. Terror is near at hand: the danger is great. In front is a vast expanse of sea; no haven for a refuge, no boats at hand; behind, the menace of the enemy's troops, which march along in unresting pursuit. Whither can one turn or swim for safety? Everything has attacked us suddenly from every side—earth, sea, man, the elements of nature. Yet *be of good courage*, faint not. Stand with unshaken minds, look for the invincible *help* which God will send. Self-sent it will be with you anon, invisible it will *fight before you*" (*De Vita Mosis*, II, 249-52).[18]

We observe the suppression of offensive details: the staff of Moses or the Jews' desire to return to Egypt. Above all Philo strives to underline the pathos of the scene. We have the very type of exercise that young Alexandrian Jews must have done in school.

Scientific culture in turn comprised arithmetic, geometry, music, and astronomy. In arithmetic reflections on the properties of numbers stands out. They occupy an important place in Philo. Thus, on the number seven, he writes in a text we have quoted:

> Some have given to it the name of virgin, having before their eyes its surpassing chastity. They also call her the 'motherless,' begotten by the father of the universe alone, the ideal form of the male sex . . . Some give it the name of the 'season' [καιρός], judging its conceptual nature from its manifestations in the realm of sense. For seven is a factor common to all the

---

18. Ibid., 575, 577. [Translator: Daniélou has italicized the words found in the book of *Exodus*.]

phenomena which stand highest in the world of sensible things and serve to consummate in due order transitions of the year and recurring seasons. Such are the seven planets, the Great Bear, the Pleiades, and the cycles of the moon, as it waxes and wanes" (*De Specialibus Legibus*, II, 56–57).[19]

Indeed, elsewhere we meet again the explanations of the number seven's mysterious attributes. Why is it a virgin and without mother? Let us read *De Opificio*, 99–100:

For of these [tr. numbers] some beget without being begotten, some are begotten but do not beget, some to both these, both beget and are begotten . . . Well then, one begets all the subsequent numbers while it is begotten by none whatever: eight is begotten by twice four, but begets no number within the decade . . . For this reason other philosophers liken this number to the motherless and virgin Nikè, who is said to have appeared out of the head of Zeus.[20]

Likewise the *Allegory of the Laws* tells us: "By reason of this the Pythagoreans, indulging in myth, liken seven to the motherless and ever-virgin Maiden, because neither was she born of he womb nor shall she ever bear" (*Legum Allegoriae*, I, 15).[21]

In fact we know that Pythagorean practice established a correspondence between the numbers and the gods, and that seven was consecrated to Athena. Moreover, we find all this again in Lydus, *De Mensibus*, II, 11, as coming from the Pythagorean Philolaos. That is fundamental for the issue of Philonic allegory. We see that an early Pythagorean allegorical tradition existed that Philo only transposed into Biblical realities.

The other feature presented by our text would suggest the same observations. In the hebdomad Philo shows the intelligible world separated from the sensible world. Indeed, *De Opificio*, 100, says:

For that which neither begets nor is begotten remains motionless; for creation takes place in movement, since there is movement both in that which begets and in that which is begotten, in the one that it may beget, in the other that it may be begotten. There is only one thing that neither causes motion nor

19. *Philo* VII, 343, 345.
20. *Philo* I, 79, 81.
21. Ibid., 155.

experiences it, the original Ruler and Sovereign. Of Him seven
may be fitly said to be a symbol."[22]

That is still Pythagorean (*De Mensibus* II, 11). Furthermore, the fact that
the sensible world is arranged according to a septenary rhythm testifies to
the sensible world's participation in the intelligible world. In *De Opificio*,
117, Philo gives other examples: the seven parts of the soul, the seven
parts of the body! Finally, the seventh day is the anniversary of creation.
Philo combined this doctrine with that of the intelligible creation corresponding to the first six days, which certainly makes the seventh day
the birthday of the sensible world.

    Quaestiones in Genesim, III, 56, offers considerations upon the
number eight and the number 10.

> In the first place, the hundred is a power of the decade. In the
> second place, the myriad is (a power) of this itself . . . In the
> fourth place, it consists of thirty and six and of sixty and of four,
> which is a cube and a square at the same time. In the fifth place,
> it consists of the several odd numbers one, three, five, seven,
> nine, eleven, thirteen, fifteen, seventeen, nineteen making 100
> (*In Genesim*, III, 56).[23]

All that is to explain why Abraham had Isaac at the age of 100. Symbolic
reflections are added to arithmetical ones. The monad is the name of God
(*Legum Allegoriae*, II, 1); five is the name of the senses; ten of perfection.
All this Pythagorean symbolism will pass through Philo to the Fathers.[24]
We also find data taken from geometry, music (that is to say the science
of musical intervals), and especially from astronomy, in particular in *De
Opificio*, 53–61.

    After that, it remains to say a word about the other disciplines:
natural sciences, history, and law were not part of the liberal arts cycle,
but were the object of special study. I will only insist on law. We have
seen that Philo knew Jewish jurisprudence. But Yizhak Heinemann,
who devoted almost his entire book to this question, shows clearly that
on a certain number of points Philo comments on the Law in function of Greek usage. That is important for literal exegesis. According
to *De Decalogo*, 141, the judge must take an oath. Now, no such thing
is found in Jewish law. The role of witnesses—and thus the question

22. Ibid., 81.

23. *Philo*, Appendix I, 257.

24. Marrou, *Histoire de l'éducation*, 249.

of false testimony—was essential in Jewish law but not in Hellenistic law. Philo gives it no importance (*De Decalogo*, 138). The doctrine on betrothal is more Greek than Jewish; the young man being freer and the young woman by contrast more dependent.[25]

Allegorical Exegesis

Cosmological interpretations

The idea of seeing cosmological myths in mythological narratives did not appear with the moderns. It is already found in Plutarch and in Philo's contemporaries. Plutarch tells us that some people claimed: "Osiris designates the lunar world and Typho the solar world" (*De Iside et Osiride*, 75). "The vestments of Isis are dyed in many colors, because her power extends over matter that receives every form" (*De Iside et Osiride*, 77). We find that Alexandrian Jews before Philo applied similar interpretations to the Bible. For Flavius Josephus the High Priest's multi-colored robe is the figure of the four elements of the cosmos, just like Isis's robe for Plutarch (*Wars of the Jews*, V, 5, 4),[26] and the seven-branched candlestick is the figure of the seven planets (V, 5, 5). Now, this kind of interpretation is frequent in Philo especially in the explanation of the Law. The Visible Temple is: "The Highest, and in the truest sense the holy, temple of God is, as we must believe, the whole universe, having for its sanctuary the most sacred part of all existence, even heaven, for its votive ornaments the stars, for its priests the angels who are servitors to His powers, unbodied souls" (*De Specialibus Legibus*, I, 66).[27] This is a Stoic theme frequent in Cicero and Seneca, which, no doubt, goes back to young Aristotle.[28]

Once the principle is posited, the different parts of the Temple are going to become different parts of the cosmos.[29] The ark of the covenant is made of imperishable wood to mark the relation of different parts of the universe (*In Exodum*, I, 54). For some, the two sides of the ark are the two equinoxes, and the four animals are the four seasons (*In Exodum*, II, 56). As for the seven branches: "It is clear to all that the seven lamps are

---

25. Heinemann, *Philons griechische und jüdische Bildung*, 306.

26. See also Wisdom 18:24.

27. *Philo* VII, 137.

28. See Festugière, *Le dieu cosmique*, 230–34.

29. See Daniélou, "Le symbolique cosmique," 1–65.

symbols of the planets" (*Quaestiones in Exodum*, II, 78).[30] We have seen this in Flavius Josephus. But Philo specifies: "The planets do not travel around all parts and sides of the celestial sphere but only in one part, in the south" (*In Exodum*, II, 79).[31] The cherubim are the two hemispheres. The veil separating the holy of holies from the rest of the temple is the firmament that separates the heaven of the stars from the sublunary world.

This traditional cosmological symbolism is also applied to the vestments of the high priest. We find it in Flavius Josephus. In Philo as in Josephus, the four colors of the robe are figures of the four elements (*De Vita Mosis*, II, 88). But Philo develops this in detail. The two onyx stones where the names of the twelve patriarchs are engraved are the two hemispheres above and below the earth. Why is this? There are two reasons: "Because the twelve stones are representations of the twelve animals which are in the zodiac, and are a symbol" (*In Exodum*, II, 114).[32] Moreover, the twelve sons of Jacob correspond to the twelve signs (*De Somniis*, II, 112). For Josephus they are the twelve loaves of proposition. Now, in old synagogues even later than Philo, paintings have been found associating the signs of the zodiac with Biblical events.[33] Accordingly, we are definitely in the presence of a customary exegesis that Philo may have extended to new details but to which he primarily bears witness.

Anthropological Exegesis

If we turn to the text of *Quaestiones in Genesim*, I, 8–10, we see that after the cosmological interrelations, Philo progresses to anthropological exegesis. The tree of life is no longer the figure of the earth or the sun or of the fourth heaven but of the *hegemonikon*, human reason (*In Genesim*, I, 10). We can give another example of this contrast. Regarding Abraham's sacrifice of an ox, a goat, a sheep, a dove, and a turtledove, (*In Genesim*, XV, 8), Philo, as we have said, starts by defending the literal sense, explaining that we are not dealing with pagan divination and that the text

---

30. *Philo*, Appendix II, 127–28.

31. Ibid., 128.

32. Ibid., 164. [Translator: This does not quite correspond to Daniélou: "D'abord l'aspect hémisphérique des pierres précieuses, ensuite la couleur de l'émeraude, semblable à celle du ciel, enfin le nombre des signes gravés égal aux signes du zodiaque." Loeb has nothing about emeralds or hemispheres.]

33. Simon, *Verus Israel*.

must be explained in the context of all of scripture. He then gives this cosmological interpretation.

> And the natures of the aforementioned five animals are related to the parts of the universe. The ox (is related) to the earth, for it ploughs and tills the soil. The goat (is related) to water, the animal being so called from its rushing about or leaping, for water is impetuous; this is attested by the currents of rivers and effusions of the wide sea and the flowing sea. The ram (is related) to air, since it is very violent and lively, whence the ram is a most useful soul and the most helpful of animals to mankind because it provides them with clothing . . . But to the birds, such as the dove and the turtledove, the whole heaven is equally appropriated, being divided into the circuits of the planets and the fixed stars. And so (Scripture) assigns the dove to the planets, for this is a tame and domesticated creature, and the planets also are rather familiar to us, as though contiguous to terrestrial places, and sympathetic. But the turtledove (is related) to the fixed stars, for this animal is something of a lover of solitude . . . Moreover, the aforesaid birds are singers, and the prophet is alluding to the music which is perfected in heaven and is produced by the harmony of the movement of the stars (*In Genesim*, III, 3).[34]

After some supplementary considerations that I skip, Philo concludes:

> Now this interpretation is most natural. But a more ethical one must be discussed. To every one of us there happen to belong these things: body and sense perception and reason. Accordingly, the heifer is related to bodily substance, for our body is tamed and driven and made to obey and is yoked to the service of life . . . And the she-goat is to be likened to the community of senses, whether because the various objects perceived are referred to their (appropriate) sense or because the impulse and movement of the soul come from the impressions made upon the senses . . . But the ram is kin to reason, first of all because this is masculine and because it is energetic, and then because it is the cause of the world and its foundation. For the ram (is necessary) because of the clothing which it yields, while reason (is necessary) in the ordering of life . . . But there are two forms of reason: there is one in nature, by which things in the sense-perception world are analyzed; and (the other is found) in those forms which are called incorporeal, by which the things of the intelligible world are analyzed. With these are compared the

34. *Philo, Supplement* I, 179–81.

dove and the turtledove. For the dove (is a symbol) of physical theory, for it is a very tame bird, and sense-perceptible things are familiar to sight. And the soul of the physicist and physiologist leaps up and grows wings and is borne aloft and travels round the heavens, viewing all its parts and their several causes. But the turtledove is likened to the intelligible and incorporeal form (of reason); for just as this creature is found of solitude, so (the reason) by an effort surpasses the forms of sense-perception and is united in essence with the invisible (*In Genesim*, III, 3).[35]

This second kind of exegesis is more frequent than the first in Philo. The traditional example is Adam, representing spirit, while Eve symbolizes sensation. The creation of Eve during Adam's sleep becomes a figure of the Aristotelian theory of knowledge.

As a matter of fact, it is when the mind has gone to sleep that perception begins, for conversely when the mind wakes up perception is quenched . . . Having said this, we must show how the terms employed accord with it. "God cast," he says, "a trance upon Adam, and he went to sleep" (Genesis 2:21). Quite correctly does he use this language. For the mind's trance and change is its sleep, and it falls into a trance when it ceases to be engaged with objects appropriate to it . . . "He took one of his sides" (Genesis 2:21). Of the many faculties of the mind he took one, the faculty of perception . . . And so he adds the words "He built it to be a woman" (*Genesis*, ii, 22), proving by this that the most proper and exact name for sense perception is "woman" (*Legum Allegoriae*, II, 25, 31, 35, 38).[36]

Here again we see how Philo bears witness to a tradition. In *De Abrahamo* he tells us that he "heard some natural philosophers who took the passage allegorically not without good reason. They said that the husband was a figure for the good mind . . . The wife they said was virtue" (*De Abrahamo*, 99).[37] Likewise in *De Josepho* he writes: "I have heard, however, some scholars give an allegorical exposition of this part of the story in a different form. . . . The king of Egypt, they said, was our mind, the ruler of the land of the body in each of us" (*De Josepho*, 151).[38] Here

---

35. Ibid., 182–84.

36. *Philo* I, 241, 245, 247, 249.

37. *Philo* VI, 53. [Translator: Daniélou here has the wife being "sensation," but the Greek reads ἀρετήν.]

38. Ibid., 213.

we are no longer in the context of Stoic allegory, which was mostly cosmological, but of moral allegory. We have a little treatise on Pythagorean
ethics from this period that recalls Philo. It describes symbolic scenes interpreting them as an allegory of the soul's powers. We refer to the *Tablet
of Cebes*. Interpretations of this type are found in *De Iside et Osiride*, 74.

Along with the soul we also see the human body symbolized. Let us
return to the tree of life. Philo writes. "But some say that it is the heart
that is called the tree of life, since it is the cause of life and has been al-
lotted the central place in the body, as it naturally would, being in their
view the dominating principle. But these people should remember that
they are setting forth a view worthy of the physician rather than of the
philosopher" (*Legum Allegoriae*, I, 59).[39] Philo rejects this interpretation.
But furthermore, he supplies analogues. Noah's ark is a figure of the body
(*Quaestiones in Genesim*, II, 1). The body indeed is inscribed in a rectan-
gular shape (*In Genesim*, II, 2). Now the ark was made of quadrangular
beams. Like the ark, the body includes spaces that are the cavern of the
senses: ear, eye, nose (*In Genesim*, II, 3). The ark is tarred with bitumen,
which corresponds to the cohesive character of the body.

Lastly, psychological allegory ends in moral allegory. Concerning
the animals led to Adam, Philo writes: "You see who are our helpers,
the wild beasts, the soul's passions . . . The passions he likens to wild
beasts and birds, because, savage and untamed as they are, they tear
the soul to pieces, and because like winged things they light upon the
understanding" (*Legum Allegoriae*. 9 and 11).[40] Here again, Philo attests
to a traditional exegesis. We have seen that in the *Letter of Aristeus*, the
impure animals are figures of the vices. We meet this again in Philo, *De
Specialibus Legibus*, IV, 105. Comparable symbolism is found in Plutarch, *De Iside et Osiride*, 75, and earlier in Plato's *Republic*, 589, where
Plato shows νοῦς commanding the passions like a herd of unchained
beasts, whether serpents, lions, or monkeys. Siegfried has noted the
principal symbols: the serpent is pleasure; the billy goat is anger.[41] This
symbolism is met again in the tradition of the seven capital sins, each
represented by an animal.

One of the most interesting aspects of this moral allegory involves
certain rites. We find the echo of a spiritualization that began in the Old

---

39. *Philo*, I, 185.

40. Ibid., 229, 231.

41. Siegfried, *Philo als Ausleger*, 182–85.

Testament: "Good sir, God does not rejoice in sacrifices even if one offers hecatombs, for all things are His possessions, yet though He possesses, He needs none of them, but He rejoices in the will to love Him and in men that practice holiness" (*De Specialibus Legibus*, I, 271).[42] Without denying the importance of the visible cult, Philo at the same time sees in it the symbol of the soul's inner disposition.

Accordingly, circumcision is good, but under the condition that circumcision of the heart accompanies it (*De Specialibus Legibus*, I, 6). The hands placed on the victim's head symbolize irreproachable actions (De *Specialibus Legibus*, I, 202). Washing of feet means that we must no longer tread upon the earth but be raised to heaven (*De Specialibus Legibus*, I, 207). The most curious thing is this: Leviticus prescribes purification by water mixed with ash. "Moses would have those who come to serve Him-that-is first know themselves and of what substance these selves are made . . . Now the substance of which our body consists is earth and water" (*De Specialibus Legibus*, I, 263).[43] This conception is completely similar to that of Christian Ash Wednesday liturgy.

Mystical exegesis

The two kinds of exegesis that we have just described are found mainly in the work Philo directed to the general public or else they are represented as coming from traditional teaching. It can be said that they constitute typical allegorical exegesis as Philo found it in contemporary Alexandria. But if Philo makes room for it as he makes room for literal exegesis, it is as testimony to a tradition, not by way of personal teaching. In reality, true Philonic allegory is what we find in the *Allegorical Interpretation*, and it no longer concerns the cosmos and man as he is in the cosmos, but the hidden mysteries of the hyper-cosmic world and the spiritual journey of the soul that rises above the visible world and attains the world of God. There dwell what Philo styles "the great mysteries", which only the initiated attain, and the heart of his teaching is there, namely the mystery of God, the Logos, and the Powers on the one hand, and on the other that of the development of perfect virtues.

We see on several occasions how Philo clearly indicates this new level and his preferences for it. Let us return to some of the examples we

42. *Philo* VII, 257.
43. Ibid., 253.

have seen. In *Quaestiones in Genesim*, dealing with the tree of life, Philo begins by recalling that some have seen the sun in it (cosmology), the νοῦς or the heart (anthropology), and he continues: "But the worthy and excellent men say that the tree of life is the best of the virtues in man, namely piety, through which pre-eminently the mind becomes immortal" (*In Genesim*, I, 10).[44] Even in *Legum Allegoriae*, Philo rejects the interpretation of those who see the heart as the tree of life as "a view worthy of the physician rather than the philosopher" and declares: "a virtue in its most generic aspect is called the tree of life" (*Legum Allegoriae*, I, 59).[45] The same occurs with the cherubim. He first recalls their cosmological interpretation as the two hemispheres and that of the sword of fire as the sun (*De Cherubim*, 25). Then he adds:

> But there is a higher thought than these. It comes from a voice in my own soul, which oftentimes is God-possessed and divines where it does not know. This thought I will record in words if I can. The voice told me that while God is indeed one, His highest and chiefest powers are two, even goodness and sovereignty . . . Of those two potencies, sovereignty and goodness the Cherubim are symbols, as the fiery sword is the symbol of reason (*De Cherubim*, 27).[46]

Elsewhere we find similar gradation. Philo interprets the statement in Genesis 25:8, about the death of Abraham, that he was "gathered to his fathers."

> By "fathers" he does not mean those whom the pilgrim soul has left behind, those who lie buried in the sepulchers of Chaldaea, but possibly, as some say, the sun, moon, and other stars to which it is held that all things on earth owe their birth and framing, or, as others think, the archetypal ideas which, invisible and intelligible *there*, are the patterns of things visible and sensible *here*— the ideas in which, as they say, the mind of the sage finds its new home. Others again have surmised that by "fathers" are meant the four first principles and potentialities from which the world has been framed, earth, water, air, and fire. For into these, they say, each thing that has come into being is duly resolved (*Quis Heres*, 280).[47]

44. *Philo, Supplement* I, 7.

45. *Philo*, I, 185

46. *Philo* II, 25. See also *In Genesim*, I, 57; *In Exodum*, II, 68; *De Vita Mosis*, II, 98.

47. *Philo* IV, 427.

Now, he chooses deliberately among these interpretations: "In the opinion of many it seems that 'the fathers' indicate all of the elements into which the dissolution (of the body) takes place. To me, however, it seems to indicate the incorporeal Logoi of the divine world, whom elsewhere it is accustomed to call 'angels'" (*In Genesim*, III, 11).[48]

We arrive here at properly Philonic exegesis that has as its object the mystery of God, the Word, and the powers—and the mystical itinerary of the soul. Is Philo the author of the exegesis? As we have said, it seems not. Here again, he appears to have had precursors. Thus in *De Somniis*, he presents a typically mystical exegesis as having been transmitted to him. He deals with Genesis 28:11: "And he came to a certain place and slept there, for the sun had gone down."

> Some supposing that in this passage "sun" is a figurative expression for sense and mind, our own accepted standards of judgment, and "place" for the divine word, have understood the passage in this way: "The Practicer [Jacob] met a divine word when the mortal and human light had gone down." For so long as mind and sense perception imagine that they get a firm grasp, mind of the objects of mind and sense of the objects of sense, and thus move aloft in the sky, the divine Word is far away. But when each of them acknowledges its weakness, and going through a kind of setting passes out of sight, right reason is forward to meet and greet at once the practicing soul, whose willing champion he is when it despairs of itself and waits for him who invisibly comes from without to its succor" (*De Somniis*, I, 118).[49]

Here we are faced with full-fledged Philonic mysticism. Now Philo presents it as coming to him from certain people. We must be dealing with the Therapeutae or other Jewish ascetics here. Although Philo rejected their anti-legalism he remained within their school of spirituality.[50] But whatever the origins of this type of exegesis, it is what Philo adopted. His interpretation is that the Torah is a mystical itinerary that leads the soul to the knowledge of the God of Revelation. The sequence of the Pentateuch describes the itinerary's stages. For Philo it is composed

---

48. *Philo, Supplement* I, 195–96.

49. *Philo* V, 361. [Translator: The Greek here translated as *word* is λόγος, and Daniélou has *logos*.]

50. Stein, *Die allegorische Exegese*, insists on this influence and denies any originality of Philo.

of two triads, followed by the supreme mystery of Moses.[51] The first and less important triad is that of Enos, Enoch, and Noah. Philo describes it especially in *De Abrahamo*, 7–47, and *De Praemiis*, 7–23. Enos is the symbol of hope, which is the first "seed" of grace (*De Praemiis*, 10)[52] and introduces the spiritual journey. Enos means man. The true man is he who seeks God. The second stage is repentance, which is gained through withdrawal and solitude (*De Praemiis*, 17). This is why its model is Enoch, "who was not found, because God translated him (Genesis 5:24). Lastly, Noah is the just man who survives the destruction of the sinful world and inaugurates the second creation (*De Praemiis*, 23).

The second triad is more important. It consists of Abraham, Isaac, and Jacob. It ranks high in Philonic symbolism. Abraham, the object of two treatises, *De Abrahamo* and *De Migratione Abrahami*, is the first level of the great triad. Supported by faith, which is his great virtue, he begins a succession of migrations, first from the body, whose figure is Chaldea, which is the world of the body (De *Migratione*, 1). Next he migrates out of sensible life (*De Abrahamo*, 72). Finally he leaves behind discourse, the realm of discursive intelligence (*De Migratione*, 2). His change of name signifies the passage from Chaldean wisdom to true spiritual wisdom. After this triple migration, he first marries Hagar, who is profane knowledge. Acquisition of knowledge of μάθησις in opposition to ignorance and illusion constitutes a first stage. From this standpoint Abraham is the figure of a διδασκαλία, acquired knowledge, which is contrasted with the infused knowledge of the perfect (*De Praemiis*, 27). After Hagar he marries Sarah, Wisdom, which is knowledge of revelation (*De Abrahamo*, 100).

In the course of this journey, God is progressively revealed to him:

> In this creed Abraham had been reared, and for a long time remained a Chaldean. Then opening the soul's eye as though after profound sleep, and beginning to see the pure beam instead of the deep darkness, he followed the ray and discerned what he had not beheld before, a charioteer and pilot presiding over the world and directing in safety his own work . . . "God," it says, "was seen by Abraham [Genesis 12:7]" (*De Abrahamo*, 70, 77).[53]

---

51. Goodenough analyzes this well in *By Light Light*, 121–235.

52. *Philo* VIII, 319.

53. *Philo* VI, 41, 43.

Still that is only a first analogical knowledge of God by means of the world. "The central place is held by the Father of the Universe, Who in the sacred scriptures is called He-that-is as His proper name, while on either side of Him are the senior potencies, the nearest to Him, the creative and the kingly" (*De Abrahamo*, 121).[54]

Abraham thus represents the first stage, that of faith and acquired virtue. Jacob symbolizes the second stage, although he comes third. Jacob represents ascetical effort. He struggles with the angel. After a soul has understood where reality is, it ought to set out towards it. This second stage constitutes progress. Jacob is the one who progresses. This stage is essentially marked by the struggle against passions and by the acquisition of virtues. It has *apatheia* as its end point. Furthermore, the name of Jacob will be changed to Israel, he who sees God. "For after the active life of youth, the contemplative life of old age is the best and most sacred" (*De Praemiis*, 51).[55]

Finally, Isaac, whose name means laughter, represents the perfect person who has infused wisdom (αὐτομαθής, αὐτοφυής). He has God alone as his father (*Quod Deterius*, 124). His marriage to Rebecca is a great mystery.

> Isaac had neither more wives than one, nor any concubine at all, but his lawful wife is the one who shares his home throughout. Why is this? It is because the virtue that comes through teaching, which Abraham pursues, needs the fruits of several studies, both those born in wedlock, which deal with wisdom, and the base-born, those of the preliminary lore of the schools. It is the same with the virtue which is perfected through practice, which Jacob seems to have made his aim . . . But the self-learnt kind, of which Isaac is a member, that joy which is the best of the good emotions, is endowed with a simple nature free from mixture and alloy, and wants neither the practice nor the teaching . . . When God rains down from heaven the good of which the self is a teacher and learner both, it is impossible that the self should still live in concubinage with the slavish arts, as though desiring to be the father of bastard thoughts and conclusions. He who has obtained this prize is enrolled as the husband of the queen and mistress of virtue. Her name in the Greek means "constancy" (ὑπομονή); in the Hebrew it is Rebecca. He who has gained the wisdom that comes without toil and trouble, because his nature is happily gifted and his soul fruitful of good, does not

54. Ibid., 63.
55. *Philo* VIII, 341.

seek for any means of betterment: for he has ready beside him in their fullness the gifts of God, conveyed by the breath of God's higher graces, but he wishes and prays that these may remain with him constantly (*De Congressu*, 34–38).[56]

This second triad conveys us toward the height of perfection. It culminates in Moses. As Goodenough has correctly seen, Moses is at the heart of Philonic symbolism. "For the Mystery, the hero, and hierophant of greatest importance is Moses."[57] His place in Philo's treatises is rather misleading. There is no treatise on the life of Moses in the *Exposition of the Law*. It is replaced by *De Vita Mosis*, but that is very literal. Nor does *Legum Allegoriae* present a life of Moses. Only the *Quaestiones in Exodum* offers a continuous exposition. But the life of Moses is so frequently treated in other treatises that in spite of everything, it is possible to reconstitute the overall Philonic symbolism of Moses. As Philo emphasizes, it will be noted that properly speaking there is no progress in Moses. He is indeed the very type of perfect man.

Let us start with his birth.

The mind called Moses, that goodly plant, given the name of goodly at his very birth (Exodus 2;2), who in virtue of his larger citizenship took the world for his township and country, weeps bitterly (Exodus, 2:6) in the days when he is imprisoned in the ark of the body bedaubed as with 'asphalt-pitch' (Exodus, 2:3) . . . He weeps for his captivity, pressed sore by his yearning for a nature that knows no body (*De Confusione Linguarum*, 106).[58]

We begin to explore the symbolic language. The cradle in which Moses is deposited is the body like the ark covered with bitumen that envelops the soul. The dispute of Moses with the Egyptian is the conflict of true philosophy with Epicureanism for which pleasure is the highest good. Having killed the Egyptian, Moses flees into the desert; that is, he withdraws into solitude. There, Moses liberates the seven daughters of Jethro, who are the five senses, speech, and sexual instinct, from evil shepherds who want to steal them from the realm of spirit. "After having driven away the shepherds, that is to say, having convinced the teachers of iniquity of the evil use to which they put education, we will lead the solitary life, all the

56. *Philo* IV, 475, 477.
57. Goodenough, *By Light, Light*, 181.
58. *Philo* IV, 67, 69.

movements of our soul being guided like a flock by the Logos" (Gregory of Nyssa, *Patrologia Graeca* XLIV, col. 332 B, following Philo).

Like the marriages of the other patriarchs, the marriage of Moses to Sephora is a great mystery, that of the union of spirit and wisdom (*De Posteritate*, 78). Like Rebecca, Sephora conceives through the action of God (*De Cherubim*, 47). These are great mysteries. "These thoughts, ye initiated, whose ears are purified, receive into your souls as holy mysteries indeed and babble not of them to any of the profane . . . I myself was initiated under Moses, yet when I saw the prophet Jeremiah and knew him to be not only himself enlightened, but a worthy minister of the holy secrets, I was not slow to become his disciple." The meaning of this mystery is that: "God is a house, the incorporeal dwelling place of incorporeal ideas, that he is the father of all things, for he begat them, and the Husband of Wisdom" (*De Cherubim*, 48–49).[59] Moses is judged worthy of being initiated into the mystery. Against Goodenough, this is not to be understood in the line of allegorical interpretation of the mystery of Isis and Osiris, but it is the dogma of the creation by God of the intelligible world pre-existing the visible world. It is Biblical Platonism.

Regarding the departure from Egypt, "To those who are accustomed to turn literal facts into allegory, the Crossing-festival suggests the purification of the soul. They say that the lover of wisdom is occupied solely in crossing from the body and the passions, each of which overwhelms him like a torrent, unless the rushing current be dammed and held back by the principles of virtue." (*De Specialibus Legibus*, II, 147).[60] Passover signifies the purification of the soul (*De Specialibus Legibus*, II, 147). The rider and horse hurled into the sea are the four passions and the guilty νοῦς. We again meet the Platonic allegory of the animals (*Legum Allegoriae*, II, 102). The twelve fountains of Elim are the little mysteries that concern the world, to which cosmological allegory corresponds. Indeed the number twelve is that of the yearly cycle. By contrast, the seventy palm trees are figures of the great mysteries and the perfect virtues (*De Fuga*, 187). The next symbols, the manna and rock of living water, are figures of the Logos. That strangely anticipates the gospel (*Legum Allegoriae*, II, 86; II, 163). Lastly, the summit of initiation is the ascent of Mt. Sinai. "So see him [tr. Moses] enter into the thick darkness where God was (Exodus 20:21), that is into conceptions regarding the Existent Being that belong to the unapproachable region where there are no material forms" (*De Posteritate*, 14).[61]

---

59. *Philo* II, 37, 39.

60. *Philo* VII, 397.

61. *Philo* II, 335.

Chapter 5

Philo's Theology

I F PHILO'S EXEGESIS IS debatable in many aspects, his theology, by contrast, represents a remarkable synthesis. It constitutes the first attempt to explain Biblical data by means of the tools of ancient philosophy. Philo takes these tools from Plato, Aristotle, and the Stoics. But his thought is not syncretistic. He assimilates these diverse elements in an original synthesis. In a recent book, Wolfson has tried to show that this synthesis was, on the one hand, perfectly coherent, and on the other, completely consistent with the demands of Biblical faith.[1] The advantage of this thesis is that it amounts to the first methodic attempt to expound Philo's thought. But we ought to say with Völker[2] that the attempt only achieves this unity at the cost of much simplification. Philo's theology certainly has a Biblical basis and is the work of a believing Jew. But it still contains inconsistencies that will be found again in the first Christian theologians.

1. Wolfson, *Philo*, vol. 2.

2. Völker, in *Theologische Literaturzeitung* of July 1950, 290. [Translator: This reference is incomplete. I have not been able to find it in *Theologische Literaturzeitung* and suspect that it is garbled.]

The Incomprehensibility of God

The first article of Philo's Biblical philosophy is the affirmation of the divine nature's transcendence. This involves several points: radical distinction of the created and uncreated, difference of the divine nature from all other natures, the mysterious incomprehensibility of the divine *ousia*. These are Biblical teachings, and Philo bases himself on Scripture to establish them. But until Philo, philosophy had not clearly affirmed them. For Plato, the contrast is between the sensible world and the intelligible world, which is divine by nature—and while it is difficult to know God, it is not impossible. For Aristotle, divine simplicity does not exclude the divine being a genus that admits clear definition.[3] For the Stoics, the whole world is divine, and man finds knowledge of God within himself. So, we can say that Philo reforms philosophy in its first and essential aspect in order to mold it according to the demands of revelation.

Divine transcendence is first of all the radical distinction between God and creation. That is the message of Moses:

> Great indeed is the profession of the founder of this tribe. He has the courage to say, God and God alone must I honor, not aught of what is below God [Exodus 20:3], neither earth nor sea nor rivers, nor the realm of air, nor the shiftings of the winds and seasons, nor the various kinds of animals and plants, nor the sun nor the moon nor the host of the stars, performing their courses in ranks of ordered harmony, no, nor yet the whole heaven and universe. A great and transcendent soul does such a boast bespeak, to soar above created being, to pass beyond [ὑπερβάλλειν] its boundaries, to hold fast to the Uncreated [ἀγένητος] alone, following the sacred admonitions in which we are told to cling to Him (Deuteronomy 30:20), and therefore to those who thus cling and serve Him without ceasing He gives Himself as portion, and this my affirmation is warranted by the oracle which says, "The Lord Himself is his portion" (Deuteronomy 10:9), (*De Congressu*, 133–34).[4]

Two things may be observed in this text. The first is transcendence in regard to all creatures. Here Philo returns to one of his fundamental themes, the criticism of any idolatry. Idolatry consists of treating created things as gods. "Some have supposed that the sun and moon and the

3. Wolfson, "The Knowability and Descriptability of God," 233–49.

4. *Philo* IV, 527. [Translator: Daniélou understands that the founder of the tribe is Moses. Loeb rejects this view, which it attributes to Wendland, in favor of Levi.]

other stars were gods with absolute powers and ascribed to them the causation of all events" (*De Specialibus Legibus*, I, 13).[5] We must say "that God is one and the framer and Maker of all things, sometimes that He is Lord of created beings, because stability and fixity and lordship are by nature vested in Him alone" (*De Specialibus Legibus*, I, 30).[6] The passage from adoring heaven to adoring the creator of heaven is Abraham's peculiar grace: "The good bestowed in the past was his departure from Chaldaean sky-lore, which taught the creed that the world was not God's work, but itself God" (*Quis Heres*, 97).[7]

It should be observed that this affirmation of God's transcendence does not at all imply his separation from man. To those who devote themselves to God, God gives himself in exchange. Accordingly, far from separating man from God, the acknowledgment of transcendence is the path that introduces him to unity with God. But this union with God is not the result of a conquest of the mind. It is a gift that God makes of himself. Therefore, transcendence and grace appear as correlatives from the outset. They define an order of things where the relation of God and man are those of a transcendent person who only gives himself freely to a created person who opens himself to the gift of God through recognition of his dependence. "What deadlier foe to the soul can there be, than he who in his vainglory claims to himself that which belongs to God alone? For it belongs to God to act, and this we may not ascribe to any created being. What belongs to the created is to suffer" (*De Cherubim*, 77).[8]

This distinction of created and uncreated implies the radical dissimilarity of man and God. God is the completely other. That reappears on different occasions. "For in reality God is not like man nor yet like the sun nor like heaven nor like the sense-perceptible world but (only) like God, if it is right to say even this. For that blessed and most happy One does not admit any likeness or comparison or parable; rather He is beyond blessedness itself and happiness and whatever is more excellent and better than these" (*In Genesim*, II, 54).[9] Or again, "God being one and alone and unique, and like God there is nothing" (*Legum Allegoriae*, II, 1).[10] Clearer still is this passage: "The Unoriginate [ἀγένητος] resembles

---

5. *Philo* VII, 107

6. Ibid., 117.

7. *Philo* IV, 329, 331.

8. *Philo* II, 55.

9. *Philo, Supplement* I, 135.

10. *Philo* I, 25.

nothing among created [γένεσις] things, but so completely transcends them, that even the swiftest understanding falls far short of apprehending Him and acknowledges its failure" (*De Somniis*, I, 184).[11]

The closing words of this passage point out the consequence of the disproportion that exists between God and creatures: the human mind is impotent to comprehend the divine essence. That essence remains entirely mysterious to our minds. This doctrine of divine incomprehensibility (ἀκατάληπτος) will play a very great role in the Church Fathers, particularly in Clement of Alexandria, Gregory of Nyssa, and John Chrysostom. We know that this doctrine appeared in different quarters during Philo's time. It is found among the Gnostics,[12] in hermetic writings. But those works are posterior to Philo. Norden's position that finds it in Acts 17:23, which alludes to the "unknown God" (ἄγνωστος) venerated at Athens has been correctly challenged by Wolfson, who shows that the expression does not mean the incomprehensibility of essence but only ignorance of name.[13] Accordingly, we must say that on a philosophical level the doctrine comes from Philo.[14]

A passage from *De Mutatione* sums up Philo's thought well:

> Do not however suppose that the Existent [ὄν] which truly exists is [καταλαμβάνεσθαι] apprehended by any man; for we have in us no organ by which we can envisage it, neither in sense, for it is not perceptible by sense, nor yet in mind [νοῦς]. So Moses the explorer of nature which lies beyond our vision [ἀειδής], Moses who, as the divine oracles tell us, entered into the darkness [γνόφος] (Exodus 20:21), by which figure they indicate existence [οὐσία] invisible and incorporeal, searched everywhere and into everything in his desire to see clearly and plainly Him, the object of our much yearning, Who alone is good. And when there was no sign of finding aught, not even any semblance [ἰδέα] of what he hoped for, in despair of learning from others, he took refuge with the Object of his search Itself and prayed in these words: "Reveal Thyself to me that I may see Thee with knowledge (Exodus 33:13)" (*De Mutatione*, 7–8).[15]

11. *Philo* V, 395.

12. Sagnard, *La gnose valentinienne*, 331–33.

13. Wolfson, *Philo*, II:113–16.

14. See Festugière, *Le dieu cosmique*, 572–75. Wolfson thinks that Albinus's and Plotinus's versions of this doctrine also comes from Philo. See Wolfson, "Albinus and Plotinus on Divine Attributes," 115.

15. *Philo* V, 145, 147.

We observe that in this passage Philo explicitly declares that the divine essence can be grasped neither by the senses nor by the intelligence. Wolfson could write that no philosopher had "ever said that so explicitly."[16] Platonic expressions about the incorporeal God may refer to it. The thought is absolutely clear. It is the radical distinction of the intelligible realm of ideas and of the realm of God that is absolutely transcendent.

Philo grounds the doctrine in the Bible. The specific instance of its articulation is the cloud into which Moses enters. Philo develops this in several passages the most important of which follows:

> But so unceasingly does he [tr. Moses] himself yearn to see God and to be seen by Him, that he implores Him to reveal clearly His own nature (Exodus 33:13), which is so hard to divine, hoping thus to obtain at length a view free from all falsehood, and to exchange doubt and uncertainty for a most assured confidence [πίστιν]. Nor will he abate the intensity of his desire, but although he is aware that he is enamored of an object which entails a hard quest, nay, which is out of reach [ἀνεφίκτου], he will nevertheless struggle on with no relaxation of his earnest endeavor, but honestly and resolutely enlisting all his faculties to co-operate for the attainment of his object. So see him enter into the thick darkness where God was (Exodus 20: 21), that is into conceptions regarding the Existent Being that belong to the unapproachable [ἀδύτους] region where there are no material forms [ἀειδεῖς]. For the Cause of all is not in the thick darkness, nor locally in any place at all, but high above both place and time . . . When therefore the God-loving soul probes the question of the essence [οὐσίαν] of the existent Being, he enters on a quest of that which is beyond matter and beyond sight. And out of this quest there accrues to him a vast boon, namely to apprehend that the God of real Being is apprehensible by no one [ἀκατάληπτος] and to see precisely this, that He is incapable of being seen" (*De Posteritate*, 13–15).[17]

These passages make us see that Philo bases his doctrine on Scripture. But he also explains it metaphysically. If human intelligence cannot attain the divine essence, it is because it is enclosed within the categories of space and time, while God transcends these categories. For Philo, God's

---

16. Wolfson, *Philo*, II:119.

17. *Philo* II, 335, 337. See Gregory of Nyssa, *Patrologia Graeca*, vol. xlv, 940 c–d; volume xliv, 404, a–d.

incomprehensibility rests upon his absolute simplicity that excludes any determination from him.[18] He is ἀειδής, without form. This implies that he cannot be defined and consequently that he cannot be named. The Being is ineffable (ἄρρητον) so that not even the powers who serve him can tell us his name (*De Mutatione Nominum*, 14). This reduction of Biblical transcendence to metaphysical transcendence was necessary. It was not without danger; it risked orienting the soul in the direction of an intellectual experience of the nakedness of concepts, instead of making it consist of the soul's passivity in relation to a personal God's action.[19]

But in Philo's case matters do not seem to be thus. The expression may be Platonic and announce Plotinus. The reality is certainly that of the living God of the Bible. Besides, for Philo, what is inaccessible is a comprehensive knowledge of God's essence, but not all knowledge of that οὐσία. Moses's advance through the cloud by faith is a true grasping of the always hidden God. Wolfson correctly saw that there could be progress in the knowledge of the divine essence although he reduced this progress to something achieved through the knowledge about God through his work.[20] More profoundly, Henri-Charles Puech sees in this a grasping of the divine essence in itself. "In this perpetual undefined pursuit of God, in this untiring, always nearer but always unfinished deeper approximation to an inexhaustible object, we will make it the highest and most vivid experience that could be granted us, the experience of the undefined and the transcendent."[21]

The Powers

If God's essence is incomprehensible, it does not follow that we can know nothing about God. God indeed reveals himself through his action in the world. For Philo, knowledge about God belongs to two orders. On the one hand, God makes himself known through the outside world, through creation. Philo takes up the Aristotelian proofs of the existence of God.[22] In addition, God reveals himself through his inner action in the soul, through prophecy. Wolfson has observed here that Philo recurs to

18. Wolfson, *Philo*, II:94, 110.

19. See Lebreton, "La nuit obscure de saint Jean de la Croix," 3–24.

20. Wolfson, *Philo*, II:148.

21. Puech, "La ténèbre mystique," 49.

22. See Festugière, *Le dieu cosmique*, 229–32.

the Platonic theory of reminiscence and the Stoic theory of innate ideas, although profoundly adapting their meaning, because this knowledge is not something that the soul possesses by nature, but comes from the gift of illumination.[23] We will meet this second mode again in the context of the action of the Logos. What interests us here is the knowledge of God's existence and his attributes. This last aspect leads us to an important point in Philo's theology, his doctrine of the divine powers (δυνάμεις). This is also one of the most complex features of Philo's thought, whose interpretation continues to be most difficult.

We can start from a passage in *De Posteritate*:

> But the Being that in reality is can be perceived and known, not only through the ears, but with the eyes of the understanding, from the powers that range the universe, and from the constant and ceaseless motion of His ineffable works. Wherefore in the great Song there come these words as from the lips of God, "See, see that I am" (Deuteronomy 32:39) . . . What He says is, "See that I am," that is "Behold My subsistence [ὕπαρξιν]." For it is quite enough for a man's reasoning faculty to advance as far as to learn that the Cause of the Universe is and subsists. To be anxious to continue his course yet further, and inquire about essence or quality in God, is a folly fit for all the world's childhood. Not even to Moses, the all-wise, did God accord this, albeit he had made countless requests, but a divine communication was issued to him, "Thou shalt behold that which is behind Me, but My Face thou shalt not see" (Exodus 30:23). This meant that all that follows in the wake of God is within the good man's apprehension [καταληπτά], while He Himself alone is beyond it [ἀκατάληπτος], beyond, that is, in the line of straight and direct approach, a mode of approach by which (had it been possible) His quality would have been made known; but brought within ken by the powers that follow and attend Him; for these make evident not His essence but His subsistence from the things which He accomplishes" (*De Posteritate*, 166–69).[24]

This passage connects with what we have said about the incomprehensibility of the *ousia*. The Biblical passage is the same, Exodus 33. Yahweh declares to Moses that he cannot see God face to face, but that he will go before Moses and that Moses will see his wake (ὀπίσθια). Philo

---

23. Wolfson, *Philo*, II:92. [Translator: I have corrected Daniélou's text here that has *Aristotelian* instead of Wolfson's *Stoic*.]

24. *Philo* II, 427, 429.

interprets this phrase about the wake of God as what God's action in the world establishes. Through this action we can know his attributes. This exegesis will persist in subsequent tradition like that of the shadow.

Philo frequently enumerates the powers. Sometimes he only names two. Thus in the interpretation of the apparition at Mambre he explains:

> The central place is held by the Father of the Universe, Who in the Sacred Scriptures is called He that is as His proper name, while on either side of Him are the senior potencies, the nearest to him, the creative and the kingly. The title of the former is God [θεός], since it made [ἔθηκε] and ordered the All; the title of the latter is Lord [κύριος], since it is the fundamental right of the maker to rule and control what he has brought into being" (*De Abrahamo*, 121).[25]

Elsewhere he distinguishes five powers, for instance in *De Fuga et Inventione*. Beside the creative and royal powers: "Third stands the gracious [ἵλεως] power, in the exercise of which the Great Artificer takes pity and compassion on his own work . . . the gracious power, the power which enjoins things that are to be done, and that which prohibits those which are not to be done (*De Fuga*, 95, 104).[26] The symbol of these five powers is the Ark of the Covenant: "Five of which were represented by symbolic figures which are in the sanctuary, the Laws laid up in the Ark being symbols of injunction and prohibition; the lid of the Ark, which he calls the Mercy-seat representing the gracious power; while the creative and kingly powers are represented by the winged Cherubim that rest upon it" (*De Fuga*, 100).[27]

This structure of the five powers is a constant element in Philo's theology. They are hierarchically ordered. In its ascent toward God, the soul first encounters the prohibition of sin, then obedience to the law, repentance in the face of mercy, acknowledgement of sovereignty, and finally adherence to the creative love. If we link this to what we have said about the divine essence, we see that the knowledge of God, which is the essential object of religion, includes a whole series of degrees for Philo: the knowledge of the powers or affirmative theology forms the small

---

25. *Philo* VI, 41, 43.

26. *Philo* V, 61, 67.

27. Ibid., 65. See *De Cherubim*, 27. In Jewish Christianity the two cherubim (or two seraphim) will be interpreted as the Word and the Holy Spirit. It seems that this supposes a common Palestinian source and not dependence on Philo. See Daniélou, *La théologie du judéo-christianisme*, 181–88.

mysteries; the knowledge in the cloud or negative theology constitutes the great mysteries.[28]

Here we must go back to the episode at Mambre:

> When, then, as at noon-tide God shines around the soul, and the light of the mind fills it though and through and the shadows are driven from it by the rays which pour all around it, the single object presents to it a triple vision, one representing the reality, the other two the shadows reflected from it . . . So the central being with each of His potencies as His squire presents to the mind which has vision the appearance sometimes of one, sometimes of three: of one, when that mind is highly purified, and passing beyond not merely the multiplicity of other numbers, but even the dyad which is next to the unit, presses on the ideal form which is free from mixture and complexity, and being self-contained needs nothing more; of three, when, as yet uninitiated into the highest mysteries, it is still a votary only of the minor rites and unable to apprehend the existent alone by itself and apart from all else, but only through Its actions, as either creative or ruling" (*De Abrahamo*, 119,122).[29]

The last three powers represent the lower degrees (*De Sacrificiis*, 131–33).

What are the origins of this theology of the powers? Here again, Philo started from Biblical data, the divine names. We know that in the Bible God is designated by two principal names, *Yahweh* and *Elohim*. The Septuagint translates them as *Kyrios* and *Theos* respectively. Philo sees the designation of two divine attributes in these two names *Theos* designates God as a creator according to an etymology found in Herodotus II, 52, which connects it with τίθημι, to establish. As for *Kyrios*, it quote naturally designates royal power. Moreover, we know that in Judaism the custom had been adopted of no longer pronouncing the sacred Tetragrammaton, but to replace it with the substitutes *Adonai* or *Elohim* (*De Somniis*, I, 230). The contrast developed by Philo between the ineffable essence and the powers is a development of that tendency.

Lastly Philo poses the question about the relation between the οὐσία and the δυνάμεις. We know that Gregory Palamas will take up this distinction again in the fifteenth century and make it the central thesis of

---

28. The first culminate with Noah who has pleased the powers; the second with Moses who has pleased "He who is in His existence alone" (*Quod Immutabilis*, 100). [Translator: Daniélou's abbreviation here is *Imm.* 100. However, *Quod Immutabilis*, 100 in *Philo* III, 59, 61, does not contain anything like the sentence quoted.]

29. *Philo* VI, 63, 65. See *De Sacrificiis Abelis et Caini*, 59.

his theology, as will Vladimir Lossky in our time.[30] For Palamas, there is a real distinction between the οὐσία and the δυνάμεις. The latter is God directly grasped in divinization and not only by way of his work. Many texts in Philo seem to justify that conception. But Wolfson has shown that this comes from the fact that the word designates two distinct realities in Philo. There are divine attributes, but they are incomprehensible like God himself (*De Sacrificiis*, 59) and are only known by their effects. Additionally, there are δυνάμεις that are grasped by the human mind: these are the intelligible archetypes of creation. But they are a created reality. We will have to speak of this below. Thus Philo does not recognize the division in the divine nature that Palamas and his works teach, any more than it receives support from the Fathers of the Church.

The Logos

The doctrine of the powers is related to our knowledge of God through his action in the world. The doctrine of the Logos concerns this action in the world in its very structure. No aspect of Philo's thought has been studied more. Indeed it is impossible to do exegesis of chapter one of John's Gospel or study the origins of the dogma of the Trinity without encountering this doctrine. It must be added that nonetheless nothing has remained more obscure. The doctrine's origins are debated, as are its relations with rabbinical speculations on the *Memra* or Greek conceptions of immanent reason.

Its meaning is far from clear. Most authors see the Logos as an intermediate hypostasis between God and the κόσμος.[31] But Wolfson devoted a great part of his monumental work to trying to show that it is no such thing. According to him one must distinguish several different realities within the Logos: an uncreated Logos that is the divine νοῦς and has no distinct existence, a created Logos that is the unity of the intelligible world, an immanent Logos that acts in intellectual creatures.[32] We will set out the data in Philo looking for what can be derived from it with certainty.

Philo designates the Logos with several expressions that constantly recur in his work:

30. Lossky, *Essai sur la théologie mystique*, 45ff.

31. Bréhier, Lebreton, Goodenough, etc.

32. Wolfson, *Philo,* I:200–204.

But if there be any as yet unfit to be called a Son of God, let him press to take his place under God's First-born [πρωτόγονος], the Word, who holds the eldership [πρεσβύτατος] among the angels, their ruler as it were. And many names are his, for he is called "the Beginning," and the Name of God and His Word, and the Man after His image, and "he that sees," that is Israel . . . For if we have not yet become fit to be thought sons of God yet we may be sons of His invisible [ἀειδής] image, the most holy Word. For the Word is the eldest-born [πρεσβύτατος] image [εἰκών] of God (*De Confusione*, 146–47).[33]

Philo derived these expressions from Palestinian Jewish theology. They are found again in Jewish Christians to designate the Word, in particular ὄνομα and ἀρχή. The same is true of ἡμέρα and τόπος, that we will discuss below. Now, Philo does not influence these Jewish Christian authors. Consequently, a common source exists. The expressions with which we will be concerned here are found again elsewhere in Philo: the Logos is "the eldest of all existences [πρεσβύτατον]" (*Quod Deterius*, 118).[34] He is the first born (προτόγονος) of God; he is his image (*Legum Allegoriae*, III, 96). All these expressions convey both a close relation to God and a clear distinction from him.

Certain passages seem to insist that the Logos is at the level of divinity. "For His word is not a sonant impact of voice upon air, or mixed with anything else at all, but it is unbodied and unclothed and in no way different from unity" (*Quod Immutabilis*, 83).[35] More precisely still we read: "The Divine Word, who is high above all these, has not been visibly portrayed, being like to no one of the objects of sense. Nay, He is himself the Image of God, chiefest of all beings intellectually perceived, placed nearest, with no intervening distance [μεθόριος] to the Alone truly existent One" (*De Fuga*, 101).[36] All these expressions, "proximity to God," "image of God," "resemblance to the monad" can signal the Logos's divine character. Like God, it is ἀειδής, as we have seen above. Like him, it is ἀκατάληπτος. "Think it not a hard saying that the Highest of all things should be unnamable when His Word has no name of its own which we

33. *Philo* IV, 89, 91.

34. *Philo* II, 281. [Translator: The Loeb translation does not make explicit that this refers to the Logos, but the Greek does.]. See *Legum Allegoriae*, III, 175.

35. *Philo* III, 51, 53.

36. *Philo* V, 65.

can speak"(*De Mutatione*, 15).[37] Here it should be observed that the word πρεσβύτατος is applied to God. Consequently, its application to the Logos does not make the latter a creature.

However, a certain number of other passages let us interpret these expressions in a way that decisively shows that the Logos is inferior to God.

> To His Word, His chief messenger, highest in age and honor, the Father of all has given the special prerogative, to stand on the border [μεθόριος] and separate the creature from the creator. This same Word both pleads with the immortal as suppliant for afflicted mortality and acts as ambassador of the ruler to the subject . . . and proudly describes it in these words "and I stood between the Lord and you" (Deuteronomy 5:5), that is neither uncreated [ἀγένητος] as God, nor created as you, but midway between the two extremes surety to both sides (*Quis Heres*, 205–6).[38]

A passage like this makes it evident that the Logos is certainly an intermediary, transcendent in relation to the world of γένεσις but still inferior to God. This is the notion that is found again in Origen. The ambiguity of the term γένεσις in Christian discourse makes the difficulty still greater. At any rate, Wolfson's interpretation seems impossible here.

In the same sense we will cite other passages where themes appear that we find again in Origen. For example, there is the distinction between ὁ θεός and θεός.[39]

> He that is truly God is One, but those that are improperly so called are more than one. Accordingly, the holy word in the present instance has indicated Him Who is truly God by means of the articles saying "I am the God [ὁ θεός]," while it omits the article when mentioning him who is improperly so called, saying "Who appeared to thee in the place" not "of the God," but simply "of God [θεός]." Here it gives the title of "God" to His chief Word, not from any superstitious nicety in applying names, but with one aim before him, to use words to express facts (*De Somniis*, I, 229).[40]

The created character of the Logos appears in a passage like the following: "God spake [λέγων] and it was done—no interval between the two—or

37. Ibid., 151.
38. *Philo*, IV, 385.
39. See Origen, *Commentary on the Gospel of St. John*, II:2.
40. *Philo* V, 419

it might suggest a truer view to say that His word was deed [ἔργον]" (*De Sacrificiis*, 65).[41] We see the thought here. God first created everything in his Logos, which contains everything and by which the cosmos will come into existence. We will find simultaneous creation again in Gregory of Nyssa, though separated from the generation of the Logos.

The last passage introduces us to the meaning of the Logos. It is the principle of all creation, intelligible and sensible. Indeed, it is the instrument by which God accompanies the creation:

> The Word who is antecedent to all that has come into existence, the Word, which the Helmsman of the Universe grasps as a rudder to guide all things on their course. Even as, when he was fashioning the world, He employed it as His instrument [ὀργάνῳ] that the fabric of His handiwork might be without reproach (*De Migratione*, 6).[42]

Likewise in another passage: "Yet He receives nothing from anyone, for besides that He has no needs, all things are His possessions, and when He gives, He employs as minister of His gifts the reason wherewith also He made the world" (*Quod Immutabilis*, 57).[43] Philo interprets Genesis 2:4 in this way: "in the day in which the Lord God made the heaven and the earth." *This day* is one of the names of the Logos. "For by His own supremely manifest and far-shining Reason God makes both of them" (*Legum Allegoriae* I, 21).[44] This exegesis is already found in Aristobulus.[45] But it comes from Palestinian Judaism, because it is found again in the Jewish Christians.[46]

This role of the Logos means first of all that it is what conceives the archetypal ideas. In this sense it is in νοῦς, God's thought, but as thought turned toward the world. This appears above all in the *Allegories of the Laws*.

41. *Philo* II, 143.

42. *Philo* IV, 135. On the Aristotelian origin of the term *organon* see Wolfson, *Philo*, I:263–66.

43. *Philo* III, 39.

44. *Philo* I, 159.

45. Eusebius, *Praeparatio Evanglica*, XIII, 12.

46. Justin, *Dialogues*, C, 4; Hippolytus, *De Benedictione Mosis*; 171. [Translator: There seems to be a separate volume *Hippolyte de Rome sur les bénédictions d'Isaac, de Jacob, et de Moïse*, translation and notes Brière, Mariès, and Mercier.] Clement of Alexandria, *Eclogae Propheticae*, 53,1. [A recent edition of the cited work is *Eclogae Propheticae. Estratti profettici*, Greek and Italian, translated and edited by Carlo Nardi.]

> God's shadow is His Word, which he made use of like and in-
> strument, and so made the world. But its shadow, and what we
> may describe as the representation, is the archetype for further
> creations. For just as God is the Pattern of the Image, to which
> the title of Shadow has just been given, even so the Image be-
> comes the pattern of other beings (*Legum Allegoriae*, III, 96).[47]

As an archetype the Logos contains the exemplar ideas of all realities. "Now place [τόπος] has a threefold meaning . . . secondly, that of the Divine Word, which God Himself has completely filled throughout with incorporeal potencies [δυνάμεις]" (*De Somniis*, I, 62).[48] The word δυνάμεις is a synonym here of ἰδέαι, as we see in a parallel passage: "The Universe that consisted of ideas would have no other location than the Divine Reason" (*De Opificio*, 20).[49] This use of τόπος is Aristotelian and Platonic.[50] We note that Philo also uses it to talk about God (*De Cherubim*, 49). We will find the same idea in Origen linked to a certain multiplicity that contrasts the Logos with the One.[51]

In so far as the Logos bears the models of created things within itself, it marks them with a seal. Under this perspective, it is designated by the name *sphragis*.

> For the world has come into being, and assuredly it has done
> so under the hand of some Cause; and the Word of Him who
> makes it is Himself the seal [σφραγίς] by which each thing that
> exists has received its shape. Accordingly, from the outset form
> [εἶδος] in perfection accompanies the things that come into be-
> ing, for it is an impress and image of the perfect Word (*De Fuga
> et Inventione*, 12).[52]

Still more precisely Philo explains:

> For this king gives the soul a seal [σφράγις] (Genesis 38:18),
> a gift all beauteous, by which he teaches it that when the sub-
> stance of the universe was without shape and figure, God gave
> it these; when it had no definite character, God molded it into

---

47. *Philo* I, 365, 367. See also *Legum Allegoriae*, I, 19; and *Quis Rerum Divinarum Heres*, 230–31.

48. *Philo* V, 329. The Logos is the γενικώτατον, the highest genus, which is symbolized by manna, whose name means τι, anything (*Legum Allegoriae*, III, 175).

49. [*Philo* I, 17.]

50. Wolfson, *Philo*, I:246.

51. Origen, *Commentary on the Gospel of St. John*, II:8.

52. [*Philo* V, 17.]

definiteness, and, when He had effected it, stamped the entire universe with His image and an ideal form, even His own Word (*De Somniis*, II, 45).[53]

The imprint engraved on the pectoral of the High Priest, himself the figure of the cosmic high priest who is the Logos depicts this *sphragis*, (*De Migratione Abrahami*, 103). The theme of the Logos as *sphragis* is found again in the Fathers. Lampe even sees it as the source of the doctrine of "sacramental" character.[54]

However, the Logos is not just God's instrument in the creation of the world. It governs, conserves, and maintains the world. We have already encountered the theme of the Logos as pilot of the world. It is also the world's driver: "While, the Word is the charioteer of the powers, He Who talks is seated in the chariot, giving directions to the charioteer for the right wielding of the reins of the Universe" (*De Fuga*, 101).[55] It is not only the instrument of creation but of Providence: "For circle-wise moves the revolution of that divine plan which most call fortune" (*Quod Immutabilis*, 176).[56] It traverses the universe with great speed: "Thus, as the Uncreated anticipates the word of the created, so the word of the Uncreated outruns the word of the created, though that ride with all speed upon the clouds . . . implying that the divine word has outrun and overtaken all things" (*De Sacrificiis Abelis et Caini*, 66).[57] As Wolfson correctly saw, this immanence of the Logos in the world falls within a Stoic tendency. But Wolfson was wrong in seeing a reality distinct from the uncreated Logos and the Intelligible Logos in this immanent Logos who illuminates the *logoi*.

This Stoic character appears in two attributes of the Philonic Logos. The first is the faculty of discerning. It is the Logos τομεύς:

> So then the two natures, the reasoning power within us and the divine Word or Reason above us, are indivisible, yet indivisible as they are, they divide other things without number. The divine Word separated and apportioned all that is in nature. Our mind deals with all the things material and immaterial which the mental process brings within its grasp, divides them to an

---

53. *Philo* V, 468.

54. Lampe, *The Seal of the Spirit*. See Dölger, *Sphragis*, 66 ff.

55. *Philo* V, 65.

56. *Philo* III, 97.

57. *Philo* II, 145.

infinity of infinities and never ceases to cleave them. This is the
result of its likeness to the Father and Maker of all. For the God-
head is without mixture or infusion or parts and yet has become
to the whole world the cause of mixture, infusion, division, and
multiplicity of parts. And thus it will be natural that these two
which are in the likeness of God, the mind within us and the
mind above us, should subsist without parts or severance and
yet be strong and potent to divide and distinguish everything
that is (*Quis Heres*, 234–36).[58]

The Logos is thus the sword of fire of Paradise "that ever moves with un-
swerving zeal, teaching thee to choose the good and eschew the evil" (*De
Cherubim*, 30).[59] This points us toward the Epistle to the Hebrews 4:12:
"For the word of God is living and efficient and keener than any two-
edged sword, and extending even to the division of soul and spirit . . . and
a discerner of the thoughts and intentions of the heart."[60]

But if the Logos discerns, it is also what unites, it is the bond of
creation. "For the Word of Him-that-is is, as has been stated, the bond
[δεσμός] of all existence, and holds and knits together all the parts, preventing them from being dissolved and separated (*De Fuga*, 112).[61] This
is taken up in a remarkable way in *De Plantatione*:

No material thing is so strong as to be able to bear the burden
of the world; and that the everlasting Word of the eternal God
is the very sure and staunch prop of the Whole. He it is, who
extending Himself from the midst to its utmost bounds and
from its extremities to the midst again, keeps up through all its
length Nature's unvanquished course, combining and compact-
ing all its parts. For the father Who began Him constituted His
Word such a Bond of the Universe as nothing can break" (*De
Plantatione*, 8–9).[62]

Here we find successively evoked before our very eyes the image of Atlas
or Anteus, the Stoics δεσμός, perhaps also the Greek Wisdom. For, the
Alexandrian who wrote the book of Wisdom already knew that Wisdom
is "subtle, lively, clear, undefiled, plain, not subject to hurt, loving the

58. *Philo* IV, 401. See also *Quis Heres*, 130–31.
59. *Philo* II, 27.
60. Spicq, "Le philonisme de l'Epître aux Hébreux," 557–58.
61. *Philo* V, 71.
62. *Philo* III, 217.

thing that is good, quick" (Wisdom 7:22) and that she "reacheth from one end to the other" (Wisdom 8:1). But he called her *Sophia* and not *Logos*.

This poses the question of the relation of these two realities in Philo. Wolfson treats the relation at length.[63] Sometimes Wisdom and Logos are identified. "This issues forth out of Eden, the Wisdom of God, and this is the Reason of God" (*Legum Allegoriae*, I, 65).[64] Similarly, the stone from which living water gushed forth in the desert is identified with Wisdom and Logos in the same passage (*Quod Deterius*, 115–18).[65] More generally, Sophia appears as prior to the Logos. She, more than the Logos, can be regarded as divine thought. In that sense she is compared to Paradise from which the Logos spring forth.

> It is this Word which one of Moses' company compared to a river, when he said in the Psalms 'the river of God is full of water' (Psalm 45/44:10); where surely it were senseless to suppose that the words can properly refer to any of the rivers of earth. No, he is representing the Divine Word as full of the stream of wisdom, with no part of it empty or devoid of itself . . . And there is another psalm which runs thus: 'The strong current of the river makes glad the city of God' (Psalm 46/45: 4) What city? For the existing holy city, where the sacred temple also is, does not stand in the neighborhood of rivers any more than of the sea. Thus it is clear that he writes to shew us allegorically something different from the obvious. It is perfectly true that the impetuous rush of the divine word borne along (swiftly) and ceaselessly with its strong and ordered current does overflow and gladden the whole universe through and through (*De Somniis*, II, 245–47).[66]

A final question is posed about the place of the Logos in the order of God's knowledge in relation to *ousia* and the powers. Speaking of the symbolism of the cities of refuge (Numbers 35), Philo writes:

> It would seem, then, that the chiefest and surest and best mother-city something more than just a city, is the divine Word, and that to take refuge first in it is supremely advantageous. The other five, colonies as it were, are powers of Him who speaks that Word, their

63. Wolfson, *Philo*, I:253–82.

64. *Philo* I, 189.

65. See also *Legum Allegoriae*, II, 86.

66. *Philo* V, 553. 555. [Translator: The more usual Hebrew numbering of the Psalm is put first with the Septuagint number—one less—second.] For Origen, Wisdom is the more elevated name and the only one peculiar to the Son (*Commentary on the Gospel of St. John*, 1:9).

leader being creative power, in the exercise of which the Creator produced the universe by a word (*De Fuga*, 94–95).[67]

Philo then enumerates the powers. We have quoted that passage. He continues by showing: "The man who is capable of running swiftly it bids stay, not to draw breath but pass forward to the supreme Divine Word, Who is the fountain of Wisdom, in order that he may draw from the stream and, released from death, gain life eternal as his prize." (*De Fuga*, 97).[68] Those incapable of this will be raised up to the creative power or merely to the royal power. We have seen that. Two things are noteworthy: on the one hand the superiority of Wisdom, identical to the Logos, to the Other powers,[69] but also the superiority of knowledge by direct illumination worked by the knowledge in the soul, over indirect knowledge starting from God's activity in the world, to which the powers correspond.[70]

Besides, Logos's knowledge is inferior to the knowledge grasped by *Ousia* in the shadow. "For it well befits those who have entered into comradeship with knowledge to desire to see the Existent if they may, but if they cannot, to see at any rate his image, the most Holy Word" (*De Confusione*, 97).[71] Thus we are told: "For this [tr. the interpreting word] must be God for us the imperfect folk, but, as for the wise and perfect, the primal Being is their God" (*Legum Allegoriae*, III, 207).[72] Also, having overcome the Logos, Joseph is "fed by God himself" (*Legum Allegoriae* III, 177).[73]

Here we come to a hierarchy that begins with the last power to rise up to the unfathomable *ousia* passing through the Logos.[74] But we must not forget that this hierarchy is constituted by the interplay of two lines of thought that do not coincide. One is the distinction between essence and powers, which is the doctrine of the divine attributes; the other tendency is the distinction of the Being and the Logos, which is the doctrine of the hypostases. The latter is found again in Justin and Origen in the contrast

67. *Philo* V, 61.

68. Ibid., 63.

69. "For the flinty rock is the wisdom of God, which he marked of highest and chiefest from his powers" (*Legum Allegoriae*, II, 86); *Philo* I, 279.

70. See *Legum Allegoriae*, III, 100.

71. *Philo* IV, 61–63.

72. *Philo* I, 443.

73. Ibid., 421.

74. See Origen, *Commentary on the Gospel of John*, 1:23.

between the knowable Logos and the unknowable Father, which will be a distortion of Trinitarian theology under Philo's influence.

What is the origin of this Philonic theology of the Logos that will bring to Trinitarian theology both so many useful kinds of expression and so many dangerous deviations? Here, as for the cloud, we are again confronted by two sources. On the one hand, the first origin is the Septuagint Logos, which translates the Hebrew *dabar*. We know that in the Old Testament, the word of God has a triple function: creative, revelatory, and judicial.[75] These diverse aspects are found again in Philo. Moreover, Jewish theology replaced the Divine Name by different expressions that, without being properly hypostases, indicated modes of divine presence or action in the world. We know the development that the Kabala will give to these doctrines. They may guide Philo, especially since the Greek book of Wisdom shows that Alexandrian Judaism knew them.

Furthermore, Philo interpreted the Biblical Logos under philosophical influences. We have given many examples of details. What seems important is that these influences are varied. The conception of Logos as thought of the creation by God is Platonic. It is the equivalent of the divine νοῦς in Aristotle. Lastly, the Logos penetrating and animating the world is Stoic. It seems that Wolfson was wrong to distinguish these three aspects as forming three levels of existence in Philo. Thereby Wolfson eliminates the notion of intermediary that he judges incompatible with Philo's monotheism. But Wolfson appears to be mistaken. By contrast, he was right to show that until then the Logos did not hold in any thinker the place that it had in Philo. It is Philo who substitutes it for Aristotle's νοῦς and the Stoic ψυχή.[76] That is why Christian theologians would seek the elements in Philo with which to elaborate their theology of the Word.[77]

The Angels

The Logos constitutes an intermediate sphere between the abyss of being and creation properly speaking. Angels fit completely within the created order. Still, they constitute a world apart that it is difficult to define

---

75. See Jacques Dupont, *Essais sur la christologie de saint Jean.*

76. Wolfson, *Philo*, I:253.

77. It would also be possible to speak of the Philonic theology of the πνεῦμα. See Verbeke, *L'évolution de la doctrine du Pneuma*, 238–60; Laurentin, "Le pneuma dans la doctrine de Philon," 490–537.

exactly. Sometimes Philo assimilates them to human souls. The only difference would be that the latter descend into bodies. "Now some of the souls have descended into bodies, but others have never deigned to be brought into union with any of the parts of earth" (*De Gigantibus*, 12).[78] In that case they will have to be studied at the same time as humans. Wolfson does this.[79] But besides that, Philo establishes a special relation between them and the Logos. They are sometimes called λόγοι. They then appear as instruments of the Logos in the administration of the world. This conception seems more fundamental, especially since there is never a question of an archetype of the angels. They seem to constitute an intelligible world of personal beings beside the intelligible world of impersonal ideas. We detain ourselves at this interpretation without overlooking the contradictions in Philo's thought.

In reality both interpretations are valuable, because they correspond to two categories of angels. In this regard a decisive text tells us:

> God is one, but He has around Him numberless Potencies [δυνάμεις], which all assist and protect created being, and among them are included the powers of chastisement. Now chastisement is not a thing of harm of mischief, but a preventive and correction of sin. Through these Potencies the incorporeal and intelligible world was framed, the archetype of this phenomenal world" (*De Confusione*, 171–72).[80]

Here we have a first group, that of the higher angels. They are not part of the cosmos, since they cooperated in its construction. Another passage shows us their relationship with the archetypes. We are dealing with the angels of the nations interpreted as parts of the soul. "When God divided and partitioned off the nations of the soul . . . then did He fix the boundaries of the offspring of virtue corresponding to the number of the angels; for there are as many forms or 'nations' of virtue as there are words [λόγοι] of God" (*De Posteritate*, 91).[81] We find equivalence here between the ideas of the virtues and the angels of the virtues.

78. *Philo* II, 451.

79. Wolfson, *Philo*, I:366ff.

80. *Philo* IV, 103–5. See also *De Somniis* I:140; *Philo* V, 371, 373: "Others there are of perfect virtue and excellence, gifted with a higher and diviner temper, that have never felt any craving after the things of earth, but are viceroys of the ruler of the universe, ears and eyes, so to speak, of the great king, beholding and hearing all things."

81. *Philo* II, 379.

The *De Confusione* text continues: "There is, too, in the air a sacred company of unbodied souls, commonly called angels in the inspired pages, who wait upon these heavenly powers" (*De Confusione Linguarum*, 174).[82] Since the former fill the divine place (*De Somniis*, I, 127), the latter fill the air. These are the ones that can be united or not to bodies:

> The air is the abode of incorporeal souls, since it seemed good to their Maker to fill all parts of the universe with living beings ... Of these souls some, such as have earthward tendencies and material tastes, descend to be fast bound in mortal bodies, while others ascend, being selected for return according to the numbers and periods determined by nature. Of these last some, longing for the familiar and accustomed ways of mortal life, again retrace their steps, while others pronouncing that life great foolery call the body a prison and a tomb, and escaping as though from a dungeon or a grave, are lifted up on light wings to the upper air and range the heights [αἰῶνα] forever" (*De Somniis*, I, 135, 138–39).[83]

We recognize the Platonic myth of the *Phaedrus* here. Furthermore, the contrast between the two categories recalls the distinction of the apocalypses concerning the bad angels, great angels, and souls of giants.

Whatever we make of the distinction, the functions of the two categories of angels are alike in their substance. They are: "servants and ministers of the primal God" (*De Abrahamo*, 115).[84]

Most especially, God confides to them tasks that are less important or unworthy of Him. "His Angels and Words [λόγους] give the secondary gifts" (*Legum Allegoriae*, III, 177),[85] while He Himself accomplishes the good. Besides their power is always derived (*De Confusione*, 181). *De Confusione* notes that clearly:

> So the whole army composed of the several contingents, each marshaled in their proper ranks, have as their business to serve and minister to the word of the Captain who marshaled them, and to follow His leadership as right and the law of service demand. For it must not be that God's soldiers should ever be

---

82. *Philo* IV, 105.

83. *Philo* V, 369, 371. See also *De Gigantibus*, 6 and 12, and *De Plantatione*, 14. Origen likewise regards men as pure spirits descended into bodies. Daniélou, *Origène*, 207–17.

84. *Philo* VI, 61.

85. *Philo* I, 421.

guilty of desertion from the ranks. Now the King may fitly hold converse with his powers and employ them to serve in matters which should not be consummated by God alone. It is true indeed that the Father of All has no need of aught, so that He should require the co-operation of others, if He wills some creative, work, yet seeing what was fitting to Himself and the world which was coming into being, He allowed his subject powers to have the fashioning of some things (*De Confusione*, 174–75).[86]

Among these functions we can note the fabrication of the human body (*De Confusione*, 179), and the punishments inflicted on humans.

Most especially, the angels help humans in their ascent toward God. They are guardians φύλακες (*De Confusione*, 27) and companions ἀκόλουθοι. "Now he that follows God has of necessity as his fellow-travelers the words and thoughts [λόγεις] that attend Him, angels as they are often called" (*De Migratione*, 173).[87] They assist humans in their struggle against the passions (*De Sobrietate*, 65). God communicates dreams by them (*De Somniis*, I, 190). This aid corresponds to the beginning of spiritual life.

The perfect deal directly with God. "In the understandings of those who have been purified to the utmost the Ruler of the universe walks [ἐμπεριπατεῖ] noiselessly, alone, invisibly, but in the understandings of those who are still undergoing cleansing and have not yet fully washed their life defiled and stained by the body's weight, there walk angels, divine words, making them bright and clean with the doctrines of all that is good and beautiful" (*De Somniis*, I, 148).[88] Christian tradition will take up this point again, especially in Clement of Alexandria and Pseudo-Dionysius.[89] Indeed humans cannot bear divine radiance.

It was a boon to us in our sad case to avail ourselves of the services of "words" acting on our behalf as mediators, so great is our awe and shuddering dread of the universal Monarch and the exceeding might of His sovereignty. It was our attainment of a conception of this that once made us address to one of those mediators the entreaty: "Speak though to us, and let not God speak to us, lest haply we die" (Exodus 20:19)" (*De Somniis* I:142–43).[90]

86. *Philo* IV, 104–5.
87. Ibid., 233.
88. *Philo*, V, 375. See also *De Somniis* I:115.
89. Daniélou, *Les anges et leur mission*.
90. *Philo* V, 373.

But if the angels transmit divine illuminations to humans, they are also charged with transmitting human prayers to God. They are the priests of the Cosmic Temple (*De Specialibus Legibus*, I, 66). Accordingly they circulate between earth and heaven. "They both convey the biddings of the Father to His children and report the children's need to their Father" (*De Somniis* I, 141).[91] Jacob's ladder is the image of this,

> Such then is that which in the universe is figuratively called stairway. If we consider that which is so called in human beings we shall find it to be soul. Its foot is sense perception, which is as it were the earthly element in it, and its head, the mind [νοῦς] which is wholly unalloyed, the heavenly element, as it may be called. Up and down throughout its whole extent are moving incessantly the "words" [λόγοι] of God, drawing it up with them when they ascend and disconnecting it with what is mortal, and exhibiting to it the spectacle of the only objects worthy of our gaze; and when they descend not casting it down, for neither does God nor does a divine Word cause harm, but condescending out of love for man [φιλανθρωπία] and compassion for our race, to be helpers and comrades, that with the healing of their breath they may quicken into new life the soul which is still borne along in the body as in a river (*De Somniis*, I, 146–47).[92]

If we compare this doctrine to that of contemporary Jewish apocalypses we observe considerable differences. We do not find any of these details: names of angels, their roles in connection to the elements of the universe, or their role at the moment of death, which characterize Palestinian angelology. Similarly, the bad angels are almost unknown.[93] If some angels are adored as gods, that is through human error (*De Fuga*, 212). In reality, Philo's angelology owes a great deal to his Greek environment. It is Plato and Plutarch's angelology. Angels are intermediaries between God and humans. They dwell in the air.[94] Philo calls them just ἄγγελοι and not δαίμονες. "It is Moses's custom to give the name of angels to those whom other philosophers call demons" (*De Gigantibus*, 6).[95] Or again: "Souls and

91. Ibid., 373.

92. Ibid., 375.

93. See only *De Gigantibus*, 16 and 17. But elsewhere Philo declares: "These are immune from wickedness" (*De Confusione Linguarum*, 177; *Philo* IV, 107).

94. Soury, *Démonologie de Plutarque*, 19–25

95. *Philo* II, 449.

demons and angels are but different names for the same one underlying object" (*De Gigantibus*, 16).[96]

The Cosmos

Angels constitute one sphere of creation. The cosmos is another. What characterizes it is the distinction between the sensible and the intelligible. The cosmos is presented in two guises. On the one hand, it subsists under the form of a collection of archetypes that Philo was the first to call κόσμος νοητός (*De Opificio*, 26). On the other hand, the cosmos exists in the particular form of the visible universe. To this distinction another is added, this time not horizontal but vertical. In its totality the universe constitutes the Great Cosmos, whose high priest is the Logos. Moreover, a man forms a microcosm whose structure is parallel to that of the universe and whose head is the νοῦς. Man is not a part of the Cosmos. He is the image of the Logos as the Cosmos is the image of the Logos. Consequently, we will study these two domains successively by viewing in each case the intelligible and sensible aspect.[97]

The distinction between κόσμος νοητός and κόσμος αἰσθητός is a Platonic theme, even though Philo puts his stamp on it. "For this universe, since we perceive it by our senses, is the younger son of God. To the elder son, I mean the intelligible universe, He assigned the place of firstborn, and purposed that it should remain in his own keeping" (*Quod Immutabilis*, 31).[98] The treatise *De Opificio* explains what the intelligible world is:

> For God, being God, assumed that a beautiful copy would never be produced apart from a beautiful pattern and that no object of perception would be faultless which was not made in the likeness of an original [ἰδέαν] discerned only by the intellect. So when He willed to create this visible world He first fully formed the intelligible world, in order that He might have the use of a pattern wholly God-like and incorporeal in producing the material world, as a later creation, the very image of an earlier, to embrace in itself objects of perception of as many kinds as the other contained objects of intelligence'" (*De Opificio*, 15–16).[99]

---

96. Ibid., 453.

97. Lindeskog, *Studien zum neutestamentlichen Schöpfungsgedanken*, 135–63

98. *Philo* III, 25, 27.

99. *Philo* I, 15.

Philo then compares God to an architect who constructs a model before building a city (*De Opificio*, 17–20. This *cosmos noetos* is conceived like a realm (πολιτεία) of incorruptible and incorporeal ideas.

The problem is to know where to situate the world of ideas and of kinds. Wolfson studied this closely. He recalls that in ancient thought we find three interpretations on this issue. For Plato there exists a created[100] world of ideas, which is the totally real world. For Aristotle, the kinds do not exist outside particular individuals in which they are realized. Lastly, a certain Platonic tendency views the ideas as existing in divine thought. Wolfson concludes that Philo has retained this threefold interpretation and that the ideas, like the Logos, which would only be their unity, would exist on three levels at the same time, in so far as thought by God and not distinct from him, in so far as created intelligible world, and in so far as realized in the sensible world.[101]

That seems to be a simplification of Philo's thought. He is sure that there is a relation between the ideas and the Logos. But no more than we can separate God's immanent Logos and a created Logos, can we distinguish a world of created ideas and a world of uncreated ideas. The world of ideas shares the same ambiguity as the Logos. We saw that the latter was called "the place of the ideas."

Other passages show this relation. "As, then, the city which was fashioned beforehand within the mind of the architect held no place in the outer world, but had been engraved in the soul of the artificer as by a seal; even so the universe that consisted of ideas would have no other location than the Divine Reason, which was the Author of this ordered frame" (*De Opificio*, 20).[102] In this sense, the world of ideas is identical to the Logos itself in so far as it thinks the world. It subsists in the Logos:

> Should a man desire to use words in a more simple and direct way, he would say that the world discerned only by the intellect is nothing else that the Word of God when He was already engaged in the act of creation. For (to revert to our illustration) the city discernible by the intellect alone is nothing else than the reasoning faculty [λογισμός] of the architect in the act of planning to found the city. It is Moses who lays down this, not I . . . when setting on record the creation of man, that he was molded after

100. [Translator: As Wolfson emphasizes *Philo*, I:204, here Philo makes "a highly significant change" in the doctrine of the *Timaeus*.]

101. Wolfson, *Philo*, I:200ff., and 290ff.

102. *Philo* I, 17.

the image of God (Genesis 1:27). Now if the part is an image of an image [εἰκών εἰκόνος], it is manifest that the whole is too, and if the whole creation, this entire world perceived by our senses (seeing that it is greater than any human image) is a copy of the Divine image, it is manifest that the archetypal seal also, which we aver to be the world described by the mind, would be the very Word of God (*De Opificio*, 24–25).[103]

But, furthermore, this intelligible world has its own reality. It belongs to the created realm. Thus we find it stands in a relation to the Logos similar to that of the Logos to the Father. It is this intelligible world that was created at the beginning:

First then, the Maker made an incorporeal heaven, and an invisible earth, and the essential form of air and void . . . Next (He made) the incorporeal essence of water and of life-breath and, to crown all, of light. This again, the seventh in order, was an incorporeal pattern, discernible only by the mind, or the sun and of all luminaries which were to come into existence through heaven . . . For the intelligible as far surpasses the visible in the brilliancy of its radiance, as sunlight assuredly surpasses darkness and day night, and mind, the ruler of the entire soul, the bodily eyes. Now that invisible light perceptible only by mind has come into being as an image [εἰκὼν] of the Divine Word Who brought it within our ken (*De Opificio*, 29–31).[104]

Likewise, there are other examples if this: "We must, however, place these, dawn and evening I mean, in the category of the incorporeal and intelligible: for there is in these nothing whatever patent to the senses, but they are simply models [ἰδέαι] and measuring-rules and patterns [τύποι] and seals [σφραγῖδες], all of these being incorporeal and serving for the creation of other bodies" (*De Opificio*, 34).[105]

This creation of the intelligible world is simultaneous. In this sense Philo comments before St. Basil on the Septuagint's μία ἡμέρα. "As a necessary consequence a measure of time was forthwith brought about, which its Maker called Day, and not 'first' [πρώτην] day but 'one,' [μίαν] an expression due to the uniqueness of the intelligible world, and to its having therefore a natural kinship to the number 'One' [μοναδικὴν]" (*De Opificio*, 35).[106]

103. Ibid., 21.
104. Ibid., 23, 25.
105. Ibid., 27.
106. Ibid., 27.

We recall that "day" is one of the names of the Logos for Philo. Thus, the order in which Genesis describes the stage of creation is not to be taken in a chronological sense for what concerns the intelligible world, but in a logical sense. "For, even if the Maker made all things simultaneously, order was nonetheless an attribute of all that came into existence in fair beauty, for beauty is absent where there is disorder. Now order [τάξις] is a series [ἀκολουθία] of things going on before and following after, in due sequence, a sequence which, though not seen in the finished productions, yet exists in the designs of the contrivers" (*De Opificio*, 28).[107] We encounter these ideas and terms again in Gregory of Nyssa.

Thus, we can conclude in what regards the intelligible world: it is impossible to distinguish several levels there. The apparently conflicting terms that describe the intelligible world show that it can neither be reduced to the Logos nor contrasted with it. It constitutes an order apart, that of subsistent ideas, whose connection is certainly the Logos, but which also correspond to an action of the Logos that constitutes them in it or in which God constitutes them. Consequently, they are posterior in regard to the generation of the Logos, at least in the logical order. But at the same time, they are not perfectly distinct from it. Just as the Logos is the terminus of an action of God that is not properly creation but an act of thought, so also the intelligible world is the terminus of an action of the Logos in so far as object of thought. Wolfson was right to see in these three items three aspects of God: νοῦς, νοητός, νοητόν. But he goes too far when he thinks that these three operations constitute distinct levels of reality. The same κόσμος νοητός is the object of divine thought and subsists in its own reality.

The sensible world that is created next is contrasted with the intelligible world. "The incorporeal world, then, was now finished and firmly settled in the divine Reason, and the world patent to sense was ripe for birth after the pattern of the incorporeal" (*De Opificio*, 36).[108] *De Opificio* describes the stages of this real creation. Here we are dealing with a strictly cosmological exposition. In it Philo follows the philosophy of his time more than anywhere else, in particular that of Aristotle and the Stoics. In particular, we will only observe that to this doctrine of the superiority of the intelligible world, Philo adds very great admiration for the sensible world, in particular the heavens. If pagan phi-

107. Ibid., 23.
108. Ibid., 27.

losophers were wrong to adore them, it nonetheless remains true that contemplation of them was to lead to knowledge of God's existence and attributes. Contemplation of the cosmos represents the first stage here in the ascent of the intellect toward God, just as it is the last stage in the order of the issuing forth of these realities.[109]

Man

The parallelism between κόσμος and ἄνθρωπος is a constant theme in Philo. In his exegesis, cosmological and psychological interpretation are paired again and again. Thus, the tree of life is simultaneously the figure of the sun and the νοῦς. The city of God that the river delights is firstly the Cosmos that has received the divine liquor in its fullness and exalts in eternal joy. Next, it is the soul of the sage in which God is said to circulate as in a city (De Somniis, II, 247–48). Jacob's ladder upon which the angels go up and down is "the air symbolized by a stairway as firmly set on earth . . . so that the earth is air's foot and root and heaven its head . . . Such then is that which in the universe is figuratively called stairway. If we consider that which is so-called in human beings we shall find it to be soul. Its foot is sense perception, which is as it were the earthly element in it, and its head, the mind" (De Somniis, I, 144, 146).[110] Macrocosm and microcosm are the two parts of creation in a mutual state of dependence, yet distinct and presenting a similar structure.

Just as the creation of the κόσμος νοητός precedes that of the κόσμος αἰσθητός, likewise the creation of man in image precedes that of man modeled with earth.

> There is a vast difference between the man thus formed and the man that came into existence earlier after the image of God: for the man so formed is an object of sense-perception, partaking already of such or such quality, consisting of body and soul, man or woman, by nature mortal; while he that was after the (Divine) image was an idea [ἰδέα] or type or seal [σφραγίς], an object of thought (only), incorporeal, neither male nor female, by nature incorruptible (De Opificio, 134–35).[111]

---

109. See Festugière, Le dieu cosmique, 554–72, which translates a large number of these passages.

110. Philo V, 373, 375.

111. Philo I, 107.

Besides,

> There are two types of men; the one a heavenly man, the other
> an earthly. The heavenly man, being made after the image of
> God, is altogether without part or lot in corruptible and ter-
> restrial substance; but the earthly one was compacted out of
> the matter scattered here and there, which Moses calls "clay."
> For this reason he says that the heavenly man was not molded,
> but was stamped with the image of God; while the earthly is
> a molded work of the Artificer, but not His offspring (*Legum
> Allegoriae*, I, 31–32).[112]

This commentary is founded on the distinction apparent when we
compare two passages in Genesis: 1:26, and 2:7. Philo's interpretation will
enjoy extraordinary favor. In particular we know that it was to be taken up
by Gregory of Nyssa whose treatise *On the Creation of Man* acknowledges
its inspiration by Philo's *De Opificio*. But the contrast between the two men
admits several interpretations. Philo's interpretation leaves no doubt after
what we have already seen. Man created in image is the archetypal idea of
man pre-existing in the Logos. It does not correspond to a particular stage
of humanity, as Origen will think in admitting real human pre-existence in
an ideal world. The idea of man is in the same relation to the Logos as the
idea of χόσμος. A phrase that we have left aside up to now explains that to
us, when among the titles of the Logos, Philo mentions that of "the Man
after His image" (*De Confusione*, 146).[113] In fact, man as image is an aspect
of the Logos *qua* place of archetypal ideas.

Still, though man presents an analogy with the χόσμος, he has a peculiar structure. Indeed, it is essential to him to be constituted by two elements, one corporeal the other intellectual, the σῶμα and the νοῦς. Each
of these components has its archetypal idea. "As before the particular
and individual mind there subsists a certain original as an archetype and
·pattern of it, and again before the particular sense-perception, a certain
original of sense-perception related to the particular as a seal [σφραγῖδος]
making impression is to the form which it makes" (*Legum Allegoriae*,
I, 22).[114] They are next realized in particular, a symbol of which is the
creation of man and woman: "For it was requisite that the creation of
mind should be followed immediately by that of sense-perception, to be

112. Ibid., 167.
113. *Philo* IV, 9.
114. *Philo* I, 161.

a helper and ally to it. Having then finished the creation of the mind He fashions the product of creative skill that comes next to it alike in order and in power, namely active sense-perception, with a view to the completeness of the whole soul" (*Legum Allegoriae*, II, 24).[115]

But there is a hierarchy between these two parts of man. The νοῦς is made to command the sensations and passions. Here Philo takes up Plato's image of the driver (*De Sacrificiis*, 49). This hierarchy is based on a difference in nature. The νοῦς possesses higher dignity. "It is in respect of the Mind [νοῦν], the sovereign element of the soul, that the word *image* is used" (*De Opificio*, 69).[116] Because of this relation, the mind has an analogy with God. Like Him, it is not comprehensible. "And why should we wonder that the Existent cannot be apprehended [ἀκατάληπτον] by men when even the mind [νοῦς] in each of us is unknown [ἄγνωστος] to us?" (*De Mutatione*, 10).[117] Besides, "The mind that is in each one of us can apprehend other objects, but is incapable of knowing itself" (*Legum Allegoriae*, I, 91).[118] In man there is kinship, συγγένεια, with God (*De Opificio*, 145). Man is "a copy or fragment or ray of that blessed nature" (*De Opificio*, 146).[119]

As a result, the relation between man and the Cosmos is modified. What the Logos is to the Cosmos the νοῦς is to the σῶμα. There is an analogy between the directive function of the Logos in regard to the Cosmos and that of the νοῦς in regard to sensation and passion That is based on a real kinship. "He breathed into him from above of His own Deity. The invisible Deity stamped on the invisible soul the impress of Itself, to the end that not even the terrestrial region should be without a share in the image of God. But the Archetype is, of course, so devoid of visible form that even His image could not be seen" (*Quod Deterius*, 86–87).[120]

Thus we see a new hierarchy appear. The Logos is, on the one hand, in relation with the angels, who are also called *logoi*. It is in relation with the archetypal ideas of the Cosmos, who are also called *logoi*. Lastly, it is in relation with the human mind which is itself also a logos. But these three relations are distinct, and while the three relations are connected to the Logos, that does not imply hierarchy among them.

115. Ibid., 241.
116. Ibid., 55.
117. *Philo* V, 147.
118. *Philo* I, 207.
119. Ibid., 115.
120. *Philo* II, 261.

By interpreting the Genesis narrative as he did and by seeing the human νοῦς in the εἰκών, Philo achieved an authentic revolution and inaugurated a theology. Giblet has noted this well: "Whereas for all Greek thought image remains on the side of the sensible and visible world, a revolution suddenly takes place. The image of God about which Moses speaks becomes the paradigmatic expression of the invisible and spiritual character of intelligence. The perspective has changed. The basic contrast is no longer between two universes, one sensible and the other intelligible. It is certainly rather between God and the Created."[121] We need to complete that by saying that the Philonic concept of εἰκών first marks the difference between created mind and uncreated mind, but second, marks their kinship. Consequently, we see that through this ambiguity, the distinction will create the same difficulties for the Christian theology of grace and nature that the ambiguousness of the Logos will create for Trinitarian theology.

Grace

The studies we have made of different aspects of creation in Philo may have given the impression that the boundaries between the divine world and the created world were not perfectly determined and that consequently, the absolute character of transcendence that we have posited as characterizing Philo's thought was threatened. This impression needs to be corrected by one final observation. It is perfectly true that Philo admits certain connaturality between God and creation. But this συγγένεια is something that does not belong to the creation by nature, but is a pure gift of God. Between God and his creation an essential abyss exists, which is precisely creation. We have seen that what characterizes Biblical transcendence is here. It does not mean that man has no kinship with God, but that this kinship is a free gift from God.

Impiety is to make oneself the issue, to attribute something to oneself. "By the only true God I deem nothing so shameful as supposing that I exert my mind and senses" (*Legum Allegoriae*, II, 68).[122] "Whoever dares to say that anything is his own will thereby have registered himself a slave in perpetuity" (*Legum Allegoriae*, III, 198).[123] "What deadlier foe

---

121. Giblet, "L'homme image de Dieu," 99.
122. *Philo* I, 267. See *Legum Allegoriae*, III, 81.
123. *Philo* I, 435.

to the soul can there be than he who in his vainglory claims to himself that which belongs to God alone? For it belongs to God to act, and this we may not ascribe to any created being. What belongs to the created is to suffer" (*De Cherubim*, 77).[124] That is the sin of Cain. "It is a fact that there are two opposite and contending views of life, one which ascribes all things to the mind [τῷ νῷ] as our master, whether we are using our reason or our senses, in motion or at rest, the other which follows God, whose handiwork it believes itself to be. The first of these views is fig-ured by Cain who is called Possession, because he thinks he possesses all things, the other by Abel, whose name means "one who refers (all things) to God" (*De Sacrificiis*, 2).[125]

Philo further analyzes the different aspects of this sin of φιλαυτία in the same works:

> Those who fail in this fall into three classes. The first are those who through forgetfulness of their blessings have lost that great treasure, the spirit of thankfulness. The second are those who though overweening pride think that they themselves have caused the good things which have fallen to them, and not He who is the true cause. But there is also a third class who are guilty of an error less blameworthy than these last, but more so than the first named. They accept the Ruling Mind as the cause of the good, yet they say that these good things are their natural inheritance. They claim that they are prudent, courageous, tem-perate, and just, and are therefore in the sight of God counted worthy of His favors (*De Sacrificiis*, 54).[126]

The attitude envisaged is very close to Pharisaism, and shows a sense in Philo of the gratuitousness of God's gifts, close to St. Paul's. The same picture is found again in *De Posteritate*:

> Those who assert that everything that is involved in thought or perception or speech is a free gift of their own soul, seeing that they introduce an impious and atheistic opinion, must be as-signed to the race of Cain, who, while incapable even of ruling himself, made bold to say that he had full possession of all other things as well. But those who do not claim as their own all that is fair in creation, but acknowledge all as due to the gift of God,

124. *Philo* II, 55.
125. Ibid., 95, 97.
126. Ibid.. 135.

being men of real nobility . . . must remain enrolled under Seth
as the head of their race (*De Posteritate*, 42).[127]

Indeed, the truth is: "For all things are God's possessions [θεοῦ γὰρ
τὰ πάντα κτήματα], so that he who assigns anything to himself is appropriating what is another's, and he receives a blow grievous and hard to
be healed, even self-conceit, a thing akin to boorish ignorance" (*Legum
Allegoriae*, III, 33).[128] *De Cherubim* especially insists on this doctrine.
"Since then it has been shown that no mortal can in solid reality be lord
of anything . . . this true prince and lord must be one, even God, who
alone can rightly claim that all things are His possessions" (*De Cherubim*,
83).[129] Moreover, commenting on Leviticus 25:23, "The land shall not be
sold permanently, for the land is Mine; for you are strangers and sojourners with Me," Philo writes:

> A clear proof surely that in possession all things are God's, and
> only as a loan to they belong to created beings. For nothing,
> he [tr. Moses] means, will be sold in perpetuity to any created
> being, because there is but One, to whom in a full and complete sense the possession of all things is assured. For all created things are assigned as a loan [χρῆσις as opposed to κτῆσις]
> to all from God, and He has made known of these particular
> things complete in itself, so that it should have no need at all of
> another. Thus through the desire to obtain what it must, it must
> perforce approach that which can supply its need, and this approach must be mutual and reciprocal. Thus through reciprocity and combination, even as a lyre is formed of unlike notes,
> God meant that they should come to fellowship and concord
> [κοινωνίαν καὶ συμφωνίαν] and form a single harmony, and that
> a universal give and take should govern them, and lead them
> up to the consummation of the whole world. (*De Cherubim*,
> 108–10).[130]

A description of universal sympathy follows in the style of Posidonius (and of Cicero):

> Thus love draws . . . heaven to earth, earth to heaven, air to water, and water to air . . . Thus each, we may say, wants and needs
> each; all need all, that so this whole of which each is a part,

127. Ibid., 351, 353.
128. *Philo* I, 323.
129. *Philo* II, 59.
130. Ibid., 73, 75.

might be that perfect work worthy of its architect, this world. In this way combining all things He claimed the sovereignty of all for Himself; to His subjects He assigned the use and enjoyment of themselves and each other. . . . Yet I find that none of them is really mine. Where was my body before birth, and whither will it go when I have departed? . . . Whence came the soul, wither will it go, how long will it be our mate and comrade? Can we tell its essential nature? When did we get it? Before birth? But then there was no "ourselves." What of it after death? But then we who are here joined to the body, creatures of composition and quality, shall be no more, but shall go forward to our rebirth, to be with the unbodied, without composition and without quality. Even now in this life, we are the ruled rather than the rulers, known rather than knowing. The soul knows us, though we know it not; it lays on us commands, which we must fain obey, as a servant obeys his mistress. And when it will, it will claim its divorce in court and depart, leaving our home desolate of life. Press it as we may to stay, it will escape from our hands . . . All this surely makes it plain that what we use are the possessions of another . . . And if we recognize that we have but their use, we shall tend them with care as God's possessions, remembering from the first, that it is the master's custom, when he will, to take back his own (*De Cherubim*, 111–15, 118).[131]

This passage is remarkable in itself in its force and fullness. It is interesting in making us feel Philo's method. The core is Biblical—it is the thought of Leviticus. But around that core, Stoic, Platonic, and Cynic themes came into play. There are Stoic ideas of universal συμπάθεια, of total mixture, of harmony of opposites. This is the doctrine of Posidonius that we meet again in Cicero's *De Natura Deorum*. The idea of the spirit as a stranger in the body that one day returns to its origin is Platonic. The diatribe method that forces man to acknowledge his indigence and his situation as a temporary guest is Cynic. We also see how this synthesis is already being formed in Philo. It will be the whole of western thought and will let Harnack say that Philo was the first theologian.

This doctrine especially developed here appears throughout Philo and always inspires him.

First it says to us, "You have no good thing of your own, but whatever you think you have, Another has provided." Hence we infer that all things are the possession of Him who gives, not of creation the beggar, who ever holds out her hand to take. The

131. Ibid., 75, 77.

second is, "Even if you take, take not for yourself, but count that which is given a loan or trust and render it back to Him who entrusted and leased it to you, thus as is fit and just requiring good will with goodwill." . . . For vast is the number of those who repudiate the sacred trusts and in their unmeasured greed use up what belongs to another as though it was their own, but thou, my friend, try with all thy might, not merely to keep unharmed and unalloyed what thou hast taken, but also deem it worthy of all carefulness, that He who entrusted it to thee may find nothing to blame in thy guardianship of it (*Quis Heres*, 103).[132]

It follows that when we return to God, through spiritual sacrifice and thanksgiving, what belongs to him, we only render unto him what he has given to us.

For unless He gives, thou shalt not have, since all things are His possessions, all things outside thee, and the body, the senses, the reason, the mind, and the functions of them all; and not thyself only, but this world also. And whatsoever thou severest or dividest from it for thy use, thou shalt find to be not thine but Another's. Earth and water, air, sky, stars, all forms of living creatures and plants, things that perish and things that perish not, thou does not hold in ownership. Therefore whatsoever thou bringest as an offering, thou wilt offer God's possession and not thine own (*De Sacrificiis*, 97).[133]

Therefore to acknowledge that everything comes from God is wisdom. In the *Allegories of the Laws* Philo shows Adam hiding in the midst of the forest of Paradise:

He that runs away from God takes refuge in himself. There are two minds, that of the universe, which is God, and the individual mind. He that flees from his own mind flees for refuge to the Mind of all things. For he that abandons his own mind acknowledges all that makes the human mind its standard to be naught, and he refers all things to God. On the other hand, he that runs away from God declares Him to be the cause of nothing, and himself to be the cause of all things that come into being . . . For it behooves the mind that would be led forth and let go free to withdraw itself from the influence of everything, the needs of the body, the organs of sense, specious arguments, the plausibilities of rhetoric, last of all itself (*Legum Allegoriae*, III, 29 and 41).[134]

132. *Philo* IV, 333, 335.
133. *Philo* II, 167.
134. *Philo* I, 321, 329.

Also, Isaac, the joy of the soul, when he converses with God and takes refuge close to him, goes forth abandoning himself and his own intelligence:

> "Isaac went forth into the plain to meditate as evening was drawing near" (Genesis 24:63). Yes, and Moses the word of prophecy, says, "When I go forth out of the city," the soul to wit (for this too is the city of the living being giving him laws and customs), "I will spread out my hands" (Exodus 9:29), and I will spread open and unfold all my doings to God, calling Him to be witness and overseer of each one of them, from whom evil cannot hide itself, but is to be forced to remove all disguises and be plainly seen.
>
> When the soul in all utterances and all actions has attained to perfect sincerity and godlikeness [ἐκθειασθῇ] the voices of the senses cease and all those abominable sounds that used to vex it. For the visible calls and summons the sense of sight to itself, and the voice calls the sense of hearing, and the perfume that of smell, and all round the object of sense invites the sense to itself. But all these cease when the mind goes forth from the city of the soul and finds in God the spring and aim of its own doings and intents. For truly are "the hands of Moses heavy" (Exodus 17:12), (*Legum Allegoriae*, III, 43–45).[135]

---

135. [Ibid., 329.]

Chapter 6

Philo's Spirituality

WE HAVE SEEN THAT Philo was a scriptural theologian of great stature. However, what strikes his readers most of all is the ardent mystical spirit that permeates his work. Moreover, his own testimony informs us that early in life he devoted himself to contemplation. His work offers the valuable testimony of experience.[1] At the same time Philo is a speculative thinker who attempted to articulate his experience theoretically. We find in him simultaneously personal testimony and an effort to give a doctrinal systematization. The essential book on this facet of Philo is by Völker.[2] The author has tried to show that Philo's experience was Biblical but his formulation of it was Hellenistic. Völker's conclusion about Philo's spiritual life is exactly the same as Wolfson's about his doctrine.

This side of Philo is interesting for two reasons. In the first place, Philo's spirituality presents points of contact with the New Testament, especially St. Paul. Words of faith, hope, charity, and humility appear in it frequently. This does not indicate influence of one of these writings on the other, but that we are put in contact with a background of both, with the Jewish pietistic current to which Hoskyns rightly draws our attention. In the second place, and this time there is certain dependence, Philo is

---

1. On prayer in Philo see Larson, "Prayer of Petition by Philo," 185–203.

2. Völker, *Fortschritt und Vollendung bei Philo von Alexandrien.*

the first person to elaborate the spirituality of the θεωρία and ἀπάθεια, that Clement of Alexandria, Origen Evagrius, and Cassian will transmit to the Middle Ages. This spirituality has been the object of much criticism. It has been seen as a distortion of the gospel ideal in the direction of Platonic idealism. We would say that it rather appears to be an embodiment of the spirit of the gospel in the structures of Hellenistic asceticism, without deforming that spirit. Still, we must acknowledge with Völker that Greek and Biblical currents are mixed in Philo, without ever being confused, in a way that gives rise to some uncertainty regarding the interpretation of his thought.

According to Philo, the study of spiritual life is expressed quite naturally in the schemes that he provides for it and that describe its stages. These stages correspond to his vision of the world and the link between ontology and spirituality is one of the most interesting aspects of his theory. At the very bottom there is the world of sin, of the souls who let themselves be seduced by the appearances of pleasure and discourse, and whose symbol is Egypt inhabited by earthly men: "The earth-born are those who take the pleasures of the body for their quarry, who make it their practice to indulge in them." Next comes the world of spirit that man discovers within himself when he becomes aware of his spiritual nature and that restores him to the intelligible world: that is the world of heavenly men: "The heaven-born are the votaries of the arts and of knowledge, the lovers of learning. For the heavenly element in us is the mind." Finally comes the world of God, to which man accedes going beyond himself: "But the men of God are priests and prophets who have refused to accept membership in the commonwealth of the world and to become citizens therein, but have risen wholly above the sphere of sense-perception and have been translated into the world of the intelligible and dwell there" (*De Gigantibus*, 60–61).[3]

Moreover, here again we encounter a hierarchy similar to the hierarchy in the meanings of Scripture, from the purely material sense to the mystical sense passing though the anthropological sense. Philo designates the different stages of this ascent with a group of expressions that recur constantly and are taken from Aristotle. The threefold source of virtue is nature, asceticism, and instruction. But Philo establishes a hierarchy among these three terms: instruction is the first stage that corresponds to conversion and to the first initiation received from the outside. This is

---

3. *Philo* II, 475.

the literal practice of the Law, the θέσις. Next comes asceticism that corresponds to the period of progress and covers the journey from the sensible world to the intelligible world and from the intelligible world to God. Lastly, nature corresponds to perfection, to the virtue that is no longer learned by instruction or acquired by effort but received from God. We know that to these three stages correspond Abraham, Jacob, and Isaac.

a. The first stage of spiritual life is the conversion by which the soul is turned away from sin to be converted to virtue. *De Migratione Abrahami* presents this conversion as a triple migration:

> Depart, therefore, out of the earthly matter that encompasses thee: escape, man, from the foul prison-house, thy body, with all thy might and main, and from the pleasures and lusts that act as its jailers; every terror that can vex and hurt them, leave none of them unused; menace the enemy with them all united and combined. Depart also out of sense-perception thy kin. For at present thou hast made a loan of thyself to each sense, and art become the property of others, a portion of the goods of those who have borrowed thee, and hast thrown away the good thing that was thine own. Yes, thou knowest, even though all men should hold their peace, how eyes draw thee, and ears, and the whole crowd of thine other kinsfolk, toward what they themselves love. But if thou desire to recover the self that thou hast lent and to have thine own possessions about thee, letting no portion of them be alienated and fall into other hands, thou shall claim instead a happy life, enjoying in perpetuity the benefit and pleasure derived from good things not foreign to thee but thine own. Again, quit speech also, "thy father's house," as Moses calls it, for fear thou shouldst be beguiled by beauties of mere phrasing, and be cut off from the real beauty, which lies in the matter expressed. Monstrous is it that shadow should be preferred to substance or a copy to originals (*De Migratione*, 9–12).[4]

Taken literally, this text has a Platonic character. The body is considered a prison that pollutes the soul according to the teaching of the *Phaedo*. The senses are tyrants, and the soul has fallen into slavery to these tyrants. Lastly, discourse, the third aspect, is connected to the Platonic critique of the sophists and is enamored of beautiful speeches and corresponds to the type of rhetorician given to the purely aesthetic use of language, which we see criticized by all of ancient philosophy.

---

4. *Philo* IV, 137, 139.

Still, it is necessary not to exaggerate this Platonic character. Indeed, we see Philo recall that sensation in itself is something indifferent (*Legum Allegoriae*, III, 67). The same goes for discourse. We have seen that Philo considers rhetoric as entering within the wise man's education. What is blameworthy is, therefore, for the mind to let itself be dominated by the body, sensation or discourse, although they are useful auxiliaries to the spirit, like Eve to Adam.

> Sense has two husbands, the one lawful, the other a seducer. After the fashion of a seducing husband the thing seen acts on the sight, the sound on the hearing, the flavor on the palate, and so with the rest one by one. And these turn away and invite to themselves the irrational sense and get the mastery of it and domineer over it . . . Look at that glutton, what a slave he is to the dishes prepared by the skill of cooks and confectioners. Mark that one wild with excitement over music, how he is swayed and held spellbound by harp or flute or it may be by a good singer. But to sense that has been turned from all else to Mind, her lawful husband, vast benefit befalls (*Legum Allegoriae*, III, 220–21).[5]

The seducer's name is pleasure, αἴσθησις, which is symbolized by the serpent. "The reason pleasure is likened to a serpent is this. The movement of pleasure like that of the serpent is tortuous and variable. To begin with, take its gliding course in five ways, for pleasures are occasioned by sight and by hearing and by taste and by smell and by touch" (*Legum Allegoriae*, II, 74).[6] These are the pleasures that bind the soul and make it a captive. "But the serpent, pleasure, is bad of itself; and therefore it is not found at all in a good man" (*Legum Allegoriae*, III, 68).[7] Philo takes up the myth from Plato's *Phaedo* to exhibit the spirit as a slave to the senses.

> When the charioteer is in command and guides the horses with the reins, the chariot goes the way he wishes, but if the horses have become unruly and got the upper hand, it has often happened that the charioteer has been dragged down and that the horses have been precipitated into a ditch by the violence of their motion . . . Just so, when Mind, the charioteer or helmsman of the soul, rules the whole living being as a governor does a city, the life holds a straight course, but when irrational

5. *Philo*, I, 451.
6. Ibid., 271.
7. Ibid., 347.

sense gains the chief place, a terrible confusion overtakes it
(*Legum Allegoriae*, III, 223–24).[8]

For Philo the essential character of the world is its instability—this
is still very Platonic. It is the world without consistency that Philo compares to the agitation in which Cain fled from the face of God.

> The lawgiver indicates that the foolish man, being a creature
> of wavering and unsettled impulses, is subject to tossing and
> tumult, like the sea lashed by contrary winds when a storm is
> ranging, and has never even in fancy had experience of quiet-
> ness and calm. And as at a time when a ship is tossing at the
> mercy of the sea, it is capable neither of sailing nor of riding at
> anchor, but pitched about this way and that it rolls in turn to
> either side and moves uncertainly swaying to and fro; even so
> the worthless man, with a mind reeling and storm-driven, pow-
> erless to direct his course with any steadiness, is always tossing,
> ready to make shipwreck of his life (*De Posteritate*, 22).[9]

This unstable changing world is contrasted with the world of spirit,
the world of stability. "Now that which is unwaveringly stable is God, and
that which is subject to movement is creation. He therefore that draws
nigh to God longs for stability, but he that forsakes Him, inasmuch as he
approaches the unresting creation is, as we might expect, carried about"
(*De Posteritate Caini*, 23).[10] On the contrary, "the soul that loves God,
having disrobed itself of the body and the objects dear to the body and
fled abroad far away from these, gains a fixed and assured settlement in
the perfect ordinances of virtue" (*Legum Allegoriae*, II, 55).[11]

The vision of the world of the senses as unstable can be connected
to the vision of its unreality. The life of the senses is an illusory realm,
inconsistent appearance that Philo compares to a dream.

> And that deep and abysmal sleep which holds fast all the
> wicked robs the mind of true apprehensions, and fills it with
> false phantoms and untrustworthy visions and persuades it to
> approve of the blameworthy as laudable: thus in the present case
> the dreamer treats sorrow as a joy and does not perceive that

---

8. Ibid., 453
9. *Philo*, II, 341.
10. Ibid.
11. *Philo* I, 259.

the vine of his vision is the plant which (produces) folly and madness"(*De Somniis*, II, 162).[12]

Philo uses a similar expression when he speaks of "the soft enchantments of pleasure" (*De Posteritate*, 101).[13]

All these expressions describe the unreality of the lives of the wicked. They are related to the Platonic view of the unreality of the sensible world and will be found again in Plotinus and in Gregory of Nyssa, who will speak of "this sleep that comes upon the minds of those buried in untruth, those illusory dreams that are the powers, wealth power, the magic of voluptuousness, the love of pleasure."[14]

The soul must emerge from the world of sense to enter the life of faith. Indeed, for Philo, faith is essentially the act by which the soul adheres to God's immutable realm, turning away from the unstable world of sensible life. Völker correctly observed that faith is closely related to solidity (βεβαιότης).[15] "Faith in God, then, is the one sure and infallible good " (*De Abrahamo*, 268).[16] Faith is contrasted to trust placed in apparent goods. "The best thing is to believe in God and not trust obscure impulses and unstable fantasies" (*Legum Allegoriae*, I, 164).[17] Philo's concept of faith is very original in this regard. The term does not have the same meaning as in Plato in whom faith involves δόξα and is opposed to knowledge. Moreover, the term sometimes has the Biblical meaning of faith in the firmness of the divine promise (*De Migratione Abrahami*, 43). But its precise meaning is the mind's adhesion to intelligible realities that are stable and establish the mind in the realm of immutability.

b. The abandonment of the senses and entrance into the life of faith are the first step, Abraham's step, and the beginning. They start the path of progress that will lead the soul to perfection. Progress is presented in two forms—that again is characteristic of Philo. It is at once progress in knowledge and progress in works, πράξις and θεορία or μάθησις. The

---

12. *Philo* V, 517.

13. *Philo* II, 385.

14. Gregory of Nyssa, *In Cantica Canticorum, Homilia XI*, col. 996 B.

15. Völker, *Fortschritt und Vollendung bei Philo von Alexandrien*, 249.

16. *Philo* VI, 268.

17. [Translator: There is no *Legum Allegoriae*, I, 164 or II, 164 either, and the passage quoted does not appear in obvious alternatives like I, 14 or 16, II, 64, etc., nor in III, 164, which at least is about faith. It certainly sounds like Philo. For example: "So then it is best to trust God and not our dim reasonings and insecure conjectures" (*Legum Allegoriae*, III, 228; *Philo*, I, 457.)]

way of knowledge, μάθησις, whose model is Abraham, will bring the soul through different stages that may be extracted from the totality of Philo's writings. The first stage is worldly knowledge, which corresponds to liberal studies considered as the preliminary to wisdom and symbolized by the marriage of Abraham to Hagar. We have discussed this παιδεία in connection with literal exegesis, and I will not return to it. The preliminary stage appears as progress in relation to the illusory world of senses, but at the same time it is insignificant in comparison to subsequent progress. This will be true of each stage, which explains how Philo can both praise and criticize the παιδεία. It is a first progression in the life of knowledge. Even in the perfect man who no longer needs it, it continues to be the means of communicating wisdom. This means of communicating is what Abel did not know.

From the knowledge of the world, we must go on to the knowledge of ourselves. After having studied the heavens in Chaldea, Abraham goes to Haran, which designates the caverns of the senses, which are the beginning of self-knowledge. A passage in *De Somniis* describes these successive states:

> Terah left the land of Chaldea and migrated to Haran . . . The Chaldeans are astronomers, while the citizens of Haran busy themselves with the place of the senses. Accordingly Holy Writ addresses to the explorer of the facts of nature certain questions—"Why do you carry on investigations about the sun, as to whether it is a foot in diameter, whether it is larger than the whole earth, whether it is many times its size? And about the illuminations of the moon, whether it has a borrowed light, or whether it employs one entirely its own? . . . And why treading as you do on earth, do you leap over the clouds? . . . Mark, my friend, not what is above and beyond your reach but what is close to yourself, or rather make yourself the object of your impartial scrutiny. What form, then will your scrutiny take? Go in spirit to Haran, *excavated* land, the openings and cavities of the body, and hold an inspection of eyes, ears, nostrils, and other organs of sense . . . And there is a weightier charge which I do not as yet lay upon you, namely to see your own soul . . . But bring the explorer down from heaven and away from these researches draw the Know thyself . . . This character Hebrews call *Terah*, Greeks *Socrates*. For they say that *Know thyself* was likewise the theme of life-long pondering to Socrates" (*De Somniis*, I, 52–57).[18]

18. *Philo* V, 325, 327.

Knowledge of the world and self-knowledge are only considered in the measure in which they are on a path toward knowledge of God. Knowledge of the world, which particularly includes knowledge of the movement of heavenly bodies, connects with the cosmological proof of the existence of God. This knowledge makes us know God's existence through the contingency of the visible world and God's wisdom through the order that holds sway in the world. Knowledge of self goes further. It elevates the soul above the sensible world and reintroduces it into the intelligible world to which it belongs by its νοῦς. This stage corresponds to the Platonic account of the ideas and of the *Cosmos Noetos*, where the soul encounters the archetypal ideas of things, far from the changing world. This stage brings the soul to a knowledge that is already closer to God, of whom the intelligible world is the image.

At the same time as this increasing knowledge, the life of the soul in progress includes asceticism, whose model is Jacob. The asceticism essentially consists of the effort, πόνος, a term we meet again in the Desert Fathers. At the same time, the virtues are considered graces of God. This combination of grace and effort is found at every level of the spiritual journey. It starts with the conversion, which is not possible without God's graces. All progress is God's gift. "For the mind of man would never have ventured to soar so high as to grasp the nature of God, had God Himself drawn it up to Himself, so far as it was possible that the mind of man should be drawn up, and stamped it with the impress of the powers that are within the scope of its understanding" (*Legum Allegoriae*, I, 39).[19] At the beginning the effort is laborious. "(The way leading to virtue is) rough and steep and difficult" (*De Posteritate*, 154).[20] For, the soul is intoxicated by sensible joys. In the measure that spiritual goods become more real to the soul: "(God renders it a highway,) transforming the bitterness of their toil into sweetness" (*De Posteritate*, 154).[21] In what would remain the standard image, the transformation of Marra's waters represents the change of the soul. "But there are others who, facing the terrors and dangers of the wilderness with all patience and stoutness of heart, carry through to its finish the contest of life, keeping it safe from failure and defeat . . . But this result is brought about not by toil unaided, but by toil with sweetening. He says 'the water was sweetened,'"(*De Con-*

---

19. *Philo* I, 171.

20. *Philo* II, 419.

21. Ibid., 149.

gressu, 165–66).[22] What gives the πόνος this sweetness is the awakening of the thirst for God, the divine ἔρως (*De Congressu*, 166).

The ascetic endeavor has two parts. One is the struggle against the passions, the πάθη. Philo retains the Platonic theory of passions, the θυμός and the ἐπιθυμία. The first is anger, the second desire. Still, we must observe that these terms are sometimes taken in a favorable sense *qua* faculties of the soul and other times in an unfavorable sense *qua* reprehensible dispositions. In the first instance, only their abuse can be condemned, and the ideal is Platonic and Aristotelian measure, *metriopathy*. In the second, the passions themselves are bad, and the ideal is Stoic apathy. Philo seems to waver between the two. The core of his position seems to be that moderation is appropriate for the person in progress. He cannot destroy passion and must be content to master it.

> Many a time have I been present at a gathering with little that was sociable about it or at costly suppers. When I did not arrive with reason for my companion, I found myself the slave of the enjoyments provided, at the mercy of harsh masters, entertainments for the eye and ear and all that brings pleasure by way of taste or smell. But whenever I arrive with convincing reason at my side, I find myself a master not a slave (*Legum Allegoriae*, III, 156).[23]

Apathy is reserved for the perfect man. "He [tr. Moses] lays further stress upon the mere moderating of passion in the man of gradual advance, by representing the wise man as declining without any bidding all the pleasures of the belly, while the man of gradual advance acts under orders" (*Legum Allegoriae*, III, 144).[24] This is the ideal of Moses, about whom Philo declares that in order to receive divine oracles: "But first he had to be clean, as in soul so also in body, to have no dealings with any passion, purifying himself form all the calls of mortal nature" (*De Vita Mosis*, II, 68).[25]

The acquisition of virtues corresponds to the struggle against the passions. The characteristic of virtue, ἀρετή, for Philo is to be a configuration toward God. The soul ceases to conform itself to the sensible in order to conform itself to the intelligible. "God sows and plants earthly excellence for the race of mortals as a copy and reproduction of the heavenly.

22. *Philo* IV, 545.

23. *Philo* I, 405.

24. Ibid., 397.

25. *Philo* VI, 483.

For pitying our race and noting that it is compact of a rich abundance of ills, He caused earthly excellence to strike root, to bring succor and aid to the diseases of the soul. It is, as I said before, a copy of the heavenly and archetypal excellence" (*Legum Allegoriae*, I, 45).[26] This again relates to the Platonic concept of resemblance to God, which combines with the Biblical doctrine of εἰκών καὶ ὁμοίωσις. The theme of following God, which is a Biblical translation of the Stoic doctrine of following nature, is associated with the idea of imitating God. We see here this synthesis of Biblical and Platonic theories being carried out.

As for the virtues in detail, we are dealing with moral virtues here. Philo integrates into the Biblical account the Stoic doctrine of the four virtues, whose symbol Philo sees in the four rivers of Paradise. Still, in general, he sees first of all a generic virtue that is sometimes piety, sometimes goodness (*Legum Allegoriae*, I, 59), whose symbol is the tree of life. "By these rivers his purpose is to indicate the particular virtues. These are four in number, prudence, self-mastery, courage, justice. The largest river, of which the four are effluxes, is generic virtue, which we have called 'goodness'" (*Legum Allegoriae*, I, 63).[27] Besides these fundamental virtues, Philo acknowledges a whole moral psychology that combines Greek and Biblical elements. Continence is connected to temperance, ἐγκράτεια. Measure and humility (ταπεινοφροσύνη) are connected with justice, ἰσότης. Love of neighbor is connected to love of God, φιλανθροπία to εὐσέβεια (*De Abrahamo*, 208), and Philo speaks of "loving others as oneself" (*In Genesim*, II, 25).[28]

c. After his conversion, which is a break with the unreal world of appearance, the person in progress enters into himself and progressively discovers the life of the mind. Now a final stage remains to be surmounted, the search for God beyond the mind, going out from oneself. This, strictly speaking, is the entrance into perfect life, whose model is Isaac:

> Therefore, my soul, if thou feelest any yearning to inherit the good things of God, leave not only thy land, that is the body, thy kinsfolk, that is the senses, thy father's house (Genesis 12:1), that is speech, but be a fugitive from thyself also and issue forth from thyself [ἔκστησι]. Like persons possessed [κατεχόμενοι] and corybants, be filled with inspired frenzy [ἐνθουσιώσης], even as the prophets are inspired. For it is the mind which is

26. *Philo* I, 175.
27. Ibid., 189.
28. [Translator: This does not appear in *Philo, Supplement* II, 25, 103–4.]

under the divine afflatus, and no longer in its own keeping, but
is stirred to its depths and maddened by heavenward yearning
[ἔροτι οὐρανίῳ], drawn by the truly existent and pulled upward
thereetoo, with truth to lead the way and remove all obstacles
before its feet, that its path may be smooth to tread—such is the
mind, which has this inheritance (*Quis Heres*, 69–70).[29]

This extraordinary text certainly introduces us to the third path.
Just as the person in progress is on the level of the mind and thus restored to the intelligible world, the perfect person goes out of himself
and from the intelligible world to enter the world of God in the shadow.
Here the principle of spiritual life is no longer knowledge, ἐπιστημή,
but ἔρως, love. We pass from the illuminative life to the unitive life.
Moreover, the life of the person in progress is an effort to acquire the
virtues. Here, God fills the soul with his infused graces, αὐτομαθεῖς. Ultimately this culminates in the spiritual experience of ecstasy, of going
forth from oneself; the soul is possessed by God, as it were. Again we
encounter the Platonic vocabulary of *enthusiasm*. This constitutes the
royal road (ὁδὸς βασιλική) where the soul advances.[30]

What characterizes this road is the replacement of human effort by
God's action:

"Turn back to the land of thy father and thy kindred, and I will
be with thee" (Genesis, 31: 3) . . . but now it is time for thee to
have done with strife, lest thou be ever toiling and have no power to reap the fruits of thy toil. This thou wilt never find while
thou remainest where thou art, dwelling still with the objects of
sense-perception, and spending thy days surrounded by bodily
existence in its varied aspects, whose head and chief is Laban,
bearing a name meaning variety of character. Nay, thou must
change thine abode and betake thee to thy father's land, the land
of the Word that is holy and in some sense father of those who
submit to training: and that land is Wisdom, abode most choice
of virtue-loving souls. In this country there awaiteth thee the
nature which is its own pupil its own teacher, that needs not to
be fed on milk [αὐτομαθεῖς], as children are fed . . . For the perpetual abundance of good things ever ready to the hand gives
freedom from toil. And the fountain [πηγή] from which the
good things are poured forth is the companionship [σύνοδος] of
the bountiful [φιλοδώρου] God. He shews this to be so when to

29. *Philo* IV, 317.
30. Pascher, Βασιλική ὁδός, 113.

set His seal about the flow of His kindnesses, He says "I will be with thee." What fair thing, then, could fail when there was present God the Perfecter, with gifts of grace, His virgin daughters, whom the Father that begat them rears up uncorrupted and undefiled? Then are all forms of studying, toiling, practicing at rest; and without interference of art by contrivance of Nature there come forth all things in one outburst . . . For the offspring of the soul's own travail are for the most part poor abortions, things untimely born; but those which God waters with the snows of heaven come to the birth perfect, complete, and peerless (*De Migratione*, 27–31, 33).[31]

The important thing here is that we are really dealing with the entrance into a new world. As *Quis Rerum Divinarum Heres* says: "Now wise men take God for their guide and teacher, but the less perfect take the wise man" (*Quis Heres*, 69).[32] What characterizes wisdom is that God and God alone communicates it. That is what Philo understands when he applies the classical division of knowledge which is possessed through ἄσκησις, μάθησις, and φύσις. Knowledge possessed by φύσις is wisdom, which is a gift—and not acquired by effort. The wise man is αὐτομαθής, αὐτοδίδιακτος, according to terms that frequently recur; he is instructed directly by God. Is this an innate disposition? Certain texts would seem to suggest that.

Every wise man [αὐτομαθής] who learns directly from no teacher but himself . . . does not by searchings and practicings and toilings gain improvement, but as soon as he comes into existence he finds wisdom placed read to his hand, shed from heaven above, and of this he drinks undiluted draughts, and sits feasting, and cease not to be drunken with the sober drunkenness which right reason brings (*De Fuga*, 166).[33]

We would thus have two races of men in those who are perfect and those who are in progress, the race of those who possess knowledge innately and others who only acquire it laboriously. That was certainly the position of the Gnostics when they distinguished the carnal from the spiritual as two races of men. It seems that we must interpret Philo differently. We are certainly dealing with different stages and the word αὐτομαθής merely signifies the divine origin of wisdom and its immediate character.

31. Ibid., 147, 149, 151.
32. Ibid., 293.
33. *Philo* V, 101.

This is what we find in a passage from *De Congressu Quaeredae Eruditiones Gratiae*:

> But the self-learnt kind, of which Isaac is a member, that joy [χαρά] which is the best of the good emotions, is endowed with a simple nature free from mixture and alloy, and wants neither the practice [ἀσκήσεως] nor teaching [διδασκαλίας] which entails the need of the concubine as well as the legitimate forms of knowledge. When God rains down from heaven the good of which the self is a teacher and learner both, it is impossible that the self should still live in concubinage with the slavish arts . . . He who has gained the wisdom that comes without toil and trouble, because his nature is happily gifted and his soul fruitful of good, does not seek any form of betterment: for he has ready beside him in their fullness the gifts of God, conveyed by the breath of God's higher races, but he wishes and prays that these may remain with him constantly . . . (*De Congressu*, 36–38).[34]

Here we note the idea that the person who has found σοφία no longer has progress to make, an idea that comes from the Stoic tradition. Again, it is quite explicit that σοφία has the character of grace.

This is the entrance into the royal road. *Quod Deus Sit Immutabilis* tells us:

> Shall we on whom God pours as in snow or rain-shower the fountains of His blessing from above, drink of a well and seek for the scanty springs that lie beneath the earth, when heaven rains upon us ceaselessly the nourishment which is better than the nectar and ambrosia of the myths? Or shall we draw up with ropes the drink which has been stored by the devices of men and accept as our haven and refuge a task which argues our lack of true hope; we to whom the Savior of all has opened His celestial treasure for our use and enjoyment? . . . So then brooking no delay should we essay to march by the king's high road, we who hold it our duty to pass by earthly things. And that is the king's road of which the lordship rests with no common citizen but with Him alone who is now alone is king in real truth. This road is, as I said but now, wisdom [σοφία], by which alone suppliant souls can make their escape to the Uncreated, for we may well believe that he who walks unimpeded along the king's way will never flag or faint, till he comes into the presence of the king (*Quod Immutabilis*, 155–56, 159–60).[35]

34. *Philo* IV, 477.
35. *Philo* III, 91, 93.

Under its highest forms the seizure of the soul by God tears the soul out from itself. This is the possession κατόχη about which Philo so often speaks.

> Be a fugitive from thyself also and issue forth from thyself. Like persons possessed [κατεχόμενοι] and corybants, be filled with inspired frenzy, even as the prophets are inspired. For it is the mind which is under the divine afflatus, and no longer in its own keeping, but is stirred to its depths and maddened by heavenward yearning, drawn by the truly existent [ἐνθουσιώσης] and pulled upward thereto, with truth to lead the way and remove all obstacles before its feet, that its path may be smooth to tread — such is the mind, which has this inheritance (*Quis Heres*, 69).[36]

To describe this state Philo disposes of a whole range of images. It is madness (μανία), sober drunkenness (μέθη νηφάλιος), passionate love (ἐρώς)—all of them expressions that signify a divine action's invasion of the soul to tear it out of itself.[37]

First of all there is sober intoxication. In *De Fuga* Philo distinguishes four kinds of souls. The third is the soul that is avid for knowledge. This soul seeks to examine the inscrutable place, the dwelling of the divine natures. When it is about to undertake this sterile, endless labor, it is aided by the mercy of the savior God, Who says regarding his sanctuary: "'Draw not nigh hither,' as much as to say 'Enter not on such an inquiry,' for the task argues a busy, restless curiosity too great for human ability" (*De Fuga*, 162).[38] Then comes the fourth category:

> There has been no "seeking" and yet "finding" meets us unbidden. Under this head is ranged every wise man who leans directly from no teacher [αὐτομαθής, αὐτοδίδακτος] but himself; for he does not by searchings and practicings and toilings gain improvement, but as soon as he comes into existence he finds wisdom placed ready to his hand, shed from heaven above, and of this he drinks undiluted draughts, and sits feasting and ceases

---

36. *Philo* IV, 317

37. Walther Völker disputes the existence of *mystical* experience in Philo and understands these expressions as a literary device. But Thyen is right to see rather the summit of Philo's ideal (*Der Stil*, 244).

38. *Philo* V, 99.

not to be drunken with the sober drunkenness[39] which right reason brings. (*De Fuga*, 166).[40]

The theme of *eros* appears in *De Somniis*:

> When the mind is mastered by the love of the divine, when
> it strains its powers to reach the inmost shrine, when it puts
> forth every effort and ardor on its forward march, under the
> divine impelling force it forgets all else, forgets itself, and fixes
> its thoughts and memories on Him alone Whose attendant
> and servant it is, to whom it dedicates not a palpable offering,
> but incense, the incense of consecrated virtues. But when the
> inspiration is stayed, and the strong yearning abates, it hastens
> back from the divine and becomes a man and meets the hu-
> man interests which lay waiting in the vestibule (*De Somniis*, II,
> 232–33).[41]

The transitory character of this divine possession appears here. It is a sort
of ecstasy, where the soul is lifted out of itself, where the soul feels that God
acts within it, and from which the soul falls back into its normal state.

Finally, we meet again the termσ *madness* (μανία) and *ecstasy*
(ἔκστασις). Philo describes ecstasy as follows:

> So while the radiance of the mind is still all around us, when it
> ours as it were a noonday beam into the whole soul, we are self-
> contained, not possessed [οὐ κατεχόμεθα]. But when it comes
> to its setting, naturally ecstasy [ἔκστασις] and divine possession
> [κατοκωχή] and madness [μανία] fall upon us. For when the
> light of God shines, the human light sets; when the divine light
> sets, the human dawns and rises. This is what regularly befalls
> the fellowship of the prophets. The mind [νοῦς] is evicted at
> the arrival of the divine Spirit [θεῖου πνεύματος], but when that
> departs the mind returns to its tendency. Mortal and immortal
> may not share the same home (*Quis Heres*, 264–65).[42]

---

39. The expression is found again in Gregory of Nyssa (*Patrologia Graeca*, vol.
XLVI, 990 B, quoted in Daniélou, *Platonisme et théologie mystique*, 290ff.), in St Ambrose, *Patrologia Latina*, vol. XVI, 449 B quoted in Quasten "Sobria ebrietas in Ambrosii *De Sacramentis*," 118ff.). In particular see the hymn for lauds on Monday: "Laeti
bibamos sobriam ebrietatem spiritus." [Translator: In *Patrologia Latina* vol. XVI. See
De Sacramentis, book V, chapter 3. "Edite, inquit (Jesus), fratres mei, et inebriamini."]

40. *Philo* V, 101. See *De Ebrietate*, 145, and *Legum Allegoriae*, II, 82.

41. Ibid., 547, 549. See also *De Somniis*, I:164–65.

42. *Philo* IV, 419. See also *De Somniis*, II, 250–54, and *De Confusione*, 59.

This certainly seems to reflect Philo's personal experience.

> I feel no shame in recording my own experience, a thing I know
> from its having happened to me a thousand times. On some occa-
> sions, after making up my mind to follow the usual course of writ-
> ing on philosophical tenets, and knowing definitely the substance
> of what I was to set down, I have found my understanding inca-
> pable of giving birth to a single idea, and have given it up without
> accomplishing anything, reviling my understanding for its self-
> conceit, and filled with amazement at the might of Him that is
> to Whom is due the opening and closing of the soul-wombs. On
> other occasions, I have approached my work empty and suddenly
> become full, the ideas falling in a shower from above and being
> sown invisibly, so that under the influence of the Divine posses-
> sion [ὑπο κατοχῆς ἐνθέου κορυβαντιᾶν] I have been filled with
> corybantic frenzy and been unconscious of anything, place, per-
> sons present, myself, words spoken, lines written. For I obtained
> language, ideas, and enjoyment of light, keenest vision, pellucid
> distinctness of objects, such as might be received through the eyes
> as the result of clearest shewing (*De Migratione*, 34–35).[43]

Here we can clearly see the elements that make up Philo's doctrine
of inspiration. There is the Greek notion of poetic inspiration as we find
it in Plato, but considered as a divine visit where the soul goes out of
itself, is expelled, and where the divine πνεῦμα replaces it. But here again
the Greek theme only comes to elucidate the Biblical idea of prophecy.[44]
Philo often talks about the perfect race, which is the prophetic race (*De
Gigantibus*, 63). Accordingly, it is the Jewish doctrine of prophecy that
is expressed in the Greek clothing of inspiration. Indeed this theory
contains all of the characteristics of the traditional Jewish theory. The
coming of the Spirit is not a stable condition in that theory, but a sud-
den arrival, a visit during which the prophet's soul is seized by the Spirit
to carry out a divine work. Still, the Greek influence distorts Biblical
thought. In consequence, that leads to two deviations. On the one hand,
at the spiritual level, mystical life as possession of the soul by the Spirit
will be considered the soul's pursuit of itself. On the other hand, at the
theological level, scriptural inspiration will be viewed as the Spirit dictat-
ing to the writer in a state of ecstasy.

43. Ibid., 151, 153.

44. Thyen, *Der Stil*, 245, is guided by debatable prejudices when he affirms that the
Philonic experience of ecstatic vision of God is purely Hellenistic and foreign to the
Jewish faith. In virtue of this same prejudice, in order to assure Philo's Jewish authen-
ticity Walther Völker denies the existence of this ecstasy.

Chapter 7

Philo and the New Testament

SEVERAL TIMES DURING OUR journey through the works of Philo we have emphasized points of contact with New Testament writings. By way of conclusion it remains for us to assemble several essential points where these coincidences are found and to specify their meaning. It is not a question of the New Testament's influence on Philo, or of Philo's influence upon the New Testament. We will see that the alleged examples of this are not valid. But several essential New Testament passages, the writings of John, the Pauline writings, the Epistle to the Hebrews, were written in Greek and contain theological reflections that strikingly resemble Philo's thought. That is not surprising, because our authors have placed conceptions from Jewish theology at the service of revelation. Behind Philo and the New Testament writers cited we will find a common background.[1]

Philo and the Pauline Writings

We will note first note some similarities of detail. We read: "But seeing that for babes [νηπίοις] milk is food, but for grown men [τελείοις]

---

1. See the bibliography in Goodenough, *The Politics of Philo*, 290–97.

wheaten bread, there must also be soul-nourishment, such as is milk-like suited to the time of childhood, in the shape of the preliminary stages of school-leaning, and such as is adapted to grown men in the shape of instructions leading the way through wisdom and temperance and all virtue" (*De Agricultura*, 9).[2] Formally, this completely parallels to I Corinthians 3:1–2: "And I brethren could not speak to you as to spiritual men but only as carnal, as to little ones in Christ. I fed you with milk, not with solid food, for you were not yet ready for it. Nor are you now ready for it, for you are still carnal." The comparison is still clearer in Hebrews 5:12, where we have a contrast between the νήπιοι and the τέλειοι: "You have become such as have need of milk and not of solid food."[3]

Another contrast, with more profound significance, is that of flesh and spirit. Its origin is Biblical. Like Paul, Philo notes the link between sin and flesh:

> But the chief cause of ignorance is the flesh [σάρξ], and the tie which binds us so closely to the flesh. And Moses himself affirms this when he says that "because they are flesh" the divine spirit cannot abide [Genesis 6:3] ... But those which bear the burden of the flesh, oppressed by the grievous load, cannot look up to the heavens as they revolve, but with necks bowed downwards are constrained to stand rooted to the ground like four-footed beasts (*De Gigantibus*, 29).[4]

So, St. Paul tells us: "When we were in the flesh, the sinful passions ... were at work in our members" (Romans 7:5). Still, it will be noted that behind the similarity in vocabulary, Philo's thought is more Platonic and more closely connects sin to the body and to matter.

A characteristic feature of Paul and Philo is long lists of virtues, vices, and tribulations. In this sense, we can compare *De Sacrificiis Abelis et Caini*, 3, and Galatians 5:20. The descriptions of the tribulations of the just man according to Philo and of the apostle according to Paul are close in its details. "The so-called lovers of virtue are almost without exception obscure [ἄδοξοι] people, looked down upon, of mean estate, destitute of the necessities of life, not enjoying the privileges of subject peoples or even of slaves, filthy, sallow, reduced to skeletons, with a hungry look from want of food, the prey of disease, in training for dying"

---

2. *Philo* III, 113. See *De Migratione*, 24; *De Sobrietate*, 8, etc.

3. See Collins, "Tentatur Nova Interpretatio Hebr. 5:11—6:8," 144–51.

4. *Philo* II, 459, 461.

(*Quod Deterius*, 34).[5] We might think of II Corinthians 6:4, where Paul talks about the servants of God "in much patience, in tribulations, in hardships, in distresses." Here again, under the literary similarity the difference appears. Philo's prototype is the emaciated ascetic; Paul's is the apostle who lives dangerously.

Some passages concerning knowledge about God are more characteristic. Philo speaks of knowing God "as in a mirror, the mind has a vision of God as acting and creating the world and controlling all that is" (*De Decalogo*, 105).[6] But Moses aspires to surpass this knowledge and know God face to face: "For I would not that Thou shouldst be manifested to me by means of heaven or earth or water or air or any created thing at all, nor would I find the reflection of thy being in aught else than in Thee Who art God, for the reflections in created things are dissolved, but those in the Uncreate will continue abiding and sure and eternal" (*Legum Allegoriae*, III, 101).[7] Now, this greatly resembles St. Paul: "We see now through a mirror in an obscure manner, but then face to face. Now I know in part, but then I shall know even as I have been known" (I Corinthians, 13:12). Or again: "But we all, with faces unveiled, reflecting as in a mirror the glory of the Lord, we are being transformed into his very image" (II Corinthians, 3:18). We would observe that the theme of Moses on Mt. Sinai is the background of both passages.

It is curious to juxtapose to the first of the two passages from St. Paul the following, where we again encounter another expression: "Even now in this life, we are the ruled rather than the rulers, known rather than knowing. The soul knows us, though we know it not; it lays on us commands, which we must fain obey, as a servant obeys his mistress" (*De Cherubim*, 115).[8] Furthermore, paganism is criticized in similar terms in Romans 1:23 and *De Vita Moysis*, II, 171. Philo refers to those "who have left the true God and wrought gods, falsely so-called, from corruptible and created matter, and given them a title which belongs to the Incorruptible and Uncreated" (*De Vita Mosis*, II, 171).[9]

A remarkable feature is the relation between the coming of God and sin. Philo writes:

5. Ibid., 225.
6. *Philo* VII, 61.
7. *Philo* I, 369.
8. *Philo* II, 77.
9. *Philo* VI, 533.

> For so long as the divine reason has not come into our soul, as to some dwelling-place, all its works are free from guilt . . . There is pardon for those whose sin is due to ignorance, because they have no experience to tell them what they should do . . . But when the true priest, Conviction, enters us, like a pure ray of light, we see in their real value the unholy thoughts that were stored without our soul, and the guilty and blameworthy actions to which we laid our hands in ignorance of our true interests. So, Conviction, discharging his priest-like task defiles all these and bids them all be cleared out and carried away, that he may see the soul's house in its natural bare condition, and heal whatever sicknesses have arisen in it (*Quod Immutabilis*, 134–35).[10]

We encounter this idea in the Letter to the Romans: "For until the Law sin was in the world, but sin is not imputed when there is no law" (Romans 5:13). It also appears in the gospel: "If I had not come and spoken to them, they would have no sin" (John, 15:22).

Still, these different passages can be explained by common allusions whether to the Old Testament or to Jewish theology. By contrast, there is a key passage that certainly seems to be a polemical reference to Philo or at least to similar speculation. It concerns the two Adams.[11] It is essential because it shows us the basic opposition between Philo and Paul in regard to the same topic, even when the ingredients are near neighbors. Philo writes: "There are two types of men; the one a heavenly [οὐράνιος] man, the other an earthly [γήϊνος]. The heavenly man, being made after the image of God, is altogether without part or lot in corruptible and terrestrial substance; but the earthly one was compacted out of the matter scattered here and there, which Moses calls 'clay'" (*Legum Allegoriae*, I, 31).[12] We must connect this passage to one in *De Opificio*:

> There is a vast difference between the man thus formed and the man that came into existence earlier after the image of God: for the man so formed is an object of sense perception, partaking already of such or such quality, consisting of body and soul, man or woman, by nature mortal; while he that was after the (Divine) image was an idea or type or seal, an object of thought (only), incorporeal, neither male nor female, by nature incorruptible (*De Opificio*, 134).[13]

10. *Philo* III, 77, 79.

11. See Vitti, "Christus Adam," 140–44.

12. *Philo* I, 167.

13. Ibid., 107.

Now the first letter to the Corinthians presents the contrast between the two Adams:

> And so it is written, "The first man, Adam, became a living being," the last [ἔσχατος] Adam became a life-giving spirit. However, the spiritual is not first, but the natural, and afterward the spiritual. The first man was of the earth, made of dust [χοϊκός]; the second Man is the Lord from heaven. As was the man of dust, so also are those who are made of dust; and as is the heavenly Man, so also are those who are heavenly [ἐπουράνιοι] (I Corinthians 15:45–49).

Here the resemblance between the conceptions is so evident that it is certain that we are within a problematic of the two Adams that constituted a contemporary *theologoumenon*. But we also see the radical opposition within this *theologoumenon*.

Indeed for Philo, the heavenly man is the archetype of man, the idea preexisting in the intelligible world. This idea is the true reality of which earthly man, who comes next, is only a corruptible degradation. Paul completely reverses this perspective. For him, earthly man, the less perfect one, is chronologically first. God created him first. Heavenly man is eschatological man who will appear at the end of time, the last Adam. Thus, the mythological perspective of a return to the origin has resurfaced in the historical perspective of the wait for the *parousia*. Paul's very repetition seems to reveal his polemical intent. In fact, that is certainly the background of the opposition that shows up here. For Philo, the preeminent reality is already given: it is the Law or the pre-existing Logos. For Paul, it is something future. It is the return of Christ at the end of time to usher in the future world.

Philo and St. John

Just as the two Adams are the essential point of contact between Philo and St. Paul, likewise the Logos was to be that point of contact for St. John. Still, before attacking this topic, we will note some coincidences of detail. They particularly involve several of the spiritual categories that correspond to the perfect person according to Philo and that St. John employs to characterize the union with Christ. First of all, we note the importance for Philo of the Logos's dwelling in the soul: "The Divine word dwells and walks among those for whom the soul's life is an object of honor" (*De Posteritate*, 122).[14] "Justly and rightly then shall we say that in the invisible soul the invisible God has His earthly dwelling-place" (*De Cherubim*, 101).[15] Let us recall John 14:23: "If anyone love me . . . we will come to him and make our abode with him." For both Philo and John we see the application to the soul of the Biblical theme of divine indwelling.

Coming into the soul, the Logos fills it with gifts. "God, Whose voice granted . . . the highest of blessings, peace—a gift which no human being can bestow" (*De Vita Mosis*, I, 304).[16] In John's gospel we read: "My peace I give you, not as the world gives do I give to you" (John 14:27). The same goes for joy, χαρά. "Thus should the divine Word, by manifesting Itself suddenly and offering Itself as a fellow-traveler to a lonely soul, hold out to it an unlooked-for joy—which is greater than hope" *De Somniis* I, 71).[17] "These things I have spoken to you that my joy may be in you and that your joy may be made full" (John 15:11). In I John 4:17, we see that the perfection of love is the παρρησία. Philo connects it to the joy of divine intoxication. "Now when grace fills the soul, that soul thereby rejoices and smiles and dances . . . How vast is the boldness [παρρησία] of the soul which is filled with the gracious gifts of God!" (*De Ebrietate*, 146, 149).[18]

That last passage from the first letter of John unites the παρρησία to the ἀγάπη that triumphs over fear. "In this is love perfected with us, that we may have confidence in the day of judgment. There is no fear [φόβος] in love, but perfect love casts out fear" (I John 4:18). Now, the opposition between fear and love is found in Philo. "For I observe that all the exhortations to piety in the law refer to our either loving or our fearing the Existent and thus to love [ἀγάπη] Him is the most suitable for those into whose conception of the Existent no thought of human parts or passions enters, who pay Him the honor meet for God for His own sake only. To fear is most suitable to the others" (*Quod Deus Immutabilis Sit*, 69).[19] Accordingly, ἀγάπη appears as belonging to the perfect in Philo also, to those from whose eyes the scales have fallen regarding all anthropomorphism in God, because they no longer need to be treated as children.[20]

14. *Philo* II, 399.
15. Ibid., 69.
16. *Philo* VI, 435.
17. *Philo* V, 333. 335.
18. *Philo* III, 395, 397.
19. Ibid., 45.
20. See also *De Migratione*, 169.

But the central point of comparison is the doctrine of the Logos. The similarities are striking. They involve not only Philo but also the book of Wisdom and Aristobulus. Thus, we will come to the conclusion that the prologue of John's gospel starts from the Judeo-Hellenistic theory of the Word, but in its general form and without the systematic elements that we have seen in Philo. Let us give some examples. Philo calls the Logos *beginning* (ἀρχήν): "But if there be any as yet unfit to be called a Son of God, let him press to take his place under God's First-born [πρωτόγονον], the Word, who holds the eldership among the angels, their ruler as it were. And many names are his, for he is called *the Beginning* [ἀρχή], and *the Name of God*, and *His Word*, and *the Man after His image*, and *he that sees*, that is Israel . . . For the Word is the eldest-born image [εἰκών] of God" (*De Confusione*, 146–47).[21] The language here is certainly close to St. John's for whom the Logos is ἐν ἀρχῇ The term πρεσβύτατος implies the same idea. But Wisdom had already said: "The Lord made me the beginning [αρχὴν] of his ways for his works. He established me before time was in the beginning [ἐν αρχῇ]" (Proverbs 8:22–23). The προτόγονος should be observed, which recalls the πρωτότοκος (Romans 8: 29) and the εἰκών that will reappear in *Colossians*: "He is the image of the invisible God the first born of every creature. For in him were created all things in the heavens and on earth, things visible and invisible" (Colossians 1:15–16).

As in St. John, the Philonic Logos is near to God. "The Divine Word, Who is high above all these [the powers], has not been visibly portrayed, being like to no one of the objects of sense. Nay, He is Himself the Image of God, chiefest of all beings intellectually perceived, placed nearest with no intervening distance, to the Alone truly existent One" (*De Fuga*, 101).[22] But this is found in Proverbs 8:23 and Wisdom 9:4. God has made everything by the Logos. "Its [tr. the universe's] cause is God, by whom [ὑφ᾽ οὗ] it has come into being, its material the four elements from which it was compounded its instrument [ὄργανον] the word of God, through which it was framed" (*De Cherubim*, 127).[23] We read that God uses his Logos as the messenger of his graces: "He employs as minister of His the Reason wherewith also He made the world" (*Quod Immutabilis*, 57).[24]

---

21. *Philo* IV, 89–91.

22. *Philo* V, 65. See also *Legum Allegoriae*, I:21; and *De Migratione*, 6.

23. *Philo* II, 83.

24. *Philo* III, 39.

The expression is found again in Hebrews: "[God] last of all in these days has spoken to us by his Son . . . by whom also he made the world" (Hebrews 1:2). But that is the doctrine of Biblical wisdom literature. "In the words of the Lord are his works" (Ecclesiasticus 42:15).[25]

From this group of convergences, we can conclude the following. First of all, at their base we find the text of the Septuagint and particularly the creation narrative where the expression ἐν ἀρχῇ is found, creation by the word of God. This Biblical data had been elaborated in the Biblical theology that is the common background of the book of Wisdom, Philo, and St. John. In so far as Philo is a distinguished representative of this common theology, his teaching can be represented as the Biblical theology that is the starting point for the construction of St. John's theology, without there being literal dependence. Finally, Philo represents a systematization of this common theology with its Platonic structure. That is completely alien to St. John. We can observe this on a particular point. For Philo the Logos did not come in sensible form because it has nothing in common with matter.[26] John, on the contrary, says: "And the Word was made flesh and dwelt among us" (John 1:4).

Some features of the Prologue to John's gospel can again be the object of comparison. The Logos is the source of light for both. "God is light," Philo says, "for there is a verse in one of the psalms, 'the Lord is my illumination and my Savior' (Psalm 27/26). And He is not only light, but the archetype of every other light, nay, prior to and high above every archetype holding the position of the model of a model. For the model or pattern was the Word which contained all His fullness—light in fact; for, as the lawgiver tells us, 'God said, "Let light come into being" (Genesis 1:3)'" (De Somniis, I, 75).[27] Along with the idea of light, we observe the idea of plenitude that is found again in the prologue: "full of grace and of truth" (John 1:14). The idea of becoming "a Son of God" and of having a "place under God's Firstborn the Word" (De Confusione, 146)[28] appears in Philo. The same occurs with the theory of the Logos dwelling in us. But we note that for Philo we confront different levels of existing but not the one God bursting into the

25. See also Wisdom 18:14.

26. See *Quod Immutabilis*, 31, "To the elder son, I mean the intelligible universe, He assigned the place of firstborn, and purposed that it should remain in His own keeping." *Philo* III, 27.

27. Philo V, 335, 337.

28. *Philo* IV, 89.

created world. Moreover, the place of that indwelling is exclusively "a soul that is perfectly purified" (*De Sobrietate*, 62).[29]

The Prologue's conclusion offers two interesting convergences. The first involves the expression "And of his fullness we have all received grace for grace" (John 1:16). The phrase is found again in Philo. "Wherefore God ever causes His earliest gifts to cease before their recipients are glutted and wax insolent; and storing them up for the future gives others in their stead [ἀντί], and a third supply to replace, the second, and ever new in place of, earlier boons" (*De Posteritate Caini*, 145).[30] This is a fundamental passage for Philo's spirituality. Spirituality is perpetual progress in the life of grace in such a way that the soul always remains in a relation of dependence upon God. Gregory of Nyssa will take up this idea from Philo. The wording is also very close to the letter of St. John. Some authors interpret John in the same sense as Philo. But the meaning is certainly very different. The issue is the succession of two alliances.[31] As in the case of indwelling, we are led to a historical perspective: the Christic temple succeeds the Mosaic Temple. That also holds for the expression "grace and truth came through Jesus Christ" (John 1:17). For Philo, truth (ἀλήθεια) designates the certitude of the intelligible world in opposition to the absence of certitude in human opinions.[32] By contrast, for John it is the reality opposed to the figure. That permits us to understand the cult "in spirit and truth" (John 4:23), not in the Philonic sense of merely inner cult (*Quod Deterius*, 212) but in the Christian sense of new creation. Hence we have "true bread from heaven"(John 6: 32). Hence also Christ is "the truth" (John 14: 6). With the two graces here we find a contrast that neatly parallels that of the Pauline *two men*.

To close, the last verse of the Prologue brings us a final term of comparison. We find the contrast between the Invisible God and the Logos who reveals. The first of these is very dear to Philo. We have mentioned that he was the great doctor of negative theology. "To none has He [tr. God] shown His nature, but He has rendered it invisible to our whole race" (*Legum Allegoriae*, III, 206).[33] Moreover, this is found previ-

---

29. *Philo* III, 477. See also *De Sobrietate*, 63–69.

30. *Philo* II, 413, 415. See also "Grace for Grace, new grace against old grace." (*Quis Heres*, 21, is found on *Philo* IV, 295. [Translator: I find nothing like this there, nor in the likely misreadings of 21, such as 121, 12, or paragraphs immediately preceding or following 21.]

31. See Frangipane, "Et Gratiam pro Gratia, 1–17.

32. See *Legum Allegoriae*, I, 32; *De Specialibus Legibus*, I, 89; and *De Praemiis*, 46.

33. *Philo* I, 441. See also *De Decalogo*, 120; *De Abrahamo*, 75; *De Praemiis*, 44.

ously in Hellenistic Judaism: "Who hath seen him that he might tell us?" (Ecclesiasticus 43:31). What is more remarkable is that the Logos who reveals is contrasted with the invisible Father in Philo.

> "The Lord was seen of Abraham" (Genesis 17:1) must not be understood in the sense that the Cause of all shone upon him and appeared to him, for what human mind could contain the vastness of that vision? . . . And therefore the words are "The Lord (not "The Existent") was seen of him," as though it would say, "The king has been manifested, king indeed from the first [ἐξ ἀρχῆς], but hitherto unrecognized by the soul, which so long unschooled has not remained in ignorance forever . . . But his interpreting [ὑπορήτης] word will show me . . ." (De Mutatione, 15–18).

That leads us to find a new point of contrast between John and Philo, which specifically concerns the background of the doctrine of the Logos. For Philo, the contrast between the unknowable God and the knowable Logos boils down to the contrast between the uncreated and the created. God remains entirely unknowable. Therefore, the role of the Logos as revealer does not eliminate radical divine unknowability. For St. John, matters are different. The Son is God in the strict sense of the Word. "Deus erat Verbum." Consequently, in Him the divine being truly reveals itself to us. If this revelation is appropriated to the Son, that appropriation occurs in virtue of the relations of the persons that are produced in the economy of the revelation, in which we should go to the Father through the Son. But in reality, it is one same divine nature possessed by Father and Son, and therefore Christ can say to Philip, who asks him to show the Father: "He who sees me sees also the Father" (John 14:9).

On this point, there is a moment of uncertainty among the Church Fathers with Justin, for whom the Father by nature is unknowable and the Son knowable. But Irenaeus will rectify the perspective. For him, Father and Son are equally inaccessible to human powers and equally accessible "when God, because He wills it, makes himself seen by men" (Adversus Haereses, IV, 205). Palamas will return to Philo's position, but distinguishes the question of the Logos and that of the powers, instead of contrasting Father and Logos. For Palamas, the whole Trinity, Father, Son, and Spirit, is inaccessible as divine οὐσία. What is know are the δυνάμεις, which are God himself (and not a created world or the divine attributes known through the world), but subsisting under a participable mode. It must be said that this eviscerates the paradox of Johannine revelation, where it is precisely God, inaccessible by nature, who becomes accessible by a decision of his love.

Philo and the Letter to the Hebrews

St. Paul and St. John have shown the links between the New Testament and Hellenistic Judaism in a very general sense. In the Letter to the Hebrews, without there being any question of direct dependence on Philo, we are more directly in the strictly Alexandrian Jewish milieu. Here, beside the common theological similarities, there are certain more systematic structural characteristics that seem to be shared. The issue is raised in every commentary on the Letter to the Hebrews. In the Collection *Verbum Salutis*, Fr. Joseph Bonsirven deals with the question in his introduction and gives the principal convergences as he proceeds. Whereas Fr. Ceslas Spicq admits, "the Letter's author is not unfamiliar with Philo's work,"[34] Bonsirven judges that this Epistle and Philo share the allegorical speculation about the Tabernacle that belongs to Alexandrian Judaism.[35]

Once more the comparison is essentially concerned with two factors. The first is the Logos, Indeed it seems that the Christology of the Letter to the Hebrews, unlike that of St. Paul, bears the marks of a philosophical elaboration of the Biblical conception of the Word. The opening of the letter presents a set of concepts applied to the Logos that all have a corresponding notion in Philo. "[God] last of all in these days has spoken to us by his Son, whom he appointed heir [κληρονόμου] of all things, by whom also he made the world; who, being the brightness [ἀπαύγασμα] of his glory and the image [χαρακτήρ] of his substance, and upholding [φέρων] all things by the word of his power . . ." (Hebrews 1:2–3). The theme of inheritance is a favorite of Philo, who applies it to the world.[36] The phrase "by which the universe was made" (*De Sacrificio*, 8)[37] is Philonic. The radiance is in Philo: "Every man in respect of his mind, is allied to the divine reason [tr. λόγῳ θείῳ], having come into being as a copy or fragment or ray of that blessed nature" (*De Opificio*, 146).[38] Lastly,

---

34. *Revue Biblique*, 1938, 73. [Translator: Daniélou's citation is incomplete here.] See also Spicq's article in *Revue Biblique*, 1938, 73.

35. See Spicq, "Le philonisme de l'Épître aux Hébreux."

36. *De Vita Mosis*, I:145.

37. *Philo* II, 101.

38. *Philo* I, 115. [Translator: This varies from Daniélou's quote that seems to be garbled here and refers to the relation of the Logos and God rather than the relation of

the word *stamp* (χαρακτέρ) is applied to the Logos.[39] Equally Philonic is the expression, "Thou, who givest being to what is not and generatest all things" (*Quis Rerum Divinarum Heres*, 36).[40]

But it must be observed that several of these expressions are already found in the Greek book of Wisdom, for instance ἀπαύγασμα (Wisdom 7:25). So this falls within Hellenistic Biblical theology. The fact remains that the Logos has a particularly prominent role in the creation and conservation of the world. There may be an element of Stoic influence here, because this is the peculiarly Stoic feature of the Logos. That appears even more strikingly in a later passage where the Epistle insists: "For the word of God is living and efficient and keener [τομώτερος] than any two-edged sword and extending even to the division [μερισμοῦ] of soul and spirit . . . and a discerner [διακριτικός] of the thought and intentions of the heart" (Hebrews 4:12).[41] The context here certainly seems to show traces of Stoicism. Λόγος τομεύς is a Stoic expression.[42] It is found again in Philo.

> He [tr. the author of Genesis] wishes you to think of God who cannot be shewn, as severing [τομεῖ] through the Severer of all things, that is his Word, the whole succession of things material and immaterial whose natures appear to us to be knitted together and united. That severing Word whetted to an edge of utmost sharpness never ceases to divide (*Quis Heres*, 130).[43]

Influence from that quarter also explains the comparison of the "fiery sword" (*De Cherubim*, 28)[44] to the Logos. What the Logos separates is "the soul into rational and irrational, speech into true and false" (*Quis Heres*, 132).[45] Consequently, we are dealing with perspectives that are close to each other.

The second characteristic that Philo and the Letter to the Hebrews share is the conception of the visible cult as a shadow of the invisible cult. Here, there is a whole area of speculation about the contrast between the earthly and heavenly cults connected to Alexandrian allegorism that is

---

man and Logos. The whole context demands the latter.]

39. See *Quod Deterius*, 83; *De Plantatione*, 18; *De Fuga*, 12.

40. *Philo* IV, 301.

41. [Translator: Daniélou has διακριτικός here instead of κριτικός.]

42. Plutarch *Moralia*, 695 B.

43. *Philo* IV, 347.

44. *Philo* II, 28.

45. *Philo* IV, 349.

particularly striking in Philo. The Epistle declares: "We have such a high priest, who has taken his seat at the right hand of the throne of Majesty in the heavens, a minister of the Holies and of the true tabernacle . . . If then he were on earth, he would not even be a priest, since there are already others to offer gifts according to the Law. The worship they offer is a mere copy [εἰκών][46] and shadow [σκία] of things heavenly . . ." (Hebrews 8:1–2, 4–5). Now this is completely reminiscent of Philo. "For it is the copies of which he [Bezaleel] is the chief builder, whereas Moses builds the patterns; for this reason the one drew an outline as it were of shadows [σκία], while the other fashioned no shadows, but the existences themselves that served as archetypes" (*De Somniis*, I, 206).[47] The contrast is certainly the same here, between the visible and invisible cult. What is being distinguished is the inward and outward cult (Hebrews 10:16) rather than the old and new cult.

Just as in Philo, the high priest is the figure of the Logos, so also the high priest is the figure of Christ of the Epistle. Thus in Philo we find: "We say, then, that the High Priest is not a man, but a Divine Word" (*De Fuga*, 108).[48] Elsewhere we read: "For the law desires him [the high priest] to be endued with a nature higher than the merely human and to approximate to the Divine on the order-line, we may truly say, between the two, that men may have a mediator through whom they may propitiate God and God [have] a servitor to employ in extending the abundance of His boons to men" (*De Specialibus Legibus*, I, 116).[49]

That in no way abolishes the visible priesthood, as we have seen. Now, the same holds true in the Epistle where the issue is that beside the Levitical priesthood, there is one "who has passed into the heavens" (Hebrews 4:14), who is a "mediator of a superior covenant" (Hebrews 8: 6). An especially noteworthy point of coincidence is the heavenly high priest's sinlessness: "The true high priest who is not falsely so-called is immune from sin" (*De Specialibus Legibus*, I, 230).[50] Likewise the Epistle's high priest is "holy, innocent [ἀμίαντος], undefiled, set apart from sinners" (Hebrews 7:26).

46. [Translator: the Greek here has ὑποδείγματι rather than εἰκών.]

47. *Philo* V, 409. See also *De Somniis*, I:206; *De Plantatione*, 27; *Legum Allegoriae*, III:96.

48. *Philo* V, 69.

49. *Philo* VII, 167.

50. Ibid., 235.

Along with this speculation about the Levitical high priest, both authors offer reflections about Melchizedek, which certainly rest upon shared foundations. Philo writes: "Melchizedek, too, has God made both king of peace, for that is the meaning of 'Salem,' and His own priest (Genesis 14:18) . . . For he is entitled 'the righteous king' . . . who is right principle" (*Legum Allegoriae*, III, 79–80).[51] All these expressions are encountered again in the Epistle (Hebrews 7:1–2). The expression "without a mother" (*De Ebrietate*, 61)[52] is not found in Philo in reference to Melchizedek, but it is frequent in him. Above all, the Epistle tells us: "likened to the Son of God, he continues a priest forever" (Hebrews 7:3). His priesthood is thus contrasted with the Levitical priesthood and is the figure of Christ's priesthood. It is evident that Philo's text plunges into speculations similar to those in the Letter to the Hebrews, and which are found again later. St. Ambrose will see an epiphany of the Logos in Melchizedek.[53]

All that makes evident the exact relations of terminology between the two texts. Others could be added. The issue of God's oath is treated quite similarly in *Legum Allegoriae*, III, 203 and Hebrews 6:133. Certain very Philonic philosophical terms like μετριοπαθεῖν appear in Hebrews 5:2. That demonstrates a common cultural context and not just a theological one. But the similarity stops there. For it is also clear that the Epistle turns Philonic perspectives upside down to make them fit into the Christian perspective. Melchizedek is not the Logos but the figure of Christ. The true cult is the heavenly cult as opposed to the earthly cult, but a new alliance that succeeds the old alliance (Hebrews 9:15). In the cultural context of Alexandrian Judaism, which is certainly a near neighbor, we have a second, very different theology.[54]

All these consequences allow us to render judgment on the relations between Philo and the New Testament. Any direct influence seems quite implausible. But Philo's considerable importance is that he lets us become acquainted with Hellenistic Judaism, in which are situated, not the life of Christ, about whose setting the apocalypses inform us better, but the New Testament writings. Consequently, the similarities of vocabulary,

51. *Philo* I, 353, 355.

52. *Philo* III, 347.

53. St. Ambrose, *De Sacramentis*, book IV, chapter III, paragraph 10, 438 B.

54. [Translator: Daniélou literally says that there are two very different theologies in Alexandrian Judaism, but the context is a comparison between the Letter to the Hebrews and Alexandrian Judaism.]

conceptions, and images are considerable. Above all, they hold for the common Hellenistic Judaism, not for its more systematic parts that hardly concern the Letter to the Hebrews. Later, Philo will directly influence certain Church Fathers. Clement will depend on his exegesis. Origen will take certain theological concepts. Gregory of Nyssa will represent two of his great mystical positions, that of the divine cloud and that of perpetual progress. But that would require another book.

Bibliography

Adriani, M., "Note sul Trattato περὶ κόσμου." *Rivista di Filologia* (1955) 30.

Ambrose, St. *De Sacramentis.* In *Patrologia Latina*, vol. XVI.

Armand, David. *Fatalisme et liberté dans l'antiquité grecque. Recherches sur la survivance de l'argumentation morale antifataliste de Carnéade chez les philosophes grecs et les théologiens chrétiens des quatre premiers siècles.* Louvain: Bibliothèque de la université, 1945.

Arnim, Hans Friedrich August von. *Quellenstudien zur Philo von Alexandria.* Berlin: Weidmann, 1888.

————. *Stoicorum veterum Fragmenta.* Leipzig: Teubner, 1903, 1921–24; Stuttgart: Teubner, 1964, 1968, 1978–79

Barthélémy, Dominique. "Redécouverte d'un chaînon manquant de l'histoire de la LXX." *Revue Biblique* (1953) 18–30.

Belkin, Samuel. *Philo and the Oral Law: The Philonic Interpretation of Biblical Law in Relation to the Palestinian Halakah.* Cambridge, MA: Harvard University Press, 1940.

Bell, Sir Harold Idris. *Jews and Christians in Egypt: The Jewish Troubles in Alexandria and the Athanasian Controversy.* London: The British Museum and B. Quaritch and H. Milford, 1924. Reprint, Westport, CT: Greenwood, 1972; Milan: Cisalpino, 1977.

Bonsirven, Joseph. *Le judaïsme palestinien au temps de Jésus-Christ*, translated by William Wolf. Paris: Beauchesne, 1950.

Bousset, Wilhelm. Jüdisch-christlicher Schulbetrieb in Alexandria und Rom, literarische Untersuchungen zu Philo und Clemens von Alexandria, Justin und Irenäus. Göttingen: Vandenhoeck & Ruprecht, 1915. Reprint, Hildesheim: G. Olms, 1975.

Bréhier, Émile. *Les idées philosophiques et religieuses de Philon d'Alexandrie.* Paris: Alphonse Picard, 1908; Paris: J. Vrin, 1925, 1950.

Carmignac, Jean, "L'utilité ou l'innutilité des sacrifices sanglants dans la communauté de Qumrân." *Revue Biblique* LXIII (1956).

A Catholic Commentary on Holy Scripture. Edited by Bernard Orchard et al. London: Thomas Nelson and Sons, 1953.

Clement of Alexandria. *Eclogae Propheticae.* In *Patrologia Graeca*, vol. IX.

Cohn, Leopold. "Einleitung und Chronologie der Schriften Philos." *Philologus* 7 (1899) 387–435.

Collins, B. "Tentatur Nova Interpretatio Hebr. 5:11—6:8." *Verbum Domini* (1948) 144–51.

Corsini, E. "Sources de *l'Hexameron* de St. Grégoire de Nysse." *Studia Patristica* I (1957).

Cumont, Franz, editor and translator. *Philo De Aeternitate Mundi*. Berlin: Georgii Reimeri, 1891.

Dalbert, Peter. *Die Theologie der hellenistisch-jüdischen Missionsliteratur unter Ausschluss von Philo und Josephus*. Hamburg-Volksdorf: H. Reich, 1954.

Daniélou, Jean. *Les anges et leur mission*, Paris: Éditions de Chevetogne, 1951. Translated by David Heimann as *The Angels and their Mission according to the Fathers of the Church* (Westminster, MD: Newman Press, 1957).

———. "Le comble du mal et l'eschatologie de S. Grégoire de Nysse." In *Festgabe Joseph Lortz*, edited by Erwin Isorloh and Peter Manns. Baden-Baden: Bei Bruno Brimm, 1958.

———. "Démon." In *Dictionnaire de Spiritualité*, 45 vols., IV: cols. 163–65. Paris: Beauchesne, 1932–1995.

———. "La Fête des Tabernacles dans l'exégèse patristique." *Studia Patristica* (1957) 262–79.

———. *Les manuscrits de la Mer Morte et les Orgines de Christianisme*, Paris: Éditions de l'Orante, 1957. Translated by Salvator Attanasio as *The Dead Sea Scrolls and Primitive Christianity* (Baltimore: Helicon, 1958).

———. *Origène*, Paris: La Table Ronde, 1948. Reprint, Paris: Association André Robert, 1986. Translated by Walter Mitchell as *Origen* (New York: Sheed and Ward, 1955).

———. "Le symbolique cosmique au temple de Jérusalem chez Philon et Josèphe." In *Symbolisme cosmique des monuments religieux*, 1–65. Paris: Musé Guimet, 1953.

———. *La théologie du judéo-christianisme*. Paris: Desclée, 1958. Translated and edited by John Baker as *The Theology of Jewish Christianity* (London: Darton, Longman & Todd, 1964, 1977).

Delatte, Armand. *Études sur la littérature pythagoricienne*. Paris: E. Champion, 1915.

Delatte, Louis. *Les traités de la royauté d'Ecphante, Diogène et Sthénidas*. Paris: E. Droz, 1942.

Dodd, Charles Harold. *The Bible and the Greeks*. Oxford: Hodder and Stoughton, 1935, 1964.

Dölger, Franz Joseph. *Sphragis: eine altchristliche Taufbezeichnung in ihren Bezeinhungen Zur profanen und religiösen*. Paderborn: Ferdinand Schöningh, 1911. Reprint, New York: Johnson Reprint Company, 1967.

Drummond, James. *Philo Judaeus or the Jewish Alexandrian Philosophy in its Development and Completion*. London: Williams and Norgate, 1888. Reprint, Amsterdam: Philo, 1969.

Dupont, Jacques. *Essais sur la christologie de saint Jean; le Christ, parole, lumière, et vie, le gloire du Christ*. Bruges: Editions de l'Abbaye de Saint-André, 1951.

Eusebius. *Praeparatio Evangelica*. In *Patrologia Graeca*, vol. XXI.

Festugière, André-Jean. *Le Dieu Cosmique*. Vol. 2 of *La Révélation d'Hermès Trimegiste*, 4 vols. Paris: Lecoffre, 1944–54. Reprint, Paris: Gabalda, 1949–54; Paris: Les Belles Lettres, 1981.

Feuillet, André. "Isaiah." In *Dictionanaire de la Bible, Supplément*, edited by Louis Pirot et al., col. 653. Paris: Letouzey et Ané 1926.

Frangipane, D. "Et Gratiam pro Gratia." *Verbum Domini* (1948) 1–17.

Friedländer, Moriz. *Geschichte der jüdischen Apologetik als Vorgeschichte des Christentums*, Zurich: Caesar Schmidt, 1903. Reprint, Amsterdam: Philo, 1973.

Fuks, Alexander. "Notes on the Archive of Nicanor." *Journal of Juristic Papyrology* 5 (1951).

Gerleman, Gillis. *Studies in the Septuagint*. Vol. 1: *Job*. Lund: Gleerup, 1946.

Giblet, Jean. "L'homme image de Dieu dans les Commentaires littéraires de Philo." *Studia Hellenistica* (1948) 5.

Goodenough, Erwin Ramsdell. *By Light, Light: The Mystic Gospel of Hellenistic Judaism*. Amsterdam: Philo, 1969. First published New Haven, CT: Yale University Press, 1935.

———. *An Introduction to Philo Judaeus*. New Haven, Yale University Press, 1940, 1962, 1986.

———. *Jewish Symbols in the Greco-Roman Period*. New York: Pantheon, 1953–1968. (NB: there is an abridged version by Jacob Neusner, Princeton University Press, 1988; reprinted, 1992.)

———. *The Politics of Philo Judaeus. Theory and Practice*. New Haven, CT: Yale University Press, 1938.

Greene, William Chase. *Moira: Fate, Good, and Evil in Greek Thought*. Cambridge, MA: Harvard University Press, 1944.

Gregory of Nyssa. *De Opificio Hominis*. In *Patrologia Graeca*, vol. xliv. Paris: Migne, 1865. [Translator: Daniélou does not mention Grégoire de Nysse, *La création de l'homme*, introduction and translation de Jean Laplace, notes by Jean Daniélou, Paris: Editions du Cerf, 1944, 2002.]

———. *In Cantica Canticorum, Homilia XI* in *Patrologia Graeca*, vol. XLIV, edited by Jacques-Paul Migne, Paris: 1863.

Heinemann, Felix. *Nomos und Physis*. Darmstadt: Reinhardt, 1945. Reprint, Darmstadt: Wissenschaftliche Buchgesellschaft, 1978.

Heinemann, Yizhak. *Philons griechische und jüdische Bildung. Kulturvergleichende Untersuchungen zu Philons Darstellung der jüdischen Gesetze*. Breslau: M & H. Marcus, 1932. Reprint, Heldesheim: George Olms, 1962.

Heinisch, Paul. *Griechische Philosophie und Altes Testament*. Münster in Westfalen: Aschendorff, 1913–14.

Heyden-Zielewicz, Johan von der. *Prolegomena in Pseudocelli De Universa Natura Libellum*. Breslau: M. & H. Marcus, 1901.

Hippolytus. *De Benedictione Mosis*. In *Patrologia Orientalis*, vol. XXVII, 171. Paris: Firmin-Didot 1957. (Available in *Hippolyte de Rome sur les bénédictions d'Isaac, de Jacob, et de Moïse*, translation and notes by Maurice Brière, Louis Mariès, and Benoît-Charles Mercier, [Paris: Firmin-Didot, 1954].)

Homer. *The Iliad*. Translated by Robert Fagles. Introduction and notes by Bernard Knox. New York: Penguin, 1990.

———. *The Odyssey*. Translated by Robert Fitzgerald. New York: Vintage, 1990.

Horovitz, Jakob. *Untersuchungen über Philons und Platons lehre der Weltschöpfung*. Marburg: N. G. Elwart, 1900.

Jonas, Hans. *Gnosis und spätantiker Geist*. Vol. II. Göttingen: Vandenhoeck & Ruprecht, 1954.

Josephus, Flavius. *The Life and Works of Flavius Josephus*. Translated by William Whiston, with an introductory essay by Rev. H. Stebbing. Philadelphia: John C. Winston, 1957.

Justin. *Dialogues*. In *Patrologia Graeca*, vol. VI.

Kahle, Paul. *Die hebräischen Handschriften aus der Höhle*, Stuttgart: W. Kohlhammer, 1951.

————. "Problems of the Septuagint." *Studia Patristica* I (1957) 328–38.

Katz, Peter. *Philo's Bible*. Cambridge: Cambridge University Press, 1950.

————. "Septuaginta Studies in Mid Century." In *The Background of the New Testament and its Eschatology. Studies in Honor of C. H. Dodd*, edited by William David Davies and David Daube, 176–208. Cambridge: Cambridge University Press, 1956.

Kilpatrick, George, Dunbar. *The Origins of the Gospel according to St. Matthew*. Oxford: Clarendon, 1946, 1950.

Lacombade, Christian, trans. *Le discours sur la royaté de Synésios de Cyrène*. Paris: Les Belles Lettres, 1951.

Lagrange, Marie-Joseph. *Le judaïsme au temps du Christ*. [Translator: I have not been able to find this book. Lagrange is indeed author of *Le judaïsme avant Jésus-Christ*, Paris: Gabalda et fils, 1931].

Lampe, Geoffrey William High. *The Seal of the Spirit: A Study in the Doctrine of Baptism and Confirmation in the New Testament and the Fathers*. New York: Longmans Green, 1951. Second corrected and enlarged edition, London: SPCK, 1967.

Larson, Curtis W. "Prayer of Petition by Philo." *Journal of Biblical Literature* (1945) 185–203.

Laurentin, A. "Le pneuma dans la doctrine de Philon." *Ephemerides Theologicae Lovanienses* (1951) 490–537.

Lebreton, J. "La nuit obscure de saint Jean de la Croix." *Revue d'ascétique et de mystique* (1928) 3–24.

Lindeskog, G. *Studien zum neotestamentlichen Schöpfungsgedanken*. Upsala: Lundequistka bokhandeln, 1952

Lossky, Vladimir. *Essai sur la théologie mystique de l'Eglise d'Orient*, translated by members of the Fellowship of St. Alban and St. Sergius, London. J. Clarke. Paris: Aubier, 1944, 1960, 1996.

Macrobius. *Commentarium in Somnium Scipionis* (no edition given). [Under this title an English translation by William Harris-Stahl was published in 1990, New York: Columbia University. An edition available to Daniélou in French and Latin could have been *Macrobe (oeuvres completes), Varron (De la langue latine), Pompoinius Mela (oeuvres complètes),* edited by M. Nisard (Fermin-Didot) 1875, 1883].

Marcus, Ralph. "Pharisees, Essenes, and Gnostics." *Journal of Biblical Literature* 73 (1954).

————. "Philo, Josephus and the Dead Sea *Yahad*." *Journal of Biblical Literature* 71 (1952).

Marrou, Henri-Irenée. *Histoire de l'éducation dans l'antiquité*, Paris: Seuil, 1948. English translation by George Lamb, *A History of Education in Antiquity*. New York: Sheed and Ward, 1956. Reprint, Madison: University of Wisconsin Press, 1982.

————. *Saint Augustin et la fin de la culture antique*. Paris: E. Brocard, 1937. Fourth edition, 1958.

Massebieau, Louis, and Émile Bréhier, "Essai sur la chronologie de la vie et des oeuvres de Philon." *Revue d'histoire des Religions* (1906) 1–3, 25–64, 164–85, 167–289.

Medico, Henri del. *L'enigme des manuscrits de la Mer Morte, étude sur la date, la provenance et le conténu des mansucrits découverts dans le grotte I de Qumrân suivie de la traduction commentée des principaux texts*. Paris: Plon, 1957.

Mireaux, Émile. *La reine Bérénice*. Paris: Michel, 1951.

Musurillo, Herbert. *The Acts of Pagan Martyrs*. New York: Oxford University Press, 1953. Reprint, Salem, NH: Ayer, 1988; New York: Oxford University Press, 2000.

Norden, Eduard. *Genesiszitat in Der Schrift von Erhabenen*. Berlin: Akademie-Verlag, 1955.

The Old Testament in Greek according to the Septuagint. Edited by Henry Barclay Swete. Cambridge: Cambridge University Press 1887–94 (first edition), 1930–34 (fourth edition).

Origen. *Commentary on the Gospel of St. John*. In *Patrologia Graeca*, vol. XIV.

Pascher, Josef. Ἡ Βασιλικὴ Ὁδός *Der Königsweg zu Widergeburt und Vergottung bei Philon von Alexandreia*. Paderborn: F. Schöning, 1931. Reprint, New York: Johnson Reprint Company, 1968.

Patrologiae Cursus Completus, Series Graeca. Edited by Jacques-Paul Migne. Paris: Imprimerie Catholique, 1857–66. Index volume edited by Ferdinando Cavallera, Paris: Garnier Frères, 1912. [*Patrologia Graeca*]

Patrologiae Cursus Completus, Series Latina. Edited by Jacques-Paul Migne. Paris: Imprimerie Catholique, 1844–64. [*Patrologia Latina*]

Pedersen, Johannes. *Israel, and its Life and Culture*. Vols. I and II. Translated by Aslaug Møller. London: H Milford, 1926.

Peterson, Erik. *Theologische Traktate*. München: Kösel, 1951. Reprint with an introduction by Barbara Nichtweiss, Wurtzburg: Echter, 1994. English translation by Michael Hollerich, *Theological Tractates*, Stanford, Stanford University Press, 2011."

Philo of Alexandria. *Philo*. Loeb Classical Library. Vols. I–V translated by F. H. Colson and G. H. Whitaker; vols. VI–X translated by F. H. Colson; appendices vols. I–II translated by Ralph Marcus. Cambridge: Harvard University Press, 1971–91.

———. *The Works of Philo*. Translated by C. D. Yonge and David Scholer. Peabody, MA: Hendrickson, 1991.

———. *Paralipomena Armena*. Latin and Armenian of *Libri Quatuor in Genesim, Libri duo in Exodum*, sermo unus De Sampsone, alter de Jona, tertius de Tribus Angelis Abrahamo Apparentibus, edition and translation by Johannis Baptista Aucher, Venice: Typis Coenobii Pp. Armenonorum in Insula S. Lazari, 1826.

———. *La migration d'Abraham*. Greek text and French translation by René Cadiou,. Sources chrétiennes. Paris: Cerf, 1957.

Philonis Alexandrini Opera Quae Supersunt. 7 vols. Edited by Leopold Cohn and Paul Wendlund. Berlin: G. Reimerus, 1896–1915. Reprint, Berlin: W. de Gruyter, 1962–1963.

Piganiol, André. *Histoire de Rome*. Paris: Presses Universitaires de France, 1939.

Plato. *Theaetetus*. [Translator: Daniélou does not cite an edition.]

———. *Timaeus*. [Translator: Daniélou does not cite an edition.]

Plutarch. *De Iside et Osiride*. [Translator: Daniélou does not cite an edition. There is a recent bilingual version edited by J. Gwyn Grifiths, *On Isis and Osiris. Plutarch's De Iside et Osiride* (Cardiff: University of Wales Press, 1970).]

———. *Moralia*. [Translator: Daniélou does not cite an edition. The *Moralia* are published in the Loeb Classical Library in 17 volumes; volume 13 is divided into parts I and II; Cambridge, MA: Harvard University Press, 1927–2004.]

Puech, Henri-Charles. "La ténèbre mystique chez le Pseudo-Denys." *Études carmelitanes* (October 1938).

Quasten Johannes. "Sobria ebrietas in Ambrosii *De Sacramentis*." In *Miscellanea Liturgica in Honorem L. Cuniberti Mohlberg*. 2 vols. Rome: Edizioni liturgiche, 1948.

Reitzenstein, Richard. *Zwei religionsgeschichtliche Fragen nach ungedruckten griechischen Texten der Strassburger Bibliothek.* Strassburg: Karl J. Tübner, 1901.

Richardson, W. "The Philonic Patriarch as Νόμος ἔμψυχος." *Studia Patristica* I:515–26.

Sagnard, François-Louis-Marie. *La gnose valentinienne et la téomoinage de saint Irenée.* Paris: Vrin, 1947.

Schenck, Kenneth. *A Brief Guide to Philo.* Louisville: Westminster John Knox, 2005.

Schwartz, J. "Note sur la famille de Philon d'Alexandrie." In *Mélanges Isidore Lévy,* 595–96. Brussels: Secrétariat des Éditions de l'Institut, 1955.

Shroyer, M. J.. "Alexandrian Jewish Literalists." *Journal of Biblical Literature* 55 (1936) 261–84.

Siegfried, Carl. *Philo von Alexandria als Ausleger des Alten Testaments.* Jena: Hermann Dufft, 1875. Reprint, Aalen: Scientia, 1970.

Simon, Marcel. *Verus Israel: étude sur les relationes entre chrétiens et juifs dans l'Empire romain, 135–45.* Paris: E. de Boccard, 1948. English translation by H. McKeating as *Verus Israel: A Study of the Relations between Christians and Jews in the Roman Empire, 135–425.*

Skringar, A. "L'aveuglement final dans Isaïe." *Biblica* (1938).

Soury, Guy. *Démonologie de Plutarque; essai sur les idées religieuses et les mythes d'un platonicien éclectique.* Paris: Societé d'éditions "Les belles lettres," 1942.

Spicq, Ceslas. "Le philonisme de l'Épître aux Hébreux." *Revue Biblique* (1949) 542–72 and (1950) 212–42.

Stein, Edmund. *Die allegorische Exegese des Philo aus Alexandreia.* Giessen: Töpelman, 1929.

Stein, S. "The Dietary Laws in Rabbinic and Patristic Literature." *Studia Patristica* II (1957) 141–54.

Stendahl, Krister. *The School of St. Matthew and Its Use of the Old Testament.* Lund: C. W. K. Gleerup, 1954.

Thyen, Hartwig. *Der Stil der jüdisch-hellenistichen Homilie.* Göttingen: Vadenhoeck & Ruprecht, 1955.

———. "Die Probleme des neueren Philo-Forschung." *Theologische Rundschau* 23 (1955) 230–46.

Venard, L. "L'utilisation des Psaumes dans l'Épitre aux Hébreux." In *Mélanges Podechard.* Lyon: Facultés catholiques, 1945.

Verbeke, Gérard. *L'évolution de la doctrine du Pneuma, du stoïcisme à S. Augustin; étude philosophique.* Paris: Desclée de Brouwer/Louvain: Institut supérieur de philosophie, 1945. Reprint, New York: Garland, 1987.

Vitti, A., "Christus Adam: De Paulino hoc conceptu interprando eiusque ab extraneis fontibus independentia vindicanda." *Biblica* 7 (1926) 140–44.

Virogoux, Fulcran-Grégoire. *Dictionnaire de la Bible.* Paris: Letouzey et Ané, 1912–26.

Völker, Walther. *Fortschritt und Vollendung bei Philo von Alexandreia, eine Studie zur Geschichte der Frömmigkei.* Leipzig: J. C. Hinrich, 1938.

Witt, Reginald Eldred. *Albinus and the History of Middle Platonism.* Cambridge: Cambridge University Press, 1937.

Wolfson, Harry Austryn. "Albinus and Plotinus on Divine Attributes." *Harvard Theological Review* (1952) 115–30.

———. "The Knowability and Descriptability of God in Plato and Aristotle." *Harvard Studies in Classical Philology* (1947) 233–49.

———. *Philo.* 2 vols. Cambridge, MA: Harvard University Press, 1947, 1968.

Lightning Source UK Ltd.
Milton Keynes UK
UKOW04n2307070715

254774UK00003B/21/P